SAT Subject Test Chinese Study Guide

NTK Publishing Limited

NTK Artes Veritas Scientia

NTK Chinese Department

Authors
Wong Chau Yee (BA, MA)
Zhang Zi Xia (BA, MA)
Ling Tsz Wai (BA, MA)

Editor
Dennis Lau

Design and Artwork
Luisa Lei

Disclaimer:
Every effort has been made to publish this book as complete and accurate as possible. The information provided is on an "as is" basis. The authors and publisher shall have no liability or responsibility for any loss or damages arising from the contents of this publication.

All figures used in this book are used with the expressed agreement from independent designers that the artwork is original. The publisher is indemnified from any copyright issues related to any such artwork.

SAT is a registered trademark of the College Board, which is not involved in the production of, and does not endorse, this book.

NTK Publishing Limited
5/F
18 Hysan Avenue
Causeway Bay
Hong Kong SAR

Tel: +852 2577 7844
Fax: +852 2881 6708
E-mail: enquiry@ntk.edu.hk

ISBN 978-988-18990-3-3
First published in 2011

Foreword

Academic success can be measured in many different ways, and I often tell my students that scoring high marks in exams is only one of the rewards from diligent study. The true measures of academic success should be the enjoyment of learning and the sense of accomplishment students get when that light flicks on in their head and they think to themselves, "So that's why!" The inception of NTK's study guides and publications is based on the simple goal of making students' learning process more enjoyable and less complicated, and to deliver positive results from students' efforts.

The SATs are a rite of passage for students planning to apply to universities in the United States. In addition to the SAT Reasoning Test, an increasing number of universities are placing more emphasis on the importance of SAT Subject Tests. High scores reflect a student's focus and ability in specific subjects, and these are traits that elite universities think highly of. The SAT Chinese Subject Test has become increasingly popular since it was first administered in 1994, and is now the second most popular SAT language Subject Test. Its popularity also means that students' Chinese language ability is becoming widely recognized by universities.

NTK's SAT Chinese Subject Test Study Guide is specifically created for students who wish to excel on the test, and are looking for a no-nonsense guide that expertly helps them succeed and achieve top scores.

NTK's study guides, courses and educational services are designed to help prepare students for exam success as they continue to pursue secondary and college education. As a leading educational service provider in Southeast Asia for more than a decade, NTK has helped thousands of students reach their academic goals. Whether they are in primary, secondary, or post-graduate studies, our students have benefited greatly from our specialized academic programs and expertise in all major international curricula and exams.

As you continue on your studies, I wish you every success and most importantly, I hope you enjoy the learning process as well.

T.K. Ng

Founder and Managing Director

NTK Academic Group

Introduction

NTK's SAT Chinese Study Guide is tailor-made for students taking the SAT Chinese Subject Test. Written by NTK's highly experienced Chinese subject specialists with multi-cultural teaching backgrounds, this study guide allows students to quickly and effectively familiarize themselves with the SAT Chinese Subject Test and is an invaluable companion for achieving top scores.

This study guide is based on past SAT tests and is divided into four main sections:

- **Test Format**

  Detailed explanation of the SAT Chinese Subject Test, including regulations, question formats and test emphasis

- **Grammar**

  Detailed explanation of grammar commonly seen on the SAT Chinese Subject Test, presented in both traditional and simplified characters

- **Vocabulary**

  Vocabulary commonly seen on the SAT Chinese Subject Test, grouped into different categories and presented in traditional and simplified characters, as well as Pinyin Romanization

- **Practice Tests**

  Six carefully graded practice tests, based on past SAT tests, improve test-taking and scoring techniques and allow students to evaluate their ability

We sincerely hope that this study guide can help many students worldwide achieve top scores in the SAT Chinese Subject Test.

Contents

Test Format

Test Format

The SAT Subject Test is a set of standardized multiple-choice tests developed by the College Board for students entering colleges and universities in the US. High SAT Subject Test scores are essential elements of US college admissions.

The SAT Chinese Subject Test was introduced in 1994, and provides the opportunity for students learning Chinese to add to their SAT scores. The SAT Chinese Subject Test is aimed at high school students who have studied Chinese for two to four years. Strong Chinese language ability can be a definite advantage in gaining admission to the college of choice.

Currently, Chinese is the most popular SAT Subject Test in foreign languages behind Spanish. There is great emphasis placed on the practical use of foreign languages in daily life, and the content of SAT Chinese Subject Test closely reflects this emphasis.

The SAT Chinese Subject Test contains 85 multiple-choice questions and is divided into three sections:

- **LISTENING** (20 minutes)
- **USAGE** (15 minutes)
- **READING COMPREHENSION** (25 minutes)

Each correct answer scores one point. Points are deducted for each incorrect answer (1/2 point each for Questions 1 thru 15 and 1/3 point each for Questions 16 thru 85). Answers left blank score no points and no points are deducted for blank answers. The total number of points scored is the raw score, which is converted into the final (composite) score of 200 – 800.

The SAT Chinese Subject Test is offered only once a year, usually in early November. For further information and application procedures, please visit www.collegeboard.com.

LISTENING

The listening section is presented on an individual CD and students must bring an acceptable CD player to the test center, including batteries and earphones.

The listening section is divided into two parts. Part A consists of 15 questions which are short questions, statements or commands in Chinese. There are three responses (A), (B) and (C) to each question. Neither the questions nor responses are printed in the test booklet, so students must note down what they hear and choose the correct answer.

Part B consists of 15 questions based on several short selections, with up to four questions for each selection. The questions, each with four possible answers (A), (B), (C) and (D), are printed in the test booklet. The questions and answers in Part B are all given in English.

USAGE

This section consists of 25 questions and is designed to test students' abilities in common everyday language usage. Students have to select the correct answer from four possible completions. Questions include classifiers (or measure words), conjunctions and order of words. Each question and its possible completions are presented in simplified characters, traditional characters, Pinyin Romanization and the Chinese phonetic alphabet. Students should choose the writing form with which they are most familiar with.

READING COMPREHENSION

This section consists of 25 questions based on everyday life situations. Students are required to read different signs, posters, as well as extracts from news reports, weather reports, diaries, menus, letters, receipts and timetables and then answer the questions. The reading material is presented in both simplified characters and traditional characters while the questions and answers are given in English.

Grammar

Simplified Characters

Grammar

Simplified Characters

Conjunctions (连接词)

In a Coordinative Relationship (并列关系)

一边 …… 一边 (yībiān …… yībiān) (Page 125 Q48, page 210 Q40)

While

例：我一边听音乐，一边吃蛋糕。
他喜欢一边吃饭，一边看电视。

Examples: I was listening to music while eating some cake.
He likes to eat while watching TV.

又/既 …… 又 (yòu/jì …… yòu) (Page 208 Q35)

Not only …… but also

例：今天晚上的月亮又圆又大。
下个星期我既得复习考试，又得打工。

Examples: Tonight's moon is not only round but also big.
During next week, not only do I have to revise for exams but also work.

In an Alternative Relationship (选择关系)

不是 ……，就是 (bú shì …… jiùshì) (Page 170 Q51)

If not …… then; it is either …… or

例：放假的时候他不是去旅游，就是去做义工。
他周末在家不是看书，就是听音乐。

Examples: If he is not traveling during his holidays, then he does volunteer work.
He either reads books or listens to music at home during weekends. *("At home during weekends he either reads books, or listens to music.")*

还是 (háishì) (Page 213 Q48) [Also see Adversative Relationship]

Or

例：你想吃饭还是面条？
明天你想去踢足球还是去游泳？

Examples: Would you like to eat rice or noodles?
Do you want to play soccer or go swimming tomorrow? *("Tomorrow do you want to play soccer or go swimming?")*

要么 …… 要么 (yàome …… yàome) (Page 164 Q34)

Either …… or

例：要么你去，要么他去，总之一定要有一个人去。
他要么去了上海，要么去了北京。

Examples: Either you have to go or he has to go. Someone must go.
He has gone to either Shanghai or Beijing.

与其[A]，不如[B] (yǔqí [A]，bùrú [B]) (Page 257 Q48)

[B] rather than [A]; [B] is better than [A]

例：与其坐船去，不如坐火车去。
与其你一个人去，不如我们一起去。

Examples: Let us take the train rather than the boat.
Rather than you going alone, why don't we go together?

In a Purposive Relationship (目的关系)

为了 (wèile) (Page 80 Q40, page 255 Q42)

For; in order to; in order that

例：为了身体健康，他每个星期都打篮球。
为了演奏出好的作品，她每天都练习弹琴。

Examples: In order to stay healthy, he plays basketball every week.
In order to put on a good performance, she practices the piano everyday.

以免 (yǐmiǎn) (Page 253 Q38)

For fear that; in order to avoid

例：工人戴上了安全帽，以免发生意外。
保管好你的财物，以免被盗。

Examples: Workers wear hard hats in order to avoid accidents.
You should look after your belongings for fear that they maybe stolen.

In a Causative Relationship (因果关系)

既然 …… 就 (jìrán …… jiù) (Page 170 Q52)

Since/as ……

例：既然你今天这么忙，我们就明天再见面吧。
你既然不想去北京，那就别去了。

Examples: Since you are so busy today, let us meet again tomorrow.
As you are not willing to go to Beijing, then there is no need for you to go there.

因此（yīncǐ）(Page 297 Q37)

Therefore; hence

例：我的弟弟没温习，因此考试不及格。
我起晚了，因此没赶上公共汽车。

Examples: My younger brother did not revise and hence failed his examination.
I woke up late and therefore missed the bus.

因为/由于 …… 所以（yīnwèi/yóuyú …… suǒyǐ）(Page 83 Q49)

Because …… so

例：因为他是我的同学，所以我对他比较熟悉。
由于我去过那里，所以我记得怎么去。

Examples: Because he is my classmate, so I am more familiar with him.
Because I have been there before, so I remember how to get there.

之所以 …… 是因为（zhī suǒyǐ …… shì yīnwèi）(Page 251 Q31, page 296 Q33)

The reason …… is because

例：他之所以生气，是因为你做错了。
她之所以迟到，是因为堵车。

Examples: The reason for him getting angry is because you made a mistake.
The reason for her being late is because of a traffic jam.

In a Successive Relationship (承接关系)

接着（jiēzhe）(Page 164 Q33)

Then

例：他买了菜，接着又买了水果。
她做完了作业，接着又预习了课文。

Examples: He bought some vegetables and then bought some fruit.
She finished her homework and then did some revision.

（先）…… 然后（(xiān) …… ránhòu）

First …… and then; after that

例：你考虑一下，然后再决定吧！
你先做作业，然后帮我做家务。

Examples: You should first consider it, and then make a decision.
You should finish your homework first. After that, please help me with the housework.

于是（yúshì）(Page 251 Q32)

As a result of; consequently; thus

例：妈妈鼓励了我，于是我恢复了信心。
他吃了太多东西，于是拉肚子了。

Examples: As a result of my mother's encouragement, I regained my confidence.
He ate too much and consequently had a stomachache.

In a Progressive Relationship (递进关系)

不但/不仅 …… 而且/还 (búdàn/bùjǐn …… érqiě/hái)
(Page 78 Q35, page 171 Q55, page 209 Q36, page 257 Q49)

Not only …… but also

例：这儿不但安静，而且地方很大。
他不仅会唱歌，还会跳舞。

Examples: This location is not only quiet, but also very spacious.
Not only can he sing, but also dance.

不但不/不但没 ……，反而 (búdàn bù/búdàn méi …… fǎn'ér) (Page 212 Q47)

On the contrary; instead

例：雨不但不停，反而越下越大了。
他不但没被困难吓倒，反而更有信心了。

Examples: The rain has not stopped, instead it got even heavier.
He is not afraid of the difficulties. On the contrary, his confidence has been boosted.

何况 (hékuàng)

Let alone; moreover

例：这块石头连年轻人都抬不动，何况老人？
我不喜欢这双鞋子的颜色，何况这么贵。

Examples: This rock cannot be moved by a young person, let alone by an elderly person.
I don't like the color of these shoes. Moreover, they are very expensive.

（连）…… 都/也 ((lián) …… dōu/yě) (Page 163 Q31)

Even

例：你为什么连饭都不吃就走了？
这个暑假，他(连)一天也没有休息过。

Examples: Why did you leave without even eating your meal?
He did not even take a single day of rest during this summer. *("This summer, he did not even take a single day of rest.")*

甚至 (shènzhì) (Page 124 Q47)

Even

例：他忙得甚至没有时间睡觉。
她甚至忙得忘记吃晚饭了。

Examples: He is so busy and does not even have time to sleep.
She was so busy that she even forgot to have dinner.

In an Adversative Relationship (转折关系)

不是 …… 而是 (bú shì …… ér shì) (Page 252 Q34, page 302 Q51)

Not …… but

例：他不是美国人，而是加拿大人。
这条裤子不是我买的，而是妈妈买的。

Examples: He is not American but Canadian.
Mom bought these trousers, not me. (*"These trousers are not bought by me, but mom bought them."*)

但（是） (dàn(shì)) (Page 210 Q41)

But, still

例：工作很忙，但他仍然坚持学习。
今天天气不好，但是她心情很好。

Examples: Despite a busy workload, he is still determined to continue his studies.
The weather is not good today, but she is still in a good mood.

固然 (gùrán) (Page 127 Q55)

No doubt; it is true; admittedly

例：德文固然难学，但只要你努力认真，也是可以学好的。
工作固然重要，但健康更重要。

Examples: Learning German is no doubt very difficult, but if you put in the effort, you can do well.
It is true that work is important, but health is even more important.

还是 (háishì) (Page 259 Q55) [Also see Alternative Relationship]

Still

例：我跟他说了很多遍，但他还是不相信我。
即使那里很危险，她还是去了。

Examples: I have said it many times, but he still does not believe me.
She still went there even if it is very dangerous. (*"Even if it is very dangerous, she still went there."*)

然而 (rán'ér) (Page 299 Q43)

But; however; yet

例：实验又失败了，然而他们并不灰心。
今天天气不好，然而他的心情好极了。

Examples: The experiment has failed again, but they are not discouraged.
The weather is not good today, yet he is in a very good mood.

虽然/尽管 …… 但（是）/可（是）/不过 (suīrán/jǐnguǎn …… dàn(shì)/kě(shì)/búguò)
(Page 78 Q33, page 120 Q33, page 301 Q50)

Although …… however

例：他虽然很有钱，但是很节俭。
尽管她工作很忙，可是每天晚上都做运动。

Examples: Although he is very rich, he is a thrifty person (however).
Although she is very busy with work, she still exercises every evening (however).

则 (zé) (Page 169 Q48)

But, although

例：我很喜欢花，他则不喜欢。
这里夏天很热，冬天则很冷。

Examples: I like flowers but he does not.
It is very hot here in the summer, but in the winter it is very cold.

In a Conditional Relationship (条件关系)

不管 …… 也/都 (bùguǎn …… yě/dōu) (Page 209 Q38)

No matter how

例：不管天气多坏，他也会来学校。
不管怎么忙，她都会看书。

Examples: No matter how bad the weather is, he will still come to school.
No matter how busy she is, she still reads everyday.

不论/无论 …… 也/都 (búlùn/wúlùn …… yě/dōu)
(Page 168 Q46, page 252 Q35, page 295 Q32)

No matter (what, who, how, etc.); regardless

例：不论天气如何，他也会去打篮球。
无论她怎么说，我都不会同意。

Examples: Regardless of the weather, he will still play basketball.
No matter what she says, I will still disagree.

才 (cái) (Page 125 Q50, page 166 Q40, page 303 Q54)

Only after …… (for some time)

例：我等了她半天，她才来。
他准备了六个星期才通过考试。

Examples: I waited for half a day and she finally arrived. *("I waited for her for half a day, only after that she arrived.")*
He managed to pass the examination, but only after six weeks of preparation.

(除非) …… 不然/否则 ((chúfēi) …… bùrán/fǒuzé) (Page 84 Q52, page 120 Q35, page 211 Q44)

Unless …… or else/otherwise

例：除非你道歉，否则她不会原谅你。
我们走吧，要不然就要迟到了。

Examples: She will not forgive you, unless you apologize. (*"Unless you apologize, otherwise she will not forgive you."*)
We should go, otherwise we will be late.

就 (jiù) (Page 210 Q39, page 298 Q41)

Then; right away; already

例：我今天六点就起床了。
她昨天就把练习做完了。

Examples: She got up right away at 6 A.M. this morning.
She already finished her homework yesterday.

一 …… 就 (yī …… jiù) (Page 167 Q44)

As soon as …… (right away)

例：他一工作就忘记吃饭了。
这些汉字一不小心就会写错。

Examples: As soon as he starts working, he forgets about having lunch.
As soon as you are not careful, you will make mistakes when writing these Chinese characters. (*"These Chinese characters, when not careful, will be wrongly written."*)

只要 …… 就 (zhǐyào …… jiù) (Page 120 Q34, page 212 Q46)

As long as ……

例：只要我们坚持努力，就能成功！
只要吃了这个药，你的病很快就会好。

Examples: Success will come as long as we persevere. (*"As long as we persevere, we can be successful!"*)
Your illness will be quickly cured as long as you take this medicine. (*"As long as this medicine is taken, your illness will be quickly cured."*)

只有 …… 才 (zhǐyǒu …… cái) (Page 252 Q33)

Only (if) ……

例：只有每天练习，你才能唱得更好。
只有努力工作，你才有美好的将来。

Examples: You can sing well, but only if you practice everyday. (*"Only if you practice everyday, you can sing well."*)
Your future will be bright, but only if you work hard. (*"Only if you work hard, you will have a bright future."*)

In a Hypothetical Relationship (假设关系)

即使/就算 …… 也 (jíshǐ/jiùsuàn …… yě) (Page 80 Q41, page 302 Q53)

Even; even if; even though

例：即使你不高兴，也不应该发脾气。
就算她做得不对，你也应该原谅她。

Examples: You should not get angry even if you feel unhappy. *("Even if you are unhappy, you should not get angry.")*
You should forgive her even though she is wrong. *("Even though she has done it wrong, you should forgive her.")*

如果/要是 ……，就 (rúguǒ/yàoshì ……, jiù)
(Page 121 Q36, page 253 Q36, page 296 Q35)

If …… , then

例：如果明天天气好，我们就去爬山。
如果心情不好，我就会听音乐。

Examples: If the weather is good tomorrow, (then) we will go hiking.
I listen to music if I am in a bad mood. *("If I am not in a good mood, then I listen to music.")*

万一 (wànyī) (Page 303 Q55)

In case ……

例：不小心过马路，万一发生意外，怎么办呢？
万一现金不够，我们就用信用卡。

Examples: What can we do in case of an accident due to crossing the road carelessly?
("Crossing the road carelessly, and in case an accident happens, what can be done?")
In case we run out of cash, we can use credit cards.

一旦 ……，(就) (yídàn ……, (jiù)) (Page 82 Q45)

Once …… then

例：一旦发生意外，就要立即报警。
一旦有机会，我一定要去美国旅游。

Examples: Once an accident happens, then the police must be called.
Once given the opportunity, then I must travel to the USA.

Expressing Similarity (表示相似)

和/跟 …… 一样 (hé/gēn …… yíyàng) [Also see Prepositions for "跟"]

Is the same as ……

例：你的毛衣和我的一样。
中国人和美国人不一样。

Examples: Your sweater is the same as mine.
Chinese people are not the same as American people.

像 (xiàng) (Page 84 Q53) [Also see Verbs]

Resemble; looks like

例：我长得像爸爸。
冬天的时候，香港像北京那么冷。

Examples: I look like my father. *("I have grown to look like my father.")*
In winter, the cold weather in Hong Kong resembles that of Beijing.

Adverbs (副词)

毕竟 (bìjìng) (Page 121 Q37)

After all; all in all; when all is said and done; in the final analysis

例：毕竟是个小孩子，他肯定会淘气。
小明毕竟才学了一年日语，当然不及你说得好。

Examples: He will be naughty. After all, he is only a child. *("He is only a child after all, so he will be naughty.")*
Xiao Ming has only been learning Japanese for just one year afterall, so his Japanese will not be as good as yours.

从此 (cóngcǐ)

From this time on; from now on; from then on; henceforth; thereupon

例：地铁通车了，从此交通就更方便了。
他没有告诉任何人就离开了，从此大家再没有见过他。

Examples: The subway train is in operation. From now on, it is much more convenient to get around.
He left without telling anyone. From then on, no one ever saw him again.

差点儿 (chàdiǎnr) (Page 84 Q51)

Nearly; almost

例：我起晚了，差点儿赶不上飞机。
那天他一直领先，差点儿跑了个第一。

Examples: I woke up late and almost missed my plane.
He was leading throughout and nearly won that day. *("That day he was leading throughout and nearly won.")*

反正 (fǎnzhèng) (Page 168 Q47)

Anyway; in any case

例：反正赶不及，我们就决定不去了。
反正离那里不远，我们就走路去吧！

Examples: We decided not to go, since we would not make it in time anyway. *("Since we would not make it in time anyway, we decided not to go.")*
Since it is not that far in any case, let us walk over there.

果然 (guǒrán)

Really; as expected; sure enough

例：你果然来了！
他说星期三会下雨，果然下雨了。

Examples: Sure enough you came!
He said it would rain on Wednesday, and it really did rain in the end.

何必 (hébì) (Page 299 Q44)

Why; there is no need

例：既然他说他不来，你又何必等呢？
这么生气，何必呢？

Examples: Why are you waiting even if he said he will not come? *("Since he said he will not come, why are you waiting?")*
There is no need to be so angry. *("Being so angry, what is the need?")*

竟然/居然 (jìngrán/jūrán) (Page 119 Q31)

Unexpectedly

例：没想到这条围巾竟然是你买的。
你居然不认识他?

Examples: I really did not think you would buy this scarf. *("I really did not think this scarf is bought by you.")*
How can you not know him?

究竟 (jiūjìng) (Page 255 Q43)

Exactly; actually; what actually happened; after all

例：这件事究竟是谁的错？
究竟你去不去南京？

Examples: Whose fault is it exactly? *("This matter, actually whose fault is it?")*
Will you actually go to Nanjing?

马上/立刻/立即 (mǎshàng/lìkè/lìjí) (Page 165 Q38)

Right away; immediately

例：你马上去办这件事。
有错就应该立刻改。

Examples: You go and take care of this matter right away.
Mistakes must be corrected immediately.

难道 (nándào)

Is it possible that, could it be said that, could it be that

例：难道你忘记那件事了吗？
他难道不明白我的意思吗？

Examples: Have you forgotten about that particular issue? *("Is it possible that you have forgotten about that particular issue?")*
Does he not understand what I mean? *("Could it be that he does not understand what I mean?")*

偶尔（ǒu'ěr）

Occasionally

例：我只是偶尔去一次电影院。
我的电脑偶尔会发生这个问题。

Examples: I only go to the cinema occasionally.
My computer has this problem occasionally.

偶然（ǒurán）(Page 126 Q52)

Accidental; accidentally; by accident

例：我在路上偶然遇到了她。
他只是偶然犯错，我们要原谅他。

Examples: I met her on the street by accident.
He only makes mistakes by accident, and we should forgive him.

千万（qiānwàn）(Page 122 Q39, page 163 Q32)

Be sure to; must

例：下个星期你千万要来啊！
你千万别去那里！

Examples: Be sure to come over next week!
You must not go there!

顺便（shùnbiàn）(Page 213 Q49)

In addition to what one is already doing; without much extra effort

例：我只是下班经过超市，顺便买点东西。
你去图书馆的时候，顺便帮我还这本书吧。

Examples: I bought a few things as I went past the supermarket after work.
Please return this book for me when you go to the library.

突然/忽然（tūrán/hūrán）(Page 301 Q48)

Unexpected; all of a sudden; suddenly

例：她的病突然好了。
她忽然想起了妈妈的话。

Examples: Her illness has been cured all of a sudden.
Suddenly, she thought of her mother's words.

未必（wèibì）(Page 82 Q47)

May not

例：他未必同意你的看法。
她未必喜欢这条裙子。

Examples: He may not agree with your point of view.
She may not like this dress.

有点(儿) (yǒudiǎn(r)) (Page 168 Q45, page 207 Q32)

Some; little; somewhat

例：小明昨天有点儿不高兴。
我有点儿不喜欢那里。

Examples: Xiao Ming was a little unhappy yesterday.
I dislike that place somewhat.

尤其 (yóuqí) (Page 81 Q43, page 297 Q38)

Especially; particularly

例：他的成绩很好，中文尤其优秀。
她很喜欢小动物，尤其是猫。

Examples: His results are very good, particularly in Chinese.
She loves pets, especially cats.

又 (yòu)

Again

例：他又喝了一杯酒。
她又唱了一首歌。

Examples: He had another drink.
She sang another song.

越来越 (yuè lái yuè)

Even more

例：天气越来越冷了。
她越来越喜欢香港的生活。

Examples: The weather is getting even colder.
She is enjoying life in Hong Kong even more.

再 (zài)

Again

例：请再喝一杯茶。
请再读一遍这个句子。

Examples: Please have another cup of tea.
Please read this sentence once more.

只好 (zhǐhǎo) (Page 171 Q54)

Have no choice but to do something

例：我们不认识路，只好问人。
我不认识那个字，只好查字典。

Examples: Since we do not know the way, we have to ask someone for directions.
Since I do not know that word, I have no choice but to look it up in the dictionary.

Auxiliary Particles (助词)

啊 (a) (Page 83 Q48)

Particle that expresses surprise or admiration

例：这里真漂亮啊！
小明真棒啊！

Examples: This place is so beautiful!
Xiao Ming is really awesome!

吧 (ba)

Particle that indicates a suggestion; used when one is sure about one's conjecture

例：你快回来吧！
明天不会下雨吧？

Examples: Please come back soon!
It is not going to rain tomorrow, is it? (*"Tomorrow it's not going to rain?"*)

的 (de)

Added to nouns and pronouns (animate and inanimate) to indicate possession

例：她是妈妈的老师。
我喜欢那条蓝色的裙子。

Examples: She is my mother's teacher.
I like that blue dress.

地 (de)

Usually an objective description of the way something is done

例：她伤心地哭了起来。
爷爷高兴地笑了。

Examples: She is crying very sadly.
Grandpa is smiling happily.

得 (de) (Page 300 Q45)

Introduces the manner in which an action is carried out; or the result

例：我的哥哥帅得很。
妹妹走得很慢。

Examples: My brother is very handsome.
His sister walks very slowly.

过 (guo)

An aspect particle used after a verb as a complement

例：我去过那个书店。
我从来没有吃过北京烤鸭。

Examples: I have been to that bookshop.
I have never eaten Beijing roast duck.

了 (le) (Page 208 Q34)
An aspect particle used after a verb to indicate completion; or the change of tone in a situation

例：我喝了一杯茶。
他写了一个下午作业。

Examples: I have drunk a cup of tea.
He has done a whole afternoons' worth of homework.

吗 (ma) (Page 214 Q51)
Final interrogative particle in a sentence

例：她是你的朋友吗？
你去学校了吗？

Examples: Is she your friend?
Have you been to school?

呢 (ne) (Page 212 Q45, page 253 Q37)
Used at the end of a special, alternative, or rhetorical question

例：谁会讨厌聪明的人呢？
哪个父母不喜欢自己的孩子呢?

Examples: Who would dislike a clever person?
Would any parents not love their own children?

着 (zhe) (Page 123 Q43)
An aspect particle used after a verb to indicate a steady state

例：外面正下着雪呢！
我在写着作业的时候，电话响了。

Examples: It is snowing outside now!
As I was doing my homework, the telephone rang.

Complements (补语)

出来 (chūlai)
Come out; come up with

例：这是什么字，我看不出来。
他把这件事说出来了。

Examples: I cannot tell what word this is. *("What word is this, I cannot see it come out.")*
He has spoken out about this matter.

起来 (qǐlai) (Page 85 Q54, page 214 Q52)

Up; upwards; increasingly

例：天气冷起来了。

这个故事听起来很有意思。

Examples: The weather is getting increasingly cold.

This story is very meaningful. *("As more of this story is listened to, it becomes very meaningful")*

下去 (xiaqu) (Page 165 Q37)

Used to indicate the continuation of an action

例：坚持下去，你一定会成功！

这个分数保持下去，我们就胜利了。

Examples: You will be successful if you continue to persevere. *("Continue to persevere, you will be successful!")*

We will win if this score can be maintained. *("If this score can be maintained, we will win.")*

Prepositions (介词)

按 (àn)

According to; in accordance with; in light of; on the basis of

例：出租车是按每公里15元计算的。

他每天按计划温习，所以成绩进步很快。

Examples: The taxi fare is based on a rate of $15 per kilometer.

In light of his planned revision everyday, his results are improving very quickly.

把/将 (bǎ/jiāng) (Page 125 Q49, Page 165 Q36)

Stresses that something has been done to a particular object (the grammatical object of the verb)

例：他的弟弟把杯子打破了。

我把蛋糕吃完了。

Examples: His younger brother broke the cup.

I have finished eating the cake.

被 (bèi) (Page 170 Q53, page 215 Q55, page 256 Q45)

Similar to the passive voice (something done by somebody) in English

例：杯子被他的弟弟打破了。

蛋糕没（有）被我吃完。

Examples: The cup was broken by his younger brother.

The cake was not eaten by me.

除了 …… 以外/之外 …… (chúle …… yǐwài/zhīwài ……)

Except for; except; besides

例：除了学习之外，小明什么都喜欢。
除了英文以外，我也会中文。

Examples: Xiao Ming likes to do everything except study. *("Apart from studying, Xiao Ming likes to do everything")*
Besides English, I can also speak Chinese.

从 (cóng) (Page 297 Q36)

From; through

例：从香港坐火车去北京要24小时。
我从书上看到了你的照片。

Examples: It takes 24 hours to travel by train from Hong Kong to Beijing. *("From Hong Kong by train to Beijing requires 24 hours.")*
I saw your photos in the book. *("From the book I saw your photos.")*

对(于) (duì(yú)) (Page 124 Q46, page 169 Q49, page 208 Q33)

With regards to

例：对于这本小说，我没有兴趣。
对于这件事，我已经没什么好说的了。

Examples: I am not interested in this novel. *("With regards to this novel, I have no interest.")*
I have nothing more to say with regards to this matter. *("With regards to this matter, I have no more to say.")*

跟 (gēn) (Page 124 Q45) [Also see Expressing Similarity]

To; towards; from; with

例：我们跟她学中文。
我跟妈妈去菜市场。

Examples: We are learning Chinese from her.
I went to the market with my mother. *("I followed mother to the market.")*

关于 (guānyú) (Page 258 Q53)

About; on the subject of; with regards to; concerning

例：我想买一本关于音乐的书。
我不想再听到关于他的消息。

Examples: I want to buy a book about music.
I do not want to hear any more news about him.

让/给 (ràng/gěi)

Used in a passive sentence to introduce the person or thing doing the action

例：蛋糕都让他吃光了！
看，衣服给雨淋湿了。

Examples: All the cake has been eaten by him!
Look, the clothes have been soaked by the rain.

据（jù）(Page 77 Q31)

According to; on the grounds of

例：据天气预报，明天将会下雨。
据统计，每天有三千人使用这个服务。

Examples: According to the weather forecast, it will rain tomorrow.
According to statistics, 3,000 people use this service everyday.

凭（píng）

Depend on; go by; based on; take as the basis; with

例：凭着多年的经验，我们一定会成功。
凭你的实力，一定能通过这次考试。

Examples: Based on many years of experience, we will no doubt be successful.
With your potential, there is no doubt that you will pass this examination.

前后（qiánhòu）

Around; "before and after"

例：圣诞节前后，我们都放假。
台风到来前后，千万别去海滩游泳。

Examples: We are all on vacation around Christmas time. *("Around Christmas, we are all on vacation.")*
Do not go swimming at the beach around the time of the typhoon.
("Before and after the typhoon arrives, do not go to the beach and swim.")

向（xiàng）(Page 121 Q38)

To; towards; in the direction of

例：我向老师介绍了美国的情况。
气球飞向了天空。

Examples: I introduced the situation in the USA to my teacher.
The balloon is floating towards the sky.

以（yǐ）(Page 126 Q53)

With; by

例：我们应该以礼待人。
香港队以二比一战胜了上海队。

Examples: We should be courteous. *("We should treat people with courtesy.")*
The Hong Kong team beat the Shanghai Team by two goals to one.

由（yóu）(Page 81 Q42, page 164 Q35, page 256 Q47)

By; through

例：这件事由我去办。
这个比赛由北京主办。

Examples: I will take care of this matter. *("This matter will be taken care of by me.")*
This competition is hosted by Beijing.

于 (yú)

Indicating time, place, or direction

例：我的哥哥出生于一九九零年。
这个产品于上海制造。

Examples: My brother was born in 1990.
This product is made in Shanghai.

自从 (zìcóng) (Page 166 Q41, page 257 Q50)

Since

例：自从大学毕业以来，小明一直没找到合适的工作。
自从认识你后，我的心情变得更加开朗。

Examples: Since graduating from university, Xiao Ming has not found a suitable job.
Since I have known you, my mood has become more cheerful.

左右 (zuǒyòu)

About; around

例：晚上十一点左右他才回来。
这棵树高十米左右。

Examples: He came back at around 11 P.M.
This tree is about 10 meters tall.

Verbs (动词)

包括 (bāokuò) (Page 258 Q52)

Including

例：住宿费并不包括在内。
这次参加活动的人包括你在内有三十人。

Examples: Accommodation costs are not included.
There are 30 people taking part in this activity, including you. (*"The number of people taking part in this activity, including you, is 30."*)

使 (shǐ) (Page 211 Q43)

Make

例：电脑使我们的生活多姿多彩。
他的话使我明白了许多道理。

Examples: Computers make our lives more colorful.
His words made me understand many principles.

像 (xiàng) (Page 123 Q42) [Also see Expressing Similarity]

As; like

例：天像要下雨了。
他像有心事。

Examples: It looks like it's going to rain. (*"The sky looks like it will rain."*)
It seems like he has some concerns. (*"He looks like he has some concerns."*)

Measure Words

Measure Words for Nouns

Individual measure words

把 (bǎ)

Measure word for objects with handles or similar

例：一把扇子；三把梳子

Examples: A hand fan; three combs

杯 (bēi)

Cup; glass

Measure word for liquid in terms of the number of cups/glasses

例：一杯水；兩杯牛奶

Examples: A cup of water; two glasses of milk

本 (běn) [Also see "冊"]

Volume

Measure word for books, magazines and similar objects

例：一本书；七本杂志

Examples: A book; seven magazines

部 (bù) (Page 213 Q50)

Measure word for movies, books, etc

例：一部电影；六部词典

Examples: A movie; six dictionaries

Measure word for machines and appliances

例：一部电话；一部相机

Examples: A telephone; a camera

场 (chǎng)

Measure word for the frequency of certain activities

例：一场考试；一场面试

Examples: An examination; an interview

Measure word for recreational activities

例：一场比赛；一场音乐会

Examples: A competition; a concert

册（cè） [Also see "本"]

Volume; book; copy

Measure word for magazines and books

例：五万册杂志；六册课本

Examples: 50,000 copies of a magazine; six volumes of a textbook.

顶（dǐng）

Measure word for objects which have a top, cap, or cover

例：一顶帽子；一顶帐篷

Examples: A hat; a tent

朵（duǒ） [Also see "枝"]

Measure word for flowers

例：一朵鲜花；五朵玫瑰

Examples: A fresh flower; five roses

份（fèn） (Page 79 Q38)

Measure word for newspapers, gifts etc

例：三份报纸；一份礼物

Examples: Three newspapers; a gift

封（fēng）

Measure word for letters, telegrams, etc

例：一封信；九封电子邮件

Examples: A letter; nine e-mails

幅（fú） (Page 300 Q47)

Measure word for calligraphy, paintings

例：四幅国画；一幅图案

Examples: Four Chinese paintings; a graphic

个 (ge) (Page 209 Q37)
Measure word for people

例：两个人；一个学生

Examples: Two people/persons; a student

Measure word for geographical areas, units etc

例：一个国家；八个城市

Examples: A country; eight cities

Measure word for certain objects

例：两个苹果；一个玩具

Examples: Two apples; a toy

Measure word for some abstract nouns

例：一个想法；四个问题

Examples: A thought; four questions

间 (jiān)
Measure word for houses and buildings

例：一间屋；三间酒店

Examples: A house; three hotels

件 (jiàn) (Page 166 Q39)
Measure word for pieces of clothing

例：五件大衣；一件背心

Examples: Five coats; a vest

棵 (kē)
Measure word for plants and vegetables

例：一棵树；两棵小草

Examples: A tree; two strands of grass

辆 (liàng)
Measure word for cars and other vehicles

例：一辆公共汽车；三辆私家车

Examples: A bus; three private cars

名 (míng)
Measure word for people

例：七名士兵；一名歌手

Examples: Seven soldiers; a singer

瓶 (píng) (Page 298 Q40)
Measure word for bottles (of liquids).

例：一瓶啤酒；三瓶可乐

Examples: a bottle of beer, three bottles of cola

所 (suǒ) (Page 79 Q36)
Measure word for houses, schools, hospitals etc

例：一所房子；八所学校

Examples: A house; eight schools

条 (tiáo)
Measure word for long, narrow objects

例：一条项链；十条裙子

Examples: A necklace; ten dresses

张 (zhāng) (Page 119 Q32, page 298 Q39)
Measure word for flat objects, or objects with a surface

例：一张地图；四张车票

Examples: A map; four tickets

支 (zhī)
Measure word for songs

例：五支民歌；一支流行歌曲

Examples: Five folk songs; a pop song

枝 (zhī) (Page 256 Q46) [Also see "朵"]
Measure word for flowers (with a stem)

例：一枝花；两枝玫瑰花

Examples: A flower; two roses

Measure word for rod-shaped objects

例：三枝笔；一枝烟

Examples: Three pens; a cigarette

只 (zhī)
Measure word for single objects normally found as a pair

例：一只手套；三只袜子

Examples: A glove; three socks

Measure word for insects or animals

例：一只猫；两只狗

Examples: A cat; two dogs

座（zuò）(Page 214 Q53)

Measure word for buildings, and other similar large, immovable objects

例：一座纪念碑；四座大桥

Examples: A memorial; four bridges

Measure word for mountains and similar objects

例：一座山峰；两座冰山

Examples: A mountain; two icebergs

班（bān）

Measure word for means of transport

例：下一班飞机；最后一班地铁

Examples: The next flight; the last subway train

家（jiā）[Also see "家" in collective measure words for nouns]

Measure word for an institution, enterprise, unit, etc

例：一家银行；一家酒店

Examples: A bank; a hotel

Partial measure words

块（kuài）

Measure word for certain types of food

例：六块蛋糕；一块西瓜

Examples: Six pieces of cake; a slice of watermelon

篇（piān）

Measure word for pieces of writing, etc

例：一篇文章；一篇散文

Examples: A passage; a short story

片 (piàn)

Measure word for thin, flat objects

例：一片面包；三片树叶

Examples: A slice of bread; three leaves

Collective measure words

家（jiā）[Also see "家" in individual measure words for nouns]

Measure word for a family

例：一家人；两家亲戚

Examples: A family; two families (of relatives)

群 (qūn)

Crowd; flock; herd

Measure word for groups of people, birds or animals

例：一群人；一群羊

Examples: A crowd of people; a flock of sheep

束 (shù)

Bunch; bundle

Measure word for objects of the same kind fastened together

例：一束鲜花；两束百合花

Examples: A bunch of fresh flowers; two bunches of lilies

双 (shuāng)

Pair

Measure word for two objects of the same kind to be used together

例：两双手套；一双袜子

Examples: Two pairs of gloves; a pair of socks

Measure word for some parts of the human body

例：一双脚；一双手

Examples: A pair of feet; a pair of hands

种 (zhǒng)

Species, kind

Measure word for objects of the same kind

例：一种动物；一种游戏

Examples: A type of animal; a type of game

Measure word for abstract objects of the same kind

例：一种方法；一种情况

Examples: A kind of method; a kind of situation

Measure words for verbs

遍 (biàn) (Page 127 Q54, page 299 Q42)

Measure word for the course of an action from the beginning to the end

例：看一遍；复习一遍

Examples: Read it once; revise once

趟 (tàng) (Page 254 Q40)

Measure word for "the number of times"

例：去了一趟上海；再走一趟

Examples: Been to Shanghai once; go once again

次 (cì)

Measure word for the number of repetitions of an event or situation

例：一次讨论；一次旅游

Examples: One discussion (*"once discuss"*); one trip (*"once travel"*)

Measure word for the number of times an action is taken

例：去了一次北京；打了三次篮球

Examples: Been to Beijing once; played basketball three times

Measure Words for Both Nouns and Verbs

番 (fān)

Measure word for action which takes time and energy

例：一番努力；一番功夫

Examples: Hard work; effort

Measure word for kindness, flavors, etc

例：一番心意；一番滋味

Examples: Kindness; (good) taste

Plural measure word for the process of certain actions

例：打扮一番；检查一番

Examples: Dressing up; inspecting

顿 (dùn)

Measure word for regular meals

例：一顿饭；一顿晚餐

Examples: A meal; a dinner

Measure word to express abuse, reprimands, or criticism

例：打一顿；骂一顿

Examples: A beating; a scolding

Grammar

Traditional Characters

Grammar

Traditional Characters

Conjunctions (連接詞)

In a Coordinative Relationship (並列關係)

一邊 …… 一邊 (yìbiān …… yìbiān) (Page 125 Q48, page 210 Q40)

While

例：我一邊聽音樂，一邊吃蛋糕。
他喜歡一邊吃飯，一邊看電視。

Examples: I was listening to music while eating some cake.
He likes to eat while watching TV.

又/既 …… 又 (yòu/jì …… yòu) (Page 208 Q35)

Not only …… but also

例：今天晚上的月亮又圓又大。
下個星期我既得複習考試，又得打工。

Examples: Tonight's moon is not only round but also big.
During next week, not only do I have to revise for exams but also work.

In an Alternative Relationship (選擇關係)

不是 ……，就是 (bú shì …… jiùshì) (Page 170 Q51)

If not …… then; it is either …… or

例：放假的時候他不是去旅遊，就是去做義工。
他週末在家不是看書，就是聽音樂。

Examples: If he is not traveling during his holidays, then he does volunteer work.
He either reads books or listens to music at home during weekends. *("At home during weekends he either reads books, or listens to music.")*

還是 (háishì) (Page 213 Q48) [Also see Adversative Relationship]

Or

例：你想吃飯還是麵條？
明天你想去踢足球還是去游泳？

Examples: Would you like to eat rice or noodles?
Do you want to play soccer or go swimming tomorrow? *("Tomorrow do you want to play soccer or go swimming?")*

要麼 …… 要麼 (yàome …… yàome) (Page 164 Q34)

Either …… or

例：要麼你去，要麼他去，總之一定要有一個人去。
他要麼去了上海，要麼去了北京。

Examples: Either you have to go or he has to go. Someone must go.
He has gone to either Shanghai or Beijing.

與其[A]，不如[B] (yǔqí [A]，bùrú [B]) (Page 257 Q48)

[B] rather than [A]; [B] is better than [A]

例：與其坐船去，不如坐火車去。
與其你一個人去，不如我們一起去。

Examples: Let us take the train rather than the boat.
Rather than you going alone, why don't we go together?

In a Purposive Relationship (目的關係)

爲了 (wèile) (Page 80 Q40, page 255 Q42)

For; in order to; in order that

例：爲了身體健康，他每個星期都打籃球。
爲了演奏出好的作品，她每天都練習彈琴。

Examples: In order to stay healthy, he plays basketball every week.
In order to put on a good performance, she practices the piano everyday.

以免 (yǐmiǎn) (Page 253 Q38)

For fear that; in order to avoid

例：工人戴上了安全帽，以免發生意外。
保管好你的財物，以免被盜。

Examples: Workers wear hard hats in order to avoid accidents.
You should look after your belongings for fear that they maybe stolen.

In a Causative Relationship (因果關係)

既然 …… 就 (jìrán …… jiù) (Page 170 Q52)

Since/as ……

例：既然你今天這麼忙，我們就明天再見面吧。
你既然不想去北京，那就別去了。

Examples: Since you are so busy today, let us meet again tomorrow.
As you are not willing to go to Beijing, then there is no need for you to go there.

因此 (yīncǐ) (Page 297 Q37)

Therefore; hence

例：我的弟弟沒溫習，因此考試不及格。
我起晚了，因此沒趕上公共汽車。

Examples: My younger brother did not revise and hence failed his examination.
I woke up late and therefore missed the bus.

因爲/由於 …… 所以 (yīnwèi/yóuyú …… suǒyǐ) (Page 83 Q49)

Because …… so

例：因爲他是我的同學，所以我對他比較熟悉。
由於我去過那裏，所以我記得怎麼去。

Examples: Because he is my classmate, so I am more familiar with him.
Because I have been there before, so I remember how to get there.

之所以 …… 是因為 (zhī suǒyǐ …… shì yīnwèi) (Page 251 Q31, page 296 Q33)

The reason …… is because

例：他之所以生氣，是因為你做錯了。
她之所以遲到，是因為堵車。

Examples: The reason for him getting angry is because you made a mistake.
The reason for her being late is because of a traffic jam.

In a Successive Relationship (承接關係)

接著 (jiēzhe) (Page 164 Q33)

Then

例：他買了菜，接著又買了水果。
她做完了作業，接著又預習了課文。

Examples: He bought some vegetables and then bought some fruit.
She finished her homework and then did some revision.

（先）…… 然後 ((xiān) …… ránhòu)

First …… and then; after that

例：你考慮一下，然後再決定吧！
你先做作業，然後幫我做家務。

Examples: You should first consider it, and then make a decision.
You should finish your homework first. After that, please help me with the housework.

於是 (yúshì) (Page 251 Q32)

As a result of; consequently; thus

例：媽媽鼓勵了我，於是我恢復了信心。
他吃了太多東西，於是拉肚子了。

Examples: As a result of my mother's encouragement, I regained my confidence.
He ate too much and consequently had a stomachache.

In a Progressive Relationship (遞進關係)

不但/不僅 …… 而且/還 (búdàn/bùjǐn …… érqiě/hái)

(Page 78 Q35, page 171 Q55, page 209 Q36, page 257 Q49)

Not only …… but also

例：這兒不但安靜，而且地方很大。
他不僅會唱歌，還會跳舞。

Examples: This location is not only quiet, but also very spacious.
Not only can he sing, but also dance.

不但不/不但沒 ……，反而 (búdàn bù/búdàn méi …… fǎn'ér) (Page 212 Q47)

On the contrary; instead

例：雨不但不停，反而越下越大了。
他不但沒被困難嚇倒，反而更有信心了。

Examples: The rain has not stopped, instead it got even heavier.
He is not afraid of the difficulties. On the contrary, his confidence has been boosted.

何況 (hékuàng)

Let alone; moreover

例：這塊石頭連年輕人都抬不動，何況老人？
我不喜歡這雙鞋子的顏色，何況這麼貴。

Examples: This rock cannot be moved by a young person, let alone an by elderly person.
I don't like the color of these shoes. Moreover, they are very expensive.

（連）…… 都/也 ((lián) …… dōu/yě) (Page 163 Q31)

Even

例：你爲什麼連飯都不吃就走了？
這個暑假，他(連)一天也沒有休息過。

Examples: Why did you leave without even eating your meal?
He did not even take a single day of rest during this summer. *("This summer, he did not even take a single day of rest.")*

甚至 (shènzhì) (Page 124 Q47)

Even

例：他忙得甚至沒有時間睡覺。
她甚至忙得忘記吃晚飯了。

Examples: He is so busy and does not even have time to sleep.
She was so busy that she even forgot to have dinner.

In an Adversative Relationship (轉折關係)

不是 …… 而是 (bú shì …… ér shì) (Page 252 Q34, page 302 Q51)

Not …… but

例：他不是美國人，而是加拿大人。
這條褲子不是我買的，而是媽媽買的。

Examples: He is not American but Canadian.
Mom bought these trousers, not me. *("These trousers are not bought by me, but mom bought them.")*

但（是） (dàn(shì)) (Page 210 Q41)

But, still

例：工作很忙，但他仍然堅持學習。
今天天氣不好，但是她心情很好。

Examples: Despite a busy workload, he is still determined to continue his studies.
The weather is not good today, but she is still in a good mood.

固然 (gùrán) (Page 127 Q55)

No doubt; it is true; admittedly

例：德文固然難學，但只要你努力認真，也是可以學好的。
工作固然重要，但健康更重要。

Examples: Learning German is no doubt very difficult, but if you put in the effort, you can do well.
It is true that work is important, but health is even more important.

還是 (háishì) (Page 259 Q55) [Also see Alternative Relationship]

Still

例：我跟他說了很多遍，但他還是不相信我。
即使那裡很危險，她還是去了。

Examples: I have said it many times, but he still does not believe me.
She still went there even if it is very dangerous. *("Even if it is very dangerous, she still went there.")*

然而 (rán'ér) (Page 299 Q43)

But; however; yet

例：實驗又失敗了，然而他們並不灰心。
今天天氣不好，然而他的心情好極了。

Examples: The experiment has failed again, but they are not discouraged.
The weather is not good today, yet he is in a very good mood.

雖然/儘管 …… 但(是)/可(是)/不過 (suīrán/jǐnguǎn …… dàn(shì)/kě(shì)/búguò)
(Page 78 Q33, page 120 Q33, page 301 Q50)

Although …… however

例:他雖然很有錢,但是很節儉。
儘管她工作很忙,可是每天晚上都做運動。

Examples: Although he is very rich, he is a thrifty person (however).
Although she is very busy with work, she still exercises every evening (however).

則 (zé) (Page 169 Q48)

But, although

例:我很喜歡花,他則不喜歡。
這裡夏天很熱,冬天則很冷。

Examples: I like flowers but he does not.
It is very hot here in the summer, but in the winter it is very cold.

In a Conditional Relationship (條件關係)

不管 …… 也/都 (bùguǎn …… yě/dōu) (Page 209 Q38)

No matter how

例:不管天氣多壞,他也會來學校。
不管怎麼忙,她都會看書。

Examples: No matter how bad the weather is, he will still come to school.
No matter how busy she is, she still reads everyday.

不論/無論 …… 也/都 (búlùn/wúlùn …… yě/dōu)
(Page 168 Q46, page 252 Q35, page 295 Q32)

No matter (what, who, how, etc.); regardless

例:不論天氣如何,他也會去打籃球。
無論她怎麼說,我都不會同意。

Examples: Regardless of the weather, he will still play basketball.
No matter what she says, I will still disagree.

才 (cái) (Page 125 Q50, page 166 Q40, page 303 Q54)

Only after …… (for some time)

例:我等了她半天,她才來。
他準備了六個星期才通過考試。

Examples: I waited for half a day and she finally arrived. *("I waited for her for half a day, only after that she arrived.")*
He managed to pass the examination, but only after six weeks of preparation.

(除非) …… 不然/否則 ((chúfēi) …… bùrán/fǒuzé) (Page 84 Q52, page 120 Q35, page 211 Q44)

Unless …… or else/otherwise

例：除非你道歉，否則她不會原諒你。
我們走吧，要不然就要遲到了。

Examples: She will not forgive you, unless you apologize. (*"Unless you apologize, otherwise she will not forgive you."*)
We should go, otherwise we will be late.

就 (jiù) (Page 210 Q39, page 298 Q41)

Then; right away; already

例：我今天六點就起床了。
她昨天就把練習做完了。

Examples: She got up right away at 6 A.M. this morning.
She already finished her homework yesterday.

一 …… 就 (yī …… jiù) (Page 167 Q44)

As soon as …… (right away)

例：他一工作就忘記吃飯了。
這些漢字一不小心就會寫錯。

Examples: As soon as he starts working, he forgets about having lunch.
As soon as you are not careful, you will make mistakes when writing these Chinese characters. (*"These Chinese characters, when not careful, will be wrongly written."*)

只要 …… 就 (zhǐyào …… jiù) (Page 120 Q34, page 212 Q46)

As long as ……

例：只要我們堅持努力，就能成功！
只要吃了這個藥，你的病很快就會好。

Examples: Success will come as long as we persevere. (*"As long as we persevere, we can be successful!"*)
Your illness will be quickly cured as long as you take this medicine. (*"As long as this medicine is taken, your illness will be quickly cured."*)

只有 …… 才 (zhǐyǒu …… cái) (Page 252 Q33)

Only (if) ……

例：只有每天練習，你才能唱得更好。
只有努力工作，你才有美好的將來。

Examples: You can sing well, but only if you practice everyday. (*"Only if you practice everyday, you can sing well."*)
Your future will be bright, but only if you work hard. (*"Only if you work hard, you will have a bright future."*)

In a Hypothetical Relationship (假設關係)

即使/就算 …… 也 (jíshǐ/jiùsuàn …… yě) (Page 80 Q41, page 302 Q53)

Even; even if; even though

例：即使你不高興，也不應該發脾氣。
就算她做得不對，你也應該原諒她。

Examples: You should not get angry even if you feel unhappy. *("Even if you are unhappy, you should not get angry.")*
You should forgive her even though she is wrong. *("Even though she has done it wrong, you should forgive her.")*

如果/要是 ……，就 (rúguǒ/yàoshì ……, jiù)
(Page 121 Q36, page 253 Q36, page 296 Q35)

If …… , then

例：如果明天天氣好，我們就去爬山。
如果心情不好，我就會聽音樂。

Examples: If the weather is good tomorrow, (then) we will go hiking.
I listen to music if I am in a bad mood. *("If I am not in a good mood, then I listen to music.")*

萬一 (wànyī) (Page 303 Q55)

In case ……

例：不小心過馬路，萬一發生意外，怎麼辦呢？
萬一現金不夠，我們就用信用卡。

Examples: What can we do in case of an accident due to crossing the road carelessly? *("Crossing the road carelessly, and in case an accident happens, what can be done?")*
In case we run out of cash, we can use credit cards.

一旦 ……，(就) (yídàn ……, (jiù)) (Page 82 Q45)

Once …… then

例：一旦發生意外，就要立即報警。
一旦有機會，我一定要去美國旅遊。

Examples: Once an accident happens, then the police must be called.
Once given the opportunity, then I must travel to the USA.

Expressing Similarity (表示相似)

和/跟 …… 一樣 (hé/gēn …… yíyàng) [Also see Prepositions for "跟"]

Is the same as ……

例：你的毛衣和我的一樣。
中國人和美國人不一樣。

Examples: Your sweater is the same as mine.
Chinese people are not the same as American people.

像 (xiàng) (Page 84 Q53) [Also see Verbs]

Resemble; looks like

例：我長得像爸爸。
冬天的時候，香港像北京那麼冷。

Examples: I look like my father. *("I have grown to look like my father.")*
In winter, the cold weather in Hong Kong resembles that of Beijing.

Adverbs (副詞)

畢竟 (bìjìng) (Page 121 Q37)

After all; all in all; when all is said and done; in the final analysis

例：畢竟是個小孩子，他肯定會淘氣。
小明畢竟才學了一年日語，當然不及你說得好。

Examples: He will be naughty. After all, he is only a child. *("He is only a child after all, so he will be naughty.")*
Xiao Ming has only been learning Japanese for just one year afterall, so his Japanese will not be as good as yours.

從此 (cóngcǐ)

From this time on; from now on; from then on; henceforth; thereupon

例：地鐵通車了，從此交通就更方便了。
他沒有告訴任何人就離開了，從此大家再沒有見過他。

Examples: The subway train is in operation. From now on, it is much more convenient to get around.
He left without telling anyone. From then on, no one ever saw him again.

差點兒 (chàdiǎnr) (Page 84 Q51)

Nearly; almost

例：我起晚了，差點兒趕不上飛機。
那天他一直領先，差點兒跑了個第一。

Examples: I woke up late and almost missed my plane.
He was leading throughout and nearly won that day. *("That day he was leading throughout and nearly won.")*

反正 (fǎnzhèng) (Page 168 Q47)

Anyway; in any case

例：反正趕不及，我們就決定不去了。
反正離那裏不遠，我們就走路去吧！

Examples: We decided not to go, since we would not make it in time anyway. *("Since we would not make it in time anyway, we decided not to go.")*
Since it is not that far in any case, let us walk over there.

果然 (guǒrán)

Really; as expected; sure enough

例：你果然來了！

他說星期三會下雨，果然下雨了。

Examples: Sure enough you came!

He said it would rain on Wednesday, and it really did rain in the end.

何必 (hébì) (Page 299 Q44)

Why; there is no need

例：既然他說他不來，你又何必等呢？

這麼生氣，何必呢？

Examples: Why are you waiting even if he said he will not come? *("Since he said he will not come, why are you waiting?")*

There is no need to be so angry. *("Being so angry, what is the need?")*

竟然/居然 (jìngrán/jūrán) (Page 119 Q31)

Unexpectedly

例：沒想到這條圍巾竟然是你買的。

你居然不認識他?

Examples: I really did not think you would buy this scarf. *("I really did not think this scarf is bought by you.")*

How can you not know him?

究竟 (jiūjìng) (Page 255 Q43)

Exactly; actually; what actually happened; after all

例：這件事究竟是誰的錯？

究竟你去不去南京？

Examples: Whose fault is it exactly? *("This matter, actually whose fault is it?")*

Will you actually go to Nanjing?

馬上/立刻/立即 (mǎshàng/lìkè/lìjí) (Page 165 Q38)

Right away; immediately

例：你馬上去辦這件事。

有錯就應該立刻改。

Examples: You go and take care of this matter right away.

Mistakes must be corrected immediately.

難道 (nándào)

Is it possible that, could it be said that, could it be that

例：難道你忘記那件事了嗎？

他難道不明白我的意思嗎？

Examples: Have you forgotten about that particular issue? *("Is it possible that you have forgotten about that particular issue?")*

Does he not understand what I mean? *("Could it be that he does not understand what I mean?")*

偶爾 (ǒu’ěr)

Occasionally

例：我只是偶爾去一次電影院。

我的電腦偶爾會發生這個問題。

Examples: I only go to the cinema occasionally.

My computer has this problem occasionally.

偶然 (ǒurán) (Page 126 Q52)

Accidental; accidentally; by accident

例：我在路上偶然遇到了她。

他只是偶然犯錯，我們要原諒他。

Examples: I met her on the street by accident.

He only makes mistakes by accident, and we should forgive him.

千萬 (qiānwàn) (Page 122 Q39, page 163 Q32)

Be sure to; must

例：下個星期你千萬要來啊！

你千萬別去那裏！

Examples: Be sure to come over next week!

You must not go there!

順便 (shùnbiàn) (Page 213 Q49)

In addition to what one is already doing; without much extra effort

例：我只是下班經過超市，順便買點東西。

你去圖書館的時候，順便幫我還這本書吧。

Examples: I bought a few things as I went past the supermarket after work.

Please return this book for me when you go to the library.

突然/忽然 (tūrán/hūrán) (Page 301 Q48)

Unexpected; all of a sudden; suddenly

例：她的病突然好了。

她忽然想起了媽媽的話。

Examples: Her illness has been cured all of a sudden.

Suddenly, she thought of her mother’s words.

未必 (wèibì) (Page 82 Q47)

May not

例：他未必同意你的看法。

她未必喜歡這條裙子。

Examples: He may not agree with your point of view.

She may not like this dress.

有點(兒) (yǒudiǎn(r)) (Page 168 Q45, page 207 Q32)

Some; little; somewhat

例：小明昨天有點兒不高興。
我有點兒不喜歡那裏。

Examples: Xiao Ming was a little unhappy yesterday.
I dislike that place somewhat.

尤其 (yóuqí) (Page 81 Q43, page 297 Q38)

Especially; particularly

例：他的成績很好，中文尤其優秀。
她很喜歡小動物，尤其是貓。

Examples: His results are very good, particularly in Chinese.
She loves pets, especially cats.

又 (yòu)

Again

例：他又喝了一杯酒。
她又唱了一首歌。

Examples: He had another drink.
She sang another song.

越來越 (yuè lái yuè)

Even more

例：天氣越來越冷了。
她越來越喜歡香港的生活。

Examples: The weather is getting even colder.
She is enjoying life in Hong Kong even more.

再 (zài)

Again

例：請再喝一杯茶。
請再讀一遍這個句子。

Examples: Please have another cup of tea.
Please read this sentence once more.

只好 (zhǐhǎo) (Page 171 Q54)

Have no choice but to do something

例：我們不認識路，只好問人。
我不認識那個字，只好查字典。

Examples: Since we do not know the way, we have to ask someone for directions.
Since I do not know that word, I have no choice but to look it up in the dictionary.

Auxiliary Particles (助詞)

啊 (a) (Page 83 Q48)

Particle that expresses surprise or admiration

例：這裏真漂亮啊！
小明真棒啊！

Examples: This place is so beautiful!
Xiao Ming is really awesome!

吧 (ba)

Particle that indicates a suggestion; used when one is sure about one's conjecture

例：你快回來吧！
明天不會下雨吧？

Examples: Please come back soon!
It is not going to rain tomorrow, is it? *("Tomorrow it's not going to rain?")*

的 (de)

Added to nouns and pronouns (animate and inanimate) to indicate possession

例：她是媽媽的老師。
我喜歡那條藍色的裙子。

Examples: She is my mother's teacher.
I like that blue dress.

地 (de)

Usually an objective description of the way something is done

例：她傷心地哭了起來。
爺爺高興地笑了。

Examples: She is crying very sadly.
Grandpa is smiling happily.

得 (de) (Page 300 Q45)

Introduces the manner in which an action is carried out; or the result

例：我的哥哥帥得很。
妹妹走得很慢。

Examples: My brother is very handsome.
His sister walks very slowly.

過 (guo)

An aspect particle used after a verb as a complement

例：我去過那個書店。
我從來沒有吃過北京烤鴨。

Examples: I have been to that bookshop.
I have never eaten Beijing roast duck.

了 (le) (Page 208 Q34)

An aspect particle used after a verb to indicate completion; or the change of tone in a situation

例：我喝了一杯茶。

他寫了一個下午作業。

Examples: I have drunk a cup of tea.

He has done a whole afternoons' worth of homework.

嗎 (ma) (Page 214 Q51)

Final interrogative particle in a sentence

例：她是你的朋友嗎？

你去學校了嗎？

Examples: Is she your friend?

Have you been to school?

呢 (ne) (Page 212 Q45, page 253 Q37)

Used at the end of a special, alternative, or rhetorical question

例：誰會討厭聰明的人呢？

哪個父母不喜歡自己的孩子呢?

Examples: Who would dislike a clever person?

Would any parents not love their own children?

著 (zhe) (Page 123 Q43)

An aspect particle used after a verb to indicate a steady state

例：外面正下著雪呢！

我在寫著作業的時候，電話響了。

Examples: It is snowing outside now!

As I was doing my homework, the telephone rang.

Complements (補語)

出來 (chūlai)

Come out; come up with

例：這是什麼字，我看不出來。

他把這件事說出來了。

Examples: I cannot tell what word this is. *("What word is this, I cannot see it come out.")*

He has spoken out about this matter.

起來（qǐlai）(Page 85 Q54, page 214 Q52)

Up; upwards; increasingly

例：天氣冷起來了。
這個故事聽起來很有意思。

Examples: The weather is getting increasingly cold.
This story is very meaningful. *("As more of this story is listened to, it becomes very meaningful")*

下去（xiaqu）(Page 165 Q37)

Used to indicate the continuation of an action

例：堅持下去，你一定會成功！
這個分數保持下去，我們就勝利了。

Examples: You will be successful if you continue to persevere. *("Continue to persevere, you will be successful!")*
We will win if this score can be maintained. *("If this score can be maintained, we will win.")*

Prepositions（介詞）

按（àn）

According to; in accordance with; in light of; on the basis of

例：出租車是按每公里15元計算的。
他每天按計劃溫習，所以成績進步很快。

Examples: The taxi fare is based on a rate of $15 per kilometer.
In light of his planned revision everyday, his results are improving very quickly.

把/將（bǎ/jiāng）(Page 125 Q49, Page 165 Q36)

Stresses that something has been done to a particular object (the grammatical object of the verb)

例：他的弟弟把杯子打破了。
我把蛋糕吃完了。

Examples: His younger brother broke the cup.
I have finished eating the cake.

被（bèi）(Page 170 Q53, page 215 Q55, page 256 Q45)

Similar to the passive voice (something done by somebody) in English

例：杯子被他的弟弟打破了。
蛋糕沒（有）被我吃完。

Examples: The cup was broken by his younger brother.
The cake was not eaten by me.

除了 …… 以外/之外 …… (chúle …… yǐwài/zhīwài ……)

Except for; except; besides

例：除了學習之外，小明什麼都喜歡。
除了英文以外，我也會中文。

Examples: Xiao Ming likes to do everything except study. *("Apart from studying, Xiao Ming likes to do everything")*
Besides English, I can also speak Chinese.

從 (cóng) (Page 297 Q36)

From; through

例：從香港坐火車去北京要24小時。
我從書上看到了你的照片。

Examples: It takes 24 hours to travel by train from Hong Kong to Beijing. *("From Hong Kong by train to Beijing requires 24 hours.")*
I saw your photos in the book. *("From the book I saw your photos.")*

對(於) (duì(yú)) (Page 124 Q46, page 169 Q49, page 208 Q33)

With regards to

例：對於這本小說，我沒有興趣。
對於這件事，我已經沒什麼好說的了。

Examples: I am not interested in this novel. *("With regards to this novel, I have no interest.")*
I have nothing more to say with regards to this matter. *("With regards to this matter, I have no more to say.")*

跟 (gēn) (Page 124 Q45) [Also see Expressing Similarity]

To; towards; from; with

例：我們跟她學中文。
我跟媽媽去菜市場。

Examples: We are learning Chinese from her.
I went to the market with my mother. *("I followed mother to the market.")*

關於 (guānyú) (Page 258 Q53)

About; on the subject of; with regards to; concerning

例：我想買一本關於音樂的書。
我不想再聽到關於他的消息。

Examples: I want to buy a book about music.
I do not want to hear any more news about him.

讓/給 (ràng/gěi)

Used in a passive sentence to introduce the person or thing doing the action

例：蛋糕都讓他吃光了！
看，衣服給雨淋濕了。

Examples: All the cake has been eaten by him!
Look, the clothes have been soaked by the rain.

據 (jù) (Page 77 Q31)

According to; on the grounds of

例：據天氣預報，明天將會下雨。
據統計，每天有三千人使用這個服務。

Examples: According to the weather forecast, it will rain tomorrow.
According to statistics, 3,000 people use this service everyday.

憑 (píng)

Depend on; go by; based on; take as the basis; with

例：憑著多年的經驗，我們一定會成功。
憑你的實力，一定能通過這次考試。

Examples: Based on many years of experience, we will no doubt be successful.
With your potential, there is no doubt that you will pass this examination.

前後 (qiánhòu)

Around; "before and after"

例：聖誕節前後，我們都放假。
颱風到來前後，千萬別去海灘游泳。

Examples: We are all on vacation around Christmas time. *("Around Christmas, we are all on vacation.")*
Do not go swimming at the beach around the time of the typhoon.
("Before and after the typhoon arrives, do not go to the beach and swim.")

向 (xiàng) (Page 121 Q38)

To; towards; in the direction of

例：我向老師介紹了美國的情況。
氣球飛向了天空。

Examples: I introduced the situation in the USA to my teacher.
The balloon is floating towards the sky.

以 (yǐ) (Page 126 Q53)

With; by

例：我們應該以禮待人。
香港隊以二比一戰勝了上海隊。

Examples: We should be courteous. *("We should treat people with courtesy.")*
The Hong Kong team beat the Shanghai Team by two goals to one.

由 (yóu) (Page 81 Q42, page 164 Q35, page 256 Q47)

By; through

例：這件事由我去辦。
這個比賽由北京主辦。

Examples: I will take care of this matter. *("This matter will be taken care of by me.")*
This competition is hosted by Beijing.

於 (yú)
Indicating time, place, or direction

例：我的哥哥出生於一九九零年。
這個產品於上海製造。

Examples: My brother was born in 1990.
This product is made in Shanghai.

自從 (zìcóng) (Page 166 Q41, page 257 Q50)
Since

例：自從大學畢業以來，小明一直沒找到合適的工作。
自從認識你後，我的心情變得更加開朗。

Examples: Since graduating from university, Xiao Ming has not found a suitable job.
Since I have known you, my mood has become more cheerful.

左右 (zuǒyòu)
About; around

例：晚上十一點左右他才回來。
這棵樹高十米左右。

Examples: He came back at around 11 P.M.
This tree is about 10 meters tall.

Verbs (動詞)

包括 (bāokuò) (Page 258 Q52)
Including

例：住宿費並不包括在內。
這次參加活動的人包括你在內有三十人。

Examples: Accommodation costs are not included.
There are 30 people taking part in this activity, including you. (*"The number of people taking part in this activity, including you, is 30."*)

使 (shǐ) (Page 211 Q43)
Make

例：電腦使我們的生活多姿多彩。
他的話使我明白了許多道理。

Examples: Computers make our lives more colorful.
His words made me understand many principles.

像 (xiàng) (Page 123 Q42) [Also see Expressing Similarity]
As; like

例：天像要下雨了。
他像有心事。

Examples: It looks like it's going to rain. (*"The sky looks like it will rain."*)
It seems like he has some concerns. (*"He looks like he has some concerns."*)

Measure Words

Measure Words for Nouns

Individual measure words

把（bǎ）

Measure word for objects with handles or similar

例：一把扇子；三把梳子

Examples: A hand fan; three combs

杯（bēi）

Cup; glass

Measure word for liquid in terms of the number of cups/glasses

例：一杯水；兩杯牛奶

Examples: A cup of water; two glasses of milk

本（běn）[Also see "冊"]

Volume

Measure word for books, magazines and similar objects

例：一本書；七本雜誌

Examples: A book; seven magazines

部（bù）(Page 213 Q50)

Measure word for movies, books, etc

例：一部電影；六部詞典

Examples: A movie; six dictionaries

Measure word for machines and appliances

例：一部電話；一部相機

Examples: A telephone; a camera

場（chǎng）

Measure word for the frequency of certain activities

例：一場考試；一場面試

Examples: An examination; an interview

Measure word for recreational activities

例：一場比賽；一場音樂會

Examples: A competition; a concert

冊 (cè) [Also see "本"]

Volume; book; copy

Measure word for magazines and books

例：五萬冊雜誌；六冊課本

Examples: 50,000 copies of a magazine; six volumes of a textbook.

頂 (dǐng)

Measure word for objects which have a top, cap, or cover

例：一頂帽子；一頂帳篷

Examples: A hat; a tent

朵 (duǒ) [Also see "枝"]

Measure word for flowers

例：一朵鮮花；五朵玫瑰

Examples: A fresh flower; five roses

份 (fèn) (Page 79 Q38)

Measure word for newspapers, gifts etc

例：三份報紙；一份禮物

Examples: Three newspapers; a gift

封 (fēng)

Measure word for letters, telegrams, etc

例：一封信；九封電子郵件

Examples: A letter; nine e-mails

幅 (fú) (Page 300 Q47)

Measure word for calligraphy, paintings

例：四幅國畫；一幅圖案

Examples: Four Chinese paintings; a graphic

個（ge） (Page 209 Q37)

Measure word for people

例：兩個人；一個學生

Examples: Two people/persons; a student

Measure word for geographical areas, units etc

例：一個國家；八個城市

Examples: A country; eight cities

Measure word for certain objects

例：兩個蘋果；一個玩具

Examples: Two apples; a toy

Measure word for some abstract nouns

例：一個想法；四個問題

Examples: A thought; four questions

間（jiān）

Measure word for houses and buildings

例：一間屋；三間酒店

Examples: A house; three hotels

件（jiàn） (Page 166 Q39)

Measure word for pieces of clothing

例：五件大衣；一件背心

Examples: Five coats; a vest

棵（kē）

Measure word for plants and vegetables

例：一棵樹；兩棵小草

Examples: A tree; two strands of grass

輛（liàng）

Measure word for cars and other vehicles

例：一輛公共汽車；三輛私家車

Examples: A bus; three private cars

名（míng）

Measure word for people

例：七名士兵；一名歌手

Examples: Seven soldiers; a singer

瓶 (píng) (Page 298 Q40)
Measure word for bottles (of liquids).

例：一瓶啤酒；三瓶可樂

Examples: a bottle of beer, three bottles of cola

所 (suǒ) (Page 79 Q36)
Measure word for houses, schools, hospitals etc

例：一所房子；八所學校

Examples: A house; eight schools

條 (tiáo)
Measure word for long, narrow objects

例：一條項鏈；十條裙子

Examples: A necklace; ten dresses

張 (zhāng) (Page 119 Q32, page 298 Q39)
Measure word for flat objects, or objects with a surface

例：一張地圖；四張車票

Examples: A map; four tickets

支 (zhī)
Measure word for songs

例：五支民歌；一支流行歌曲

Examples: Five folk songs; a pop song

枝 (zhī) (Page 256 Q46) [Also see "朵"]
Measure word for flowers (with a stem)

例：一枝花；兩枝玫瑰花

Examples: A flower; two roses

Measure word for rod-shaped objects

例：三枝筆；一枝煙

Examples: Three pens; a cigarette

隻 (zhī)
Measure word for single objects normally found as a pair

例：一隻手套；三隻襪子

Examples: A glove; three socks

Measure word for insects or animals

例：一隻貓；兩隻狗

Examples: A cat; two dogs

座（zuò） (Page 214 Q53)

Measure word for buildings, and other similar large, immovable objects

例：一座紀念碑；四座大橋

Examples: A memorial; four bridges

Measure word for mountains and similar objects

例：一座山峰；兩座冰山

Examples: A mountain; two icebergs

班（bān）

Measure word for means of transport

例：下一班飛機；最後一班地鐵

Examples: The next flight; the last subway train

家（jiā） [Also see "家" in collective measure words for nouns]

Measure word for an institution, enterprise, unit, etc

例：一家銀行；一家酒店

Examples: A bank; a hotel

Partial measure words

塊（kuài）

Measure word for certain types of food

例：六塊蛋糕；一塊西瓜

Examples: Six pieces of cake; a slice of watermelon

篇（piān）

Measure word for pieces of writing, etc

例：一篇文章；一篇散文

Examples: A passage; a short story

片（piàn）

Measure word for thin, flat objects

例：一片麵包；三片樹葉

Examples: A slice of bread; three leaves

Collective measure words

家（jiā） [Also see "家" in individual measure words for nouns]

Measure word for a family

例：一家人；兩家親戚

Examples: A family; two families (of relatives)

群 (qún)

Crowd; flock; herd

Measure word for groups of people, birds or animals

例：一群人；一群羊

Examples: A crowd of people; a flock of sheep

束 (shù)

Bunch; bundle

Measure word for objects of the same kind fastened together

例：一束鮮花；兩束百合花

Examples: A bunch of fresh flowers; two bunches of lilies

雙 (shuāng)

Pair

Measure word for two objects of the same kind to be used together

例：兩雙手套；一雙襪子

Examples: Two pairs of gloves; a pair of socks

Measure word for some parts of the human body

例：一雙腳；一雙手

Examples: A pair of feet; a pair of hands

種 (zhǒng)

Species, kind

Measure word for objects of the same kind

例：一種動物；一種遊戲

Examples: A type of animal; a type of game

Measure word for abstract objects of the same kind

例：一種方法；一種情況

Examples: A kind of method; a kind of situation

Measure words for verbs

遍 (biàn) (Page 127 Q54, page 299 Q42)

Measure word for the course of an action from the beginning to the end

例：看一遍；複習一遍

Examples: Read it once; revise once

趟 (tàng) (Page 254 Q40)

Measure word for "the number of times"

例：去了一趟上海；再走一趟

Examples: Been to Shanghai once; go once again

次 (cì)

Measure word for the number of repetitions of an event or situation

例：一次討論；一次旅遊

Examples: One discussion (*"once discuss"*); one trip (*"once travel"*)

Measure word for the number of times an action is taken

例：去了一次北京；打了三次籃球

Examples: Been to Beijing once; played basketball three times

Measure Words for Both Nouns and Verbs

番 (fān)

Measure word for action which takes time and energy

例：一番努力；一番功夫

Examples: Hard work; effort

Measure word for kindness, flavors, etc

例：一番心意；一番滋味

Examples: Kindness; (good) taste

Plural measure word for the process of certain actions

例：打扮一番；檢查一番

Examples: Dressing up; inspecting

頓 (dùn)

Measure word for regular meals

例：一頓飯；一頓晚餐

Examples: A meal; a dinner

Measure word to express abuse, reprimands, or criticism

例：打一頓；罵一頓

Examples: A beating; a scolding

Vocabulary

Vocabulary

国家	國家	(guójiā)	Countries
澳洲	澳洲	(Àozhōu)	Australia
巴西	巴西	(Bāxī)	Brazil
德国	德國	(Déguó)	Germany
法国	法國	(Fǎguó)	France
韩国	韓國	(Hánguó)	Korea
加拿大	加拿大	(Jiānádà)	Canada
美国	美國	(Měiguó)	USA
墨西哥	墨西哥	(Mòxīgē)	Mexico
欧洲	歐洲	(Ōuzhōu)	Europe
日本	日本	(Rìběn)	Japan
泰国	泰國	(Tàiguó)	Thailand
新加坡	新加坡	(Xīnjiāpō)	Singapore
意大利	意大利	(Yìdàlì)	Italy
英国	英國	(Yīngguó)	UK/England
越南	越南	(Yuènán)	Vietnam
中国	中國	(Zhōngguó)	China

地方	地方	(dìfāng)	Places
公共汽车站	公共汽車站	(gōnggòngqìchēzhàn)	bus stop
办公室	辦公室	(bàngōngshì)	office
菜市场	菜市場	(càishìchǎng)	market
餐厅	餐廳	(cāntīng)	restaurant
超级市场	超級市場	(chāojí shìchǎng)	supermarket
大使馆	大使館	(dàshǐguǎn)	embassy
地铁站	地鐵站	(dìtiězhàn)	metro/subway station
电影院	電影院	(diànyǐngyuàn)	cinema
公园	公園	(gōngyuán)	public park
机场	機場	(jīchǎng)	airport
警察局	警察局	(jǐngchájú)	police station
酒店	酒店	(jiǔdiàn)	hotel
礼堂	禮堂	(lǐtáng)	hall
沙滩	沙灘	(shātān)	beach
商场	商場	(shāngchǎng)	shopping mall
商店	商店	(shāngdiàn)	store
停车场	停車場	(tíngchēchǎng)	parking lot
图书馆	圖書館	(túshūguǎn)	library
洗手间	洗手間	(xǐshǒujiān)	washroom
小卖部	小賣部	(xiǎomàibù)	tuck shop
学校	學校	(xuéxiào)	school
药店	藥店	(yàodiàn)	drug store
医院	醫院	(yīyuàn)	hospital

医务所	醫務所	(yīwùsuǒ)	clinic
银行	銀行	(yínháng)	bank
邮局	郵局	(yóujú)	post office
游泳池	游泳池	(yóuyǒngchí)	swimming pool
运动场	運動場	(yùndòngchǎng)	sports ground

运动	運動	(yùndòng)	Sports
高尔夫球	高爾夫球	(gāo'ěrfūqiú)	golf
功夫	功夫	(gōngfu)	martial arts
滑雪	滑雪	(huáxuě)	skiing
剑道	劍道	(jiǎndào)	fencing
篮球	籃球	(lánqiú)	basketball
空手道	空手道	(kōngshǒudào)	karate
排球	排球	(páiqiú)	volleyball
跑步	跑步	(pǎobù)	jogging/running
乒乓球	乒乓球	(pīngpāngqiú)	table tennis
骑自行车	騎自行車	(qízìxíngchē)	cycling
拳击	拳擊	(quánjī)	boxing
柔道	柔道	(róudào)	judo
跆拳道	跆拳道	(táiquándào)	taekwondo
跳高	跳高	(tiàogāo)	high-jump
跳远	跳遠	(tiàoyuǎn)	long-jump
网球	網球	(wǎngqiú)	tennis
游泳	游泳	(yóuyǒng)	swimming
羽毛球	羽毛球	(yǔmáoqiú)	badminton
足球	足球	(zúqiú)	football/soccer

娱乐	娛樂	(yúlè)	Entertainment
唱歌	唱歌	(chànggē)	singing
电脑游戏	電腦遊戲	(diànnǎoyóuxì)	computer game
古典音乐	古典音樂	(gǔdiǎn yīnyuè)	classical music
绘画	繪畫	(huìhuà)	painting
看电视	看電視	(kàn diànshì)	watch television
看电影	看電影	(kàn diànyǐng)	watch a movie
拉小提琴	拉小提琴	(lā xiǎotíqín)	play the violin
流行音乐	流行音樂	(liúxíng yīnyuè)	pop music
旅行	旅行	(lǚxíng)	travel
上网	上網	(shàngwǎng)	surf the Internet
摄影	攝影	(shèyǐng)	photography
书法	書法	(shūfǎ)	calligraphy
弹钢琴	彈鋼琴	(tán gāngqín)	play the piano
跳舞	跳舞	(tiàowǔ)	dancing
听音乐	聽音樂	(tīng yīnyuè)	listen to music
戏剧	戲劇	(xìjù)	drama

天气	天氣	(tiānqì)	Weather
大风雪	大風雪	(dàfēngxuě)	snowstorm
打雷	打雷	(dǎlié)	thunder
度	度	(dù)	degree (temperature)
多云	多雲	(duōyún)	cloudy
刮风	颳風	(guāfēng)	windy
冷	冷	(lěng)	cold
凉快	涼快	(liángkuai)	cool
零下	零下	(língxià)	below zero
毛毛雨	毛毛雨	(máomaoyǔ)	drizzle
暖和	暖和	(nuǎnhuo)	warm
晴天	晴天	(qíngtiān)	sunny
晴转多云	晴轉多雲	(qíng zhuǎn duō yún)	sunny, becoming cloudy
热	熱	(rè)	hot
闪电	閃電	(shǎndiàn)	lightning
台风	颱風	(táifēng)	typhoon
下雪	下雪	(xiàxuě)	snow
下雨	下雨	(xiàyǔ)	rain
阴天	陰天	(yīntiān)	cloudy/overcast
雨天	雨天	(yǔtiān)	rainy

服饰	服飾	(fúshì)	Clothing
长裤	長褲	(chángkù)	trousers
长袖	長袖	(chángxiù)	long-sleeve
衬衫	襯衫	(chènshān)	shirt
短裤	短褲	(duǎnkù)	shorts
短袖	短袖	(duǎnxiù)	short-sleeve
高跟鞋	高跟鞋	(gāogēnxié)	high-heel shoes
外套	外套	(wàitào)	jacket
汗衫	汗衫	(hànshān)	T-shirt
连衣裙	連衣裙	(liányīqún)	long dress
领带	領帶	(lǐngdài)	neck tie
毛衣	毛衣	(máoyī)	woolen sweater
帽子	帽子	(màozi)	hat
牛仔裤	牛仔褲	(niúzǎikù)	jeans
皮带	皮帶	(pídài)	leather belt
皮鞋	皮鞋	(píxié)	leather shoes
裙子	裙子	(qúnzi)	skirt
手表	手錶	(shǒubiǎo)	watch
手套	手套	(shǒutào)	gloves
睡衣	睡衣	(shuìyī)	pajamas
太阳眼镜	太陽眼鏡	(tàiyángyǎnjìng)	sunglasses
拖鞋	拖鞋	(tuōxié)	slippers
袜子	襪子	(wàzi)	socks

围巾	圍巾	(wéijīn)	scarf
西装	西裝	(xīzhuāng)	suit
校服	校服	(xiàofú)	school uniform
眼镜	眼鏡	(yǎnjìng)	glasses
游泳衣	游泳衣	(yóuyǒngyī)	swimsuit
雨衣	雨衣	(yǔyī)	raincoat
运动服	運動服	(yǔndòngfú)	sportswear
运动鞋	運動鞋	(yùndòngxié)	sports shoes

科目 科目 (kēmù) Subjects

德文	德文	(Déwén)	German
地理	地理	(dìlǐ)	Geography
电脑	電腦	(diànnǎo)	Computer studies
化学	化學	(huàxué)	Chemistry
家政	家政	(jiāzhèng)	Home economics
科学	科學	(kēxué)	Science
历史	歷史	(lìshǐ)	History
美术	美術	(měishù)	Art
日文	日文	(Rìwén)	Japanese
生物	生物	(shēngwù)	Biology
数学	數學	(shùxué)	Mathematics
体育	體育	(tǐyù)	Physical education
物理	物理	(wùlǐ)	Physics
西班牙文	西班牙文	(Xībānyáwén)	Spanish
英文	英文	(Yīngwén)	English
音乐	音樂	(yīnyuè)	Music
中文	中文	(Zhōngwén)	Chinese

颜色 顏色 (yánsè) Colors

白色	白色	(báisè)	white
粉红色	粉紅色	(fěnhóngsè)	pink
红色	紅色	(hóngsè)	red
黄色	黃色	(huángsè)	yellow
黑色	黑色	(hēisè)	black
灰色	灰色	(huīsè)	gray
蓝色	藍色	(lánsè)	blue
绿色	綠色	(lǜsè)	green
浅	淺	(qiǎn)	light
浅蓝色	淺藍色	(qiǎnlánsè)	light blue
深	深	(shēn)	dark
深蓝色	深藍色	(shēnlánsè)	dark blue
棕色	棕色	(zōngsè)	brown
紫色	紫色	(zǐsè)	purple

食物	食物	(shíwù)	Food
炒饭	炒飯	(chǎofàn)	fried rice
春卷	春卷	(chūnjuǎn)	spring roll
蛋糕	蛋糕	(dàngāo)	cake
点心	點心	(diǎnxīn)	snack/Dim Sum
豆腐	豆腐	(dòufu)	bean curd/tofu
饭	飯	(fàn)	rice
果酱	果醬	(guǒjiàng)	jam
花生	花生	(huāshēng)	peanut
黄油	黃油	(huángyóu)	butter
火腿	火腿	(huǒtuǐ)	ham
鸡蛋	雞蛋	(jīdàn)	egg
鸡肉	雞肉	(jīròu)	chicken
酱油	醬油	(jiàngyóu)	soy sauce
烤鸭	烤鴨	(kǎoyā)	roast duck
面包	麵包	(miànbāo)	bread
面条	麵條	(miàntiáo)	noodles
奶酪	奶酪	(nǎilào)	cheese
牛肉	牛肉	(niúròu)	beef
巧克力	巧克力	(qiǎokèlì)	chocolate
热狗	熱狗	(règǒu)	hot dog
肉	肉	(ròu)	meat
三明治	三明治	(sānmíngzhì)	sandwich
薯条	薯條	(shǔtiáo)	French fries
酸奶	酸奶	(suānnǎi)	yoghurt
糖	糖	(táng)	sugar
糖果	糖果	(tángguǒ)	sweets/candies
甜品	甜品	(tiánpǐn)	dessert
香肠	香腸	(xiāngcháng)	sausage
盐	鹽	(yán)	salt
羊肉	羊肉	(yángròu)	lamb/mutton
油条	油條	(yóutiáo)	fritters
鱼	魚	(yú)	fish
玉米	玉米	(yùmǐ)	corn
粥	粥	(zhōu)	congee
猪肉	豬肉	(zhūròu)	pork

饮品	飲品	(yínpǐn)	Drinks
白开水	白開水	(báikāishuǐ)	boiled water
冰水	冰水	(bīngshuǐ)	ice water
茶	茶	(chá)	tea
豆浆	豆漿	(dòujiāng)	soy bean milk
果汁	果汁	(guǒzhī)	fruit juice
红茶	紅茶	(hóngchá)	tea

红酒	紅酒	(hóngjiǔ)	red wine
橙汁	橙汁	(chéngzhī)	orange juice
咖啡	咖啡	(kāfēi)	coffee
可乐	可樂	(kělè)	Coca-cola
绿茶	綠茶	(lǜchá)	green tea
奶茶	奶茶	(nǎichá)	milk tea
牛奶	牛奶	(niúnǎi)	milk
啤酒	啤酒	(píjiǔ)	beer
汽水	汽水	(qìshuǐ)	soft drink/soda
汤	湯	(tāng)	soup

蔬菜和水果	蔬菜和水果	(shūcài hé shuǐguǒ)	Fruits and vegetables
白菜	白菜	(báicài)	cabbage
草莓	草莓	(cǎoméi)	strawberry
胡萝卜	胡蘿蔔	(húluóbo)	carrot
黄瓜	黃瓜	(huángguā)	cucumber
橙子	橙子	(chéngzi)	orange
梨	梨	(lí)	pear
李子	李子	(lǐzi)	plum
木瓜	木瓜	(mùguā)	papaya
南瓜	南瓜	(nánguā)	pumpkin
苹果	蘋果	(píngguǒ)	apple
葡萄	葡萄	(pútao)	grapes
桃子	桃子	(táozi)	peach
土豆	土豆	(tǔdòu)	potato
西瓜	西瓜	(xīguā)	watermelon
香蕉	香蕉	(xiāngjiāo)	banana
西红柿	西紅柿	(xīhóngshì)	tomato

职业	職業	(zhíyè)	Jobs
厨师	廚師	(chúshī)	cook/chef
法官	法官	(fǎguān)	judge (court)
服务员	服務員	(fúwùyuán)	waiter
歌手	歌手	(gēshǒu)	singer
护士	護士	(hùshi)	nurse
画家	畫家	(huàjiā)	artist (painting)
记者	記者	(jìzhě)	journalist
家庭主妇	家庭主婦	(jiātíngzhǔfù)	housewife
警察	警察	(jǐngchá)	policeman
经理	經理	(jīnglǐ)	manager
老板	老闆	(lǎobǎn)	boss
老师/教师	老師/教師	(lǎoshī/jiàoshī)	teacher
律师	律師	(lǜshī)	lawyer
司机	司機	(sījī)	driver

设计师	設計師	(shèjìshī)	designer
商人	商人	(shāngrén)	businessman
售货员	售貨員	(shòuhuòyuán)	salesperson
舞蹈员	舞蹈員	(wǔdǎoyuán)	dancer
消防员	消防員	(xiāofángyuán)	fireman
学生	學生	(xuésheng)	student
演员	演員	(yǎnyuán)	actor
医生	醫生	(yīshēng)	doctor
银行家	銀行家	(yínhángjiā)	banker
音乐家	音樂家	(yīnyuèjiā)	musician
邮递员	郵遞員	(yóudìyuán)	postman
运动员	運動員	(yùndòngyuán)	athlete
职员	職員	(zhíyuán)	clerk
作家	作家	(zuòjiā)	writer

动植物	動植物	(dòngzhíwù)	Animals & plants
大象	大象	(dàxiàng)	elephant
鹅	鵝	(é)	goose
狗	狗	(gǒu)	dog
花	花	(huā)	flower
鸡	雞	(jī)	chicken
老虎	老虎	(lǎohǔ)	tiger
马	馬	(mǎ)	horse
猫	貓	(māo)	cat
玫瑰花	玫瑰花	(méiguihuā)	rose
牛	牛	(niú)	cow
狮子	獅子	(shīzi)	lion
树	樹	(shù)	tree
兔	兔	(tù)	rabbit
小草	小草	(xiǎocǎo)	grass
鸭	鴨	(yā)	duck
羊	羊	(yáng)	sheep
鱼	魚	(yú)	fish
猪	豬	(zhū)	pig

病	病	(bìng)	Sickness
打针	打針	(dǎzhēn)	have an injection
动手术	動手術	(dòngshǒushù)	have an operation
发烧	發燒	(fāshāo)	fever
感冒	感冒	(gǎnmào)	cold/flu
健康	健康	(jiànkāng)	health/healthy
康复	康復	(kāngfù)	recover

咳嗽	咳嗽	(késou)	cough
拉肚子	拉肚子	(lādùzi)	diarrhea
量体温	量體溫	(liángtǐ wēn)	take the body temperature
流血	流血	(liúxuè)	bleeding
嗓子疼	嗓子疼	(sǎngziténg)	sore throat
头疼	頭疼	(tóuténg)	headache
牙疼	牙疼	(yáténg)	toothache
药片	藥片	(yàopiàn)	pills/tablets
止咳药水	止咳藥水	(zhǐkéyàoshuǐ)	cough syrup

家庭	家庭	(jiātíng)	Family
阿姨	阿姨	(āyí)	aunt
爸爸	爸爸	(bàba)	father
弟弟	弟弟	(dìdi)	younger brother
哥哥	哥哥	(gēge)	older brother
姐姐	姐姐	(jiějie)	older sister
妈妈	媽媽	(māma)	mother
妹妹	妹妹	(mèimei)	younger sister
叔叔	叔叔	(shūshu)	uncle
外祖父/外公	外祖父/外公	(wàizǔfù/wàigōng)	grandfather (mother's side)
外祖母/外婆	外祖母/外婆	(wàizǔmǔ/wàipó)	grandmother (mother's side)
祖父/爷爷	祖父/爺爺	(zǔfù/yěye)	grandfather (father's side)
祖母/奶奶	祖母/奶奶	(zǔmǔ/nǎinai)	grandmother (father's side)

身体	身體	(shēntǐ)	Parts of the body
鼻子	鼻子	(bízi)	nose
耳朵	耳朵	(ěrduo)	ear
喉咙	喉嚨	(hóulóng)	throat
脚	腳	(jiǎo)	foot
脸	臉	(liǎn)	face
舌头	舌頭	(shétou)	tongue
身体	身體	(shēntǐ)	body
手	手	(shǒu)	hand
手指	手指	(shǒuzhǐ)	finger
头	頭	(tóu)	head
头发	頭髮	(tóufa)	hair
腿	腿	(tuǐ)	leg
牙齿	牙齒	(yáchǐ)	tooth
眼睛	眼睛	(yǎnjing)	eyes
嘴巴	嘴巴	(zuǐba)	mouth

文具	文具	(wénjù)	Stationery
书包	書包	(shūbāo)	school bag
电脑	電腦	(diànnǎo)	computer
计算器	計算器	(jìsuànqì)	calculator
课本	課本	(kèběn)	textbook
铅笔	鉛筆	(qiānbǐ)	pencil
文件夹	文件夾	(wénjiànjiā)	folder
橡皮	橡皮	(xiàngpí)	eraser
圆珠笔	圓珠筆	(yuánzhūbǐ)	ball pen
字典	字典	(zìdiǎn)	dictionary

动词	動詞	(dòngcí)	verb
帮忙	幫忙	(bāngmáng)	help
保护	保護	(bǎohù)	protect
报名	報名	(bàomíng)	register/enroll
毕业	畢業	(bìyè)	graduate
表演	表演	(biǎoyǎn)	perform (in a show)
泊车	泊車	(bóchē)	park the car
播放	播放	(bōfàng)	play (a CD, video tape etc)
参加	參加	(cānjiā)	take part
称赞	稱讚	(chēngzàn)	praise
出版	出版	(chūbǎn)	publish
打扰	打擾	(dǎrǎo)	disturb
答应	答應	(dāying)	agree/promise
道歉	道歉	(dàoqiàn)	apologize
发生	發生	(fāshēng)	happen
发现	發現	(fāxiàn)	discover
发展	發展	(fāzhǎn)	develop
付款	付款	(fùkuǎn)	pay
改变	改變	(gǎibiàn)	change
感到	感到	(gǎndào)	feel
恭贺	恭賀	(gōnghè)	congratulate
关	關	(guān)	close
逛街	逛街	(guàngjiē)	go shopping
花	花	(huā)	spend
换	換	(huàn)	change/exchange
计划	計劃	(jìhuà)	plan
寄信	寄信	(jìxìn)	send a letter
践踏	踐踏	(jiàntà)	step on/trample on
建议	建議	(jiànyì)	suggest
解决	解決	(jiějué)	solve/resolve
介绍	介紹	(jièshào)	introduce
联系	聯繫	(liánxì)	contact
练习	練習	(liànxí)	practice

爬	爬	(pá)	climb
认识	認識	(rènshi)	know
扔垃圾	扔垃圾	(rēng lājī)	dispose of rubbish
庆祝	慶祝	(qìngzhù)	celebrate
欺骗	欺騙	(qīpiàn)	cheat/lie
申请	申請	(shēnqǐng)	apply for
收	收	(shōu)	receive
售	售	(shòu)	sell
探望	探望	(tànwàng)	visit
讨论	討論	(tǎolùn)	discuss
提供	提供	(tígōng)	provide
贴	貼	(tiē)	stick
退钱	退錢	(tuìqián)	refund
完成	完成	(wánchéng)	finish
忘记	忘記	(wàngjì)	forget
喜欢	喜歡	(xǐhuan)	like
吸煙（抽煙）	吸烟（抽烟）	(xīyān) (chōuyān)	smoke
休息	休息	(xiūxi)	rest
下车	下車	(xiàchē)	alight (from a bus, train etc)
相信	相信	(xiāngxìn)	believe
需要	需要	(xūyào)	need/require
询问	詢問	(xúnwèn)	enquire
喧哗	喧嘩	(xuānhuá)	shout/make noise
遗失	遺失	(yíshī)	lose (an article/object)
营业	營業	(yíngyè)	do business
遇到	遇到	(yùdào)	encounter
预订	預訂	(yùdìng)	place an (advance) order
原谅	原諒	(yuánliàng)	forgive
照顾	照顧	(zhàogu)	take care of
招聘	招聘	(zhāopìn)	recruit
找赎	找贖	(zhǎoshú)	give change
责怪	責怪	(zéguài)	blame
赚	賺	(zhuàn)	earn
准备	準備	(zhǔnbèi)	prepare
租	租	(zū)	rent

形容词 形容詞 (xíng róng cí) Adjectives

矮	矮	(ǎi)	short (person/tree etc)
安全	安全	(ānquán)	safe
笨	笨	(bèn)	stupid
长	長	(cháng)	long
丑	醜	(chǒu)	ugly
聪明	聰明	(cōngming)	clever

大	大	(dà)	big
短	短	(duǎn)	short (length)
方便	方便	(fāngbiàn)	convenient
干净	乾淨	(gānjìng)	clean
高	高	(gāo)	tall
高兴	高興	(gāoxìng)	happy
贵	貴	(guì)	expensive
健康	健康	(jiànkāng)	healthy
旧	舊	(jiù)	old
可爱	可愛	(kě'ài)	cute/lovely
快	快	(kuài)	fast
老	老	(lǎo)	old
累	累	(lèi)	tired
流行	流行	(liúxíng)	popular
满	滿	(mǎn)	full
忙	忙	(máng)	busy
美味	美味	(měiwèi)	delicious
难	難	(nán)	difficult
难过	難過	(nánguò)	sad
年轻	年輕	(niánqīng)	young
胖	胖	(pàng)	fat
漂亮	漂亮	(piàoliang)	pretty
便宜	便宜	(piányi)	cheap
轻	輕	(qīng)	light
轻松	輕鬆	(qīngsōng)	relaxed
容易	容易	(róngyì)	easy
伤心	傷心	(shāngxīn)	sad
瘦	瘦	(shòu)	thin
舒服	舒服	(shūfu)	comfortable
无聊	無聊	(wúliáo)	bored
小	小	(xiǎo)	small
新	新	(xīn)	new
严重	嚴重	(yánzhòng)	serious/severe
有趣的	有趣的	(yǒuqùde)	funny
有意思	有意思	(yǒuyìsi)	meaningful
脏	髒	(zāng)	dirty
重	重	(zhòng)	heavy
著名	著名	(zhùmíng)	famous

Practice Tests

SAT Chinese Practice Test — One

SAT 中文模拟试题 — 第一套

SAT 中文模擬試題 — 第一套

Time — 1 hour

Questions 1 - 85

PLEASE NOTE THAT YOUR ANSWER SHEET HAS FOUR ANSWER POSITIONS, MARKED A, B, C, AND D, WHILE THE QUESTIONS THROUGHOUT THIS TEST CONTAIN EITHER THREE OR FOUR ANSWER CHOICES. BE SURE NOT TO MARK YOUR ANSWERS IN COLUMN D IF THERE ARE ONLY THREE CHOICES GIVEN.

SECTION I
LISTENING

Approximate time — 20 minutes

Questions 1 - 30

Part A

Directions:

In this part of the test, you will hear short questions, statements, or commands in Mandarin Chinese, followed by three responses in Mandarin Chinese, designated (A), (B), and (C). You will hear the questions or statements, as well as the responses, only once, and they are not printed in your test booklet. Therefore, you must listen very carefully. Select the best response and fill in the corresponding circle on your answer sheet.

Question 1 Mark your answer on your answer sheet.

Question 2 Mark your answer on your answer sheet.

Question 3 Mark your answer on your answer sheet.

Question 4 Mark your answer on your answer sheet.

Question 5 Mark your answer on your answer sheet.

Question 6 Mark your answer on your answer sheet.

Question 7 Mark your answer on your answer sheet.

Question 8 Mark your answer on your answer sheet.

Question 9 Mark your answer on your answer sheet.

Question 10 Mark your answer on your answer sheet.

Question 11 Mark your answer on your answer sheet.

Question 12 Mark your answer on your answer sheet.

Question 13 Mark your answer on your answer sheet.

Question 14 Mark your answer on your answer sheet.

Question 15 Mark your answer on your answer sheet.

Part B

Directions:

You will now hear a series of dialogues. You will hear them only once, and they are not printed in your test booklet. After each selection, you will be asked to answer one or more questions about what you have just heard. These questions, each with four possible answers, are printed in your test booklet. Select the best answer to each question from among the four choices printed and fill in the corresponding circle on your answer sheet.

Questions 16-17

16. What is the relationship between the two people?
    (A) Classmates
    (B) Colleagues
    (C) Friends
    (D) Husband and wife

17. What does the woman plan to do these days?
    (A) Travel abroad
    (B) Go to work
    (C) Rest at home
    (D) Find another job

Questions 18-20

18. Which team won the game yesterday?
    (A) USA
    (B) China
    (C) U.K.
    (D) It was a draw

19. What was the final score?
    (A) 68 : 78
    (B) 86 : 66
    (C) 86 : 86
    (D) 86 : 78

20. Which one of the following statements about the dialogue is true?
    (A) The man and the woman were watching the game together.
    (B) The man was working over-time yesterday.
    (C) The woman knew the final score.
    (D) The man thinks that the Chinese team put on a satisfactory performance.

Questions 21-22

21. What are the two people planning to do tomorrow?
    (A) Borrow some books from the library
    (B) Enroll for a course
    (C) Go to a lecture
    (D) Go to class

22. When are they going to register?
    (A) This afternoon
    (B) Tomorrow afternoon
    (C) 9 A.M. today
    (D) 9 A.M. tomorrow

Questions 23-24

23. What did Wangling ask the man to buy for her?
    (A) A ticket
    (B) A book
    (C) A computer
    (D) Some furniture

24. What did the woman ask the man to do?
    (A) Leave a contact number
    (B) Call back later
    (C) Come and visit when he is free
    (D) Wait for her at home

Questions 25-26

25. What is the cost for a room without a private bathroom?
    (A) $250 per day
    (B) $200 per day
    (C) $150 per day
    (D) $100 per day

26. What kind of identification does the man have to provide?
    (A) Passport
    (B) ID card
    (C) Credit card
    (D) Driver's license

Questions 27-28

27. When is Chinese New Year's day?
    (A) 19th of this month
    (B) 20th of this month
    (C) 21st of this month
    (D) 22nd of this month

28. Where is the man planning to go on holiday?
    (A) China
    (B) Singapore
    (C) Japan
    (D) USA

Questions 29-30

29. What did the man want to order originally?
    (A) A glass of lemon juice
    (B) A glass of apple juice
    (C) A glass of pineapple juice
    (D) A glass of orange juice

30. What does the man order in the end?
    (A) A glass of lemon juice
    (B) A glass of apple juice
    (C) A glass of pineapple juice
    (D) Nothing

SECTION II
USAGE

Suggested time — 15 minutes

Questions 31 - 55

Part A

Directions:

This section consists of a number of incomplete statements, each of which has four possible completions. Select the word or phrase that best completes the sentence structurally and logically and fill in the corresponding circle on your answer sheet.

This section of the test is presented in four different ways of representing Chinese: traditional characters, simplified characters, pinyin romanization, and the Chinese phonetic alphabet. IT IS RECOMMEMD THAT YOU CHOOSE THE WRITING SYSTEM WITH WHICH YOU ARE MORE FAMILIAR WITH AND **ONLY READ THAT VERSION** AS YOU WORK THROUGH THIS SECTION OF THE TEST.

31. __C__专家介绍，这种树不太常见。
(A) 说
(B) 由
(C) 据
(D) 对

31. __C__專家介紹，這種樹不太常見。
(A) 說
(B) 由
(C) 據
(D) 對

31. _____ zhuānjiā jièshào, zhè zhǒng shù bú tài chángjiàn.
(A) Shuō
(B) Yóu
(C) Jù
(D) Duì

31. __C__ ㄓㄨㄢ ㄐㄧㄚ ㄐㄧㄝˋ ㄕㄠˋ，ㄓㄜˋ ㄓㄨㄥˇ ㄕㄨˋ ㄅㄨˊ ㄊㄞˋ ㄔㄤˊ ㄐㄧㄢˋ。
(A) ㄕㄨㄛ
(B) ㄧㄡˊ
(C) ㄐㄩˋ
(D) ㄉㄨㄟˋ

32. 妈妈_____去了。
(A) 到学校已经妹妹带
(B) 妹妹带到学校已经
(C) 学校已经到妹妹带
(D) 已经带妹妹到学校

32. 媽媽__D__去了。
(A) 到學校已經妹妹帶
(B) 妹妹帶到學校已經
(C) 學校已經到妹妹帶
(D) 已經帶妹妹到學校

32. Māma_____qùle.
(A) dào xuéxiào yǐjīng mèimei dài
(B) mèimei dài dào xuéxiào yǐjīng
(C) xuéxiào yǐjīng dào mèimei dài
(D) yǐjīng dài mèimei dào xuéxiào

32. ㄇㄚ ˙ㄇㄚ __D__ ㄑㄩˋ ˙ㄌㄜ。
(A) ㄉㄠˋ ㄒㄩㄝˊ ㄒㄧㄠˋ ㄧˇ ㄐㄧㄥ ㄇㄟˋ ˙ㄇㄟ ㄉㄞˋ
(B) ㄇㄟˋ ˙ㄇㄟ ㄉㄞˋ ㄉㄠˋ ㄒㄩㄝˊ ㄒㄧㄠˋ ㄧˇ ㄐㄧㄥ
(C) ㄒㄩㄝˊ ㄒㄧㄠˋ ㄧˇ ㄐㄧㄥ ㄉㄠˋ ㄇㄟˋ ˙ㄇㄟ ㄉㄞˋ
(D) ㄧˇ ㄐㄧㄥ ㄉㄞˋ ㄇㄟˋ ˙ㄇㄟ ㄉㄠˋ ㄒㄩㄝˊ ㄒㄧㄠˋ

33. ____出国念书要花很多钱，____他仍然要去。

(A) 无论 …… 但
(B) 即使 …… 也
(C) 哪些 …… 却
(D) 尽管 …… 但

33. ____chūguó niànshū yào huā hěnduō qián, ____tā réngrán yào qù.

(A) Wúlùn …… dàn
(B) Jíshǐ …… yě
(C) Nǎxiē …… què
(D) Jǐnguǎn …… dàn

34. 考完了一场试，____。

(A) 同学们了都下来放松
(B) 都下来放松同学们了
(C) 放松同学们都下来了
(D) 同学们都放松下来了

34. Kǎo wán le yì chǎng shì, ____.

(A) tóngxuémen le dōu xiàlai fàngsōng
(B) dōu xiàlai fàngsōng tóngxuémen le
(C) fàngsōng tóngxuémen dōu xiàlai le
(D) tóngxuémen dōu fàngsōng xiàlai le

35. 他____成绩好，运动____很好。

(A) 不仅 …… 也
(B) 不但 …… 而且
(C) 不仅 …… 不
(D) 不但 …… 反而

35. Tā____chéngjì hǎo, yùndòng____ hěn hǎo.

(A) Bùjǐn …… yě
(B) Bùdàn …… érqiě
(C) Bùjǐn …… bù
(D) Bùdàn …… fǎn'ér

33. __D__出國念書要花很多錢，____他仍然要去。

(A) 無論 …… 但
(B) 即使 …… 也
(C) 哪些 …… 卻
(D) 儘管 …… 但

33. __D__ㄔㄨ ㄍㄨㄛˊ ㄋㄧㄢˋ ㄕㄨ ㄧㄠˋ ㄏㄨㄚ ㄏㄣˇ ㄉㄨㄛ ㄑㄧㄢˊ，____ ㄊㄚ ㄖㄥˊ ㄖㄢˊ ㄧㄠˋ ㄑㄩˋ。

(A) ㄨˊ ㄌㄨㄣˋ …… ㄉㄢˋ
(B) ㄐㄧˊ ㄕˇ …… ㄧㄝˇ
(C) ㄋㄚˇ ㄒㄧㄝ …… ㄑㄩㄝˋ
(D) ㄐㄧㄣˇ ㄍㄨㄢˇ …… ㄉㄢˋ

34. 考完了一場試，__D__。

(A) 同學們了都下來放鬆
(B) 都下來放鬆同學們了
(C) 放鬆同學們都下來了
(D) 同學們都放鬆下來了

34. ㄎㄠˇ ㄨㄢˊ ㄌㄜ˙ ㄧˋ ㄔㄤˇ ㄕˋ，__D__。

(A) ㄊㄨㄥˊ ㄒㄩㄝˊ ㄇㄣ˙ ㄌㄜ˙ ㄉㄡ ㄒㄧㄚˋ ㄌㄞ˙ ㄈㄤˋ ㄙㄨㄥ
(B) ㄉㄡ ㄒㄧㄚˋ ㄌㄞ˙ ㄈㄤˋ ㄙㄨㄥ ㄊㄨㄥˊ ㄒㄩㄝˊ ㄇㄣ˙ ㄌㄜ˙
(C) ㄈㄤˋ ㄙㄨㄥ ㄊㄨㄥˊ ㄒㄩㄝˊ ㄇㄣ˙ ㄉㄡ ㄒㄧㄚˋ ㄌㄞ˙ ㄌㄜ˙
(D) ㄊㄨㄥˊ ㄒㄩㄝˊ ㄇㄣ˙ ㄉㄡ ㄈㄤˋ ㄙㄨㄥ ㄒㄧㄚˋ ㄌㄞ˙ ㄌㄜ˙

35. 他__A__成績好，運動____很好。

(A) 不僅 …… 也
(B) 不但 …… 而且
(C) 不僅 …… 不
(D) 不但 …… 反而

35. ㄊㄚ __A__ ㄔㄥˊ ㄐㄧˋ ㄏㄠˇ，ㄩㄣˋ ㄉㄨㄥˋ ____ ㄏㄣˇ ㄏㄠˇ。

(A) ㄅㄨˋ ㄐㄧㄣˇ …… ㄧㄝˇ
(B) ㄅㄨˋ ㄉㄢˋ …… ㄦˊ ㄑㄧㄝˇ
(C) ㄅㄨˋ ㄐㄧㄣˇ …… ㄅㄨˋ
(D) ㄅㄨˋ ㄉㄢˋ …… ㄈㄢˇ ㄦˊ

36. 美国有很多____世界知名的大学。
(A) 顶
(B) 张
(C) 客
(D) 所

36. Měiguó yǒu hěnduō ____ shìjiè zhīmíng de dàxué.
(A) dǐng
(B) zhāng
(C) kè
(D) suǒ

37. ____一年的学习，他的汉语有了很大进步。
(A) 已经
(B) 经过
(C) 或者
(D) 甚至

37. ____ yì nián de xuéxí, tā de Hànyǔ yǒu le hěn dà jìnbù.
(A) Yǐjīng
(B) Jīngguò
(C) Huòzh
(D) Shènzhì

38. 每天早晨，他都买一____报纸。
(A) 本
(B) 册
(C) 片
(D) 份

38. Měitiān zǎochén, tā dōu mǎi yī ____ bàozhǐ.
(A) běn
(B) cè
(C) piàn
(D) fèn

36. 美國有很多__D__世界知名的大學。
(A) 頂
(B) 張
(C) 客
(D) 所

36. ㄇㄟˇ ㄍㄨㄛˊ ㄧㄡˇ ㄏㄣˇ ㄉㄨㄛ __D__ ㄕˋ ㄐㄧㄝˋ ㄓ ㄇㄧㄥˊ ˙ㄉㄜ ㄉㄚˋ ㄒㄩㄝˊ。
(A) ㄉㄧㄥˇ
(B) ㄓㄤ
(C) ㄎㄜˋ
(D) ㄙㄨㄛˇ

37. __B__一年的學習，他的漢語有了很大進步。
(A) 已經
(B) 經過
(C) 或者
(D) 甚至

37. __B__ ㄧˋ ㄋㄧㄢˊ ˙ㄉㄜ ㄒㄩㄝˊ ㄒㄧˊ，ㄊㄚ ˙ㄉㄜ ㄏㄢˋ ㄩˇ ㄧㄡˇ ˙ㄌㄜ ㄏㄣˇ ㄉㄚˋ ㄐㄧㄣˋ ㄅㄨˋ。
(A) ㄧˇ ㄐㄧㄥ
(B) ㄐㄧㄥ ㄍㄨㄛˋ
(C) ㄏㄨㄛˋ ㄓㄜˇ
(D) ㄕㄣˋ ㄓˋ

38. 每天早晨，他都買一__D__報紙。
(A) 本
(B) 冊
(C) 片
(D) 份

38. ㄇㄟˇ ㄊㄧㄢ ㄗㄠˇ ㄔㄣˊ，ㄊㄚ ㄉㄡ ㄇㄞˇ ㄧ __D__ ㄅㄠˋ ㄓˇ。
(A) ㄅㄣˇ
(B) ㄘㄜˋ
(C) ㄆㄧㄢˋ
(D) ㄈㄣˋ

39. 认识他的人，____ 称赞他是个好人。

(A) 无非
(B) 无不
(C) 非不
(D) 别不

39. Rènshi tā de rén, ____ chēngzàn tā shì ge hǎorén.

(A) wúfēi
(B) wúbù
(C) fēibù
(D) biébù

40. 很多爱美的女生常常____ 减肥而不吃东西。

(A) 因此
(B) 为了
(C) 虽然
(D) 即使

40. Hěnduō àiměi de nǚshēng chángcháng ____ jiǎnféi ér bù chī dōngxi.

(A) yīncǐ
(B) wèile
(C) suīrán
(D) jíshǐ

41. 夏天的南极，气温仍在零下四十度左右，____ 穿上很多衣服，____ 会感到寒冷。

(A) 如果 …… 那么
(B) 尽管 …… 但是
(C) 即使 …… 也
(D) 只要 …… 就

41. Xiàtiān de Nánjí, qìwēn réng zài língxià sìshí dù zuǒyòu, ____ chuān shàng hěn duō yīfu, ____ huì gǎndào hánlěng.

(A) rúguǒ …… nàme
(B) jǐnguǎn …… dànshì
(C) jíshǐ …… yě
(D) zhǐyào …… jiù

39. 認識他的人，__B__ 稱讚他是個好人。

(A) 無非
(B) 無不
(C) 非不
(D) 別不

39. ㄖㄣˋ ㄕˋ ㄊㄚ ㄉㄜ˙ ㄖㄣˊ，__B__ ㄔㄥ ㄗㄢˋ ㄊㄚ ㄕˋ ㄍㄜ˙ ㄏㄠˇ ㄖㄣˊ。

(A) ㄨˊ ㄈㄟ
(B) ㄨˊ ㄅㄨˋ
(C) ㄈㄟ ㄅㄨˋ
(D) ㄅㄧㄝˊ ㄅㄨˋ

40. 很多愛美的女生常常__B__ 減肥而不吃東西。

(A) 因此
(B) 爲了
(C) 雖然
(D) 即使

40. ㄏㄣˇ ㄉㄨㄛ ㄞˋ ㄇㄟˇ ㄉㄜ˙ ㄋㄩˇ ㄕㄥ ㄔㄤˊ ㄔㄤˊ __B__ ㄐㄧㄢˇ ㄈㄟˊ ㄦˊ ㄅㄨˋ ㄔ ㄉㄨㄥ ㄒㄧ˙。

(A) ㄧㄣ ㄘˇ
(B) ㄨㄟˋ ㄌㄜ˙
(C) ㄙㄨㄟ ㄖㄢˊ
(D) ㄐㄧˊ ㄕˇ

41. 夏天的南極，氣溫仍在零下四十度左右，__C__ 穿上很多衣服，____ 會感到寒冷。

(A) 如果 …… 那麼
(B) 儘管 …… 但是
(C) 即使 …… 也
(D) 只要 …… 就

41. ㄒㄧㄚˋ ㄊㄧㄢ ㄉㄜ˙ ㄋㄢˊ ㄐㄧˊ，ㄑㄧˋ ㄨㄣ ㄖㄥˊ ㄗㄞˋ ㄌㄧㄥˊ ㄒㄧㄚˋ ㄙˋ ㄕˊ ㄉㄨˋ ㄗㄨㄛˇ ㄧㄡˋ，____ ㄔㄨㄢ ㄕㄤˋ ㄏㄣˇ ㄉㄨㄛ ㄧ ㄈㄨ˙，__C__ ㄏㄨㄟˋ ㄍㄢˇ ㄉㄠˋ ㄏㄢˊ ㄌㄥˇ。

(A) ㄖㄨˊ ㄍㄨㄛˇ …… ㄋㄚˋ ㄇㄜ˙
(B) ㄐㄧㄣˇ ㄍㄨㄢˇ …… ㄉㄢˋ ㄕˋ
(C) ㄐㄧˊ ㄕˇ …… ㄧㄝˇ
(D) ㄓˇ ㄧㄠˋ …… ㄐㄧㄡˋ

42. “二零零八年奥运会” ____ 中国主办。

(A) 在
(B) 被
(C) 由
(D) 自

42. “Èr líng líng bā nián Àoyùnhuì” ____Zhōngguó zhǔbàn.

(A) zài
(B) bèi
(C) yóu
(D) zì

43. 我喜欢吃中国菜，____ 是北京烤鸭。

(A) 更
(B) 而且
(C) 尤其
(D) 还

43. Wǒ xǐhuan chī Zhōngguócài, ____ shì Běijīng kǎoyā.

(A) gèng
(B) érqiě
(C) yóuqí
(D) hái

44. 中国人每年春节的时候总是很忙，就是为了能 ____ 地过年。

(A) 热闹热闹
(B) 热热闹闹
(C) 闹热闹热
(D) 闹闹热热

44. Zhōngguórén měinián Chūn Jié de shíhou zǒngshì hěn máng, jiùshì wèile néng ____ de guò nián.

(A) rè nao rè nao
(B) rè re nào nao
(C) nào rè nào rè
(D) nào nào rè rè

42. “二零零八年奧運會” __C__ 中國主辦。

(A) 在
(B) 被
(C) 由
(D) 自

42. “ㄦˋ ㄌㄧㄥˊ ㄌㄧㄥˊ ㄅㄚ ㄋㄧㄢˊ ㄠˋ ㄩㄣˋ ㄏㄨㄟˋ” __C__ ㄓㄨㄥ ㄍㄨㄛˊ ㄓㄨˇ ㄅㄢˋ。

(A) ㄗㄞˋ
(B) ㄅㄟˋ
(C) ㄧㄡˊ
(D) ㄗˋ

43. 我喜歡吃中國菜，__C__ 是北京烤鴨。

(A) 更
(B) 而且
(C) 尤其
(D) 還

43. ㄨㄛˇ ㄒㄧˇ ㄏㄨㄢ ㄔ ㄓㄨㄥ ㄍㄨㄛˊ ㄘㄞˋ，__C__ ㄕˋ ㄅㄟˇ ㄐㄧㄥ ㄎㄠˇ ㄧㄚ。

(A) ㄍㄥˋ
(B) ㄦˊ ㄑㄧㄝˇ
(C) ㄧㄡˊ ㄑㄧˊ
(D) ㄏㄞˊ

44. 中國人每年春節的時候總是很忙，就是爲了能 __B__ 地過年。

(A) 熱鬧熱鬧
(B) 熱熱鬧鬧
(C) 鬧熱鬧熱
(D) 鬧鬧熱熱

44. ㄓㄨㄥ ㄍㄨㄛˊ ㄖㄣˊ ㄇㄟˇ ㄋㄧㄢˊ ㄔㄨㄣ ㄐㄧㄝˊ ㄉㄜ˙ ㄕˊ ㄏㄡˋ ㄗㄨㄥˇ ㄕˋ ㄏㄣˇ ㄇㄤˊ，ㄐㄧㄡˋ ㄕˋ ㄨㄟˋ ㄌㄜ˙ ㄋㄥˊ __B__ ㄉㄜ˙ ㄍㄨㄛˋ ㄋㄧㄢˊ。

(A) ㄖㄜˋ ㄋㄠˋ ㄖㄜˋ ㄋㄠˋ
(B) ㄖㄜˋ ㄖㄜˋ ㄋㄠˋ ㄋㄠˋ
(C) ㄋㄠˋ ㄖㄜˋ ㄋㄠˋ ㄖㄜˋ
(D) ㄋㄠˋ ㄋㄠˋ ㄖㄜˋ ㄖㄜˋ

45. ____发生火灾，____立即打电话求救。
(A) 只有 …… 才
(B) 一旦 …… 就
(C) 无论 …… 都
(D) 不仅 …… 而且

45. ____ fāshēng huǒzāi, ____ lìjí dǎ diànhuà qiújiù.
(A) Zhǐyǒu ……cái
(B) Yīdàn …… jiù
(C) Wúlùn …… dōu
(D) Bùjǐn …… érqiě

46. 明天的晚会，把你的女朋友叫____一起玩吧。
(A) 进来
(B) 过来
(C) 到来
(D) 起来

46. Míngtiān de wǎnhuì, bǎ nǐ de nǚpéngyou jiào ____ yīqǐ wán ba.
(A) jìnlai
(B) guòlai
(C) dàolai
(D) qǐlai

47. 足球踢得好的人，篮球____打得好。
(A) 不必
(B) 未必
(C) 必定
(D) 想必

47. Zúqiú tī de hǎo de rén, lánqiú ____ dǎ de hǎo.
(A) bùbì
(B) wèibì
(C) bìdìng
(D) xiǎngbì

45. __B__發生火災，____立即打電話求救。
(A) 只有 …… 才
(B) 一旦 …… 就
(C) 無論 …… 都
(D) 不僅 …… 而且

45. __B__ ㄈㄚ ㄕㄥ ㄏㄨㄛˇ ㄗㄞ，____ ㄌㄧˋ ㄐㄧˊ ㄉㄚˇ ㄉㄧㄢˋ ㄏㄨㄚˋ ㄑㄧㄡˊ ㄐㄧㄡˋ。
(A) ㄓˇ ㄧㄡˇ …… ㄘㄞˊ
(B) ㄧ ㄉㄢˋ …… ㄐㄧㄡˋ
(C) ㄨˊ ㄌㄨㄣˋ …… ㄉㄡ
(D) ㄅㄨˋ ㄐㄧㄣˇ …… ㄦˊ ㄑㄧㄝˇ

46. 明天的晚會，把你的女朋友叫__B__一起玩吧。
(A) 進來
(B) 過來
(C) 到來
(D) 起來

46. ㄇㄧㄥˊ ㄊㄧㄢ ˙ㄉㄜ ㄨㄢˇ ㄏㄨㄟˋ，ㄅㄚˇ ㄋㄧˇ ˙ㄉㄜ ㄋㄩˇ ㄆㄥˊ ㄧㄡˇ ㄐㄧㄠˋ __B__ ㄧ ㄑㄧˇ ㄨㄢˊ ˙ㄅㄚ。
(A) ㄐㄧㄣˋ ㄌㄞˊ
(B) ㄍㄨㄛˋ ㄌㄞˊ
(C) ㄉㄠˋ ㄌㄞˊ
(D) ㄑㄧˇ ㄌㄞˊ

47. 足球踢得好的人，籃球__B__打得好。
(A) 不必
(B) 未必
(C) 必定
(D) 想必

47. ㄗㄨˊ ㄑㄧㄡˊ ㄊㄧ ˙ㄉㄜ ㄏㄠˇ ˙ㄉㄜ ㄖㄣˊ，ㄌㄢˊ ㄑㄧㄡˊ __B__ ㄉㄚˇ ˙ㄉㄜ ㄏㄠˇ。
(A) ㄅㄨˋ ㄅㄧˋ
(B) ㄨㄟˋ ㄅㄧˋ
(C) ㄅㄧˋ ㄉㄧㄥˋ
(D) ㄒㄧㄤˇ ㄅㄧˋ

48. 这是一个多么美好的夜晚 ____！
(A) 呢
(B) 啊
(C) 吧
(D) 吗

48. Zhè shì yí ge duōme měihǎo de yèwǎn ____！
(A) ne
(B) a
(C) ba
(D) ma

49. 我们____住得很远，____不常见面。
(A) 虽然 …… 但是
(B) 因为 …… 所以
(C) 即使 …… 也
(D) 无论 …… 都

49. Wǒmen____zhù de hěn yuǎn, ____bù cháng jiànmiàn.
(A) suīrán …… dànshì
(B) yīnwèi …… suǒyǐ
(C) jíshǐ …… yě
(D) wúlùn …… dōu

50. 妹妹一听到音乐，就跳 ____ 舞 ____。
(A) 下，去
(B) 过，来
(C) 起，来
(D) 回，去

50. Mèimei yì tīngdào yīnyuè, jiù tiào____wǔ____.
(A) xià, qù
(B) guò, lái
(C) qǐ, lái
(D) huí, qù

48. 這是一個多麼美好的夜晚 __B__！
(A) 呢
(B) 啊
(C) 吧
(D) 嗎

48. ㄓㄜˋ ㄕˋ ㄧˊ ˙ㄍㄜ ㄉㄨㄛ ˙ㄇㄜ ㄇㄟˇ ㄏㄠˇ ˙ㄉㄜ ㄧㄝˋ ㄨㄢˇ __B__！
(A) ˙ㄋㄜ
(B) ㄚ
(C) ˙ㄅㄚ
(D) ㄇㄚ

49. 我們__B__住得很遠，____不常見面。
(A) 雖然 …… 但是
(B) 因爲 …… 所以
(C) 即使 …… 也
(D) 無論 …… 都

49. ㄨㄛˇ ˙ㄇㄣ __B__ ㄓㄨˋ ˙ㄉㄜ ㄏㄣˇ ㄩㄢˇ，____ ㄅㄨˋ ㄔㄤˊ ㄐㄧㄢˋ ㄇㄧㄢˋ。
(A) ㄙㄨㄟ ㄖㄢˊ …… ㄉㄢˋ ㄕˋ
(B) ㄧㄣ ㄨㄟˋ …… ㄙㄨㄛˇ ㄧˇ
(C) ㄐㄧˊ ㄕˇ …… ㄧㄝˇ
(D) ㄨˊ ㄌㄨㄣˋ …… ㄉㄡ

50. 妹妹一聽到音樂，就跳 ____ 舞 __C__。
(A) 下，去
(B) 過，來
(C) 起，來
(D) 回，去

50. ㄇㄟˋ ˙ㄇㄟ ㄧˋ ㄊㄧㄥ ㄉㄠˋ ㄧㄣ ㄩㄝˋ，ㄐㄧㄡˋ ㄊㄧㄠˋ ____ ㄨˇ __C__。
(A) ㄒㄧㄚˋ，ㄑㄩˋ
(B) ㄍㄨㄛˋ，ㄌㄞˊ
(C) ㄑㄧˇ，ㄌㄞˊ
(D) ㄏㄨㄟˊ，ㄑㄩˋ

51. 昨天玩得太累了，他今天____起不了床。

(A) 差很多
(B) 几乎不
(C) 差点儿
(D) 没能

51. Zuótiān wán de tài lèi le, tā jīntiān____qǐ bu liǎo chuáng.

(A) chàhěnduō
(B) jīhūbù
(C) chàdiǎnr
(D) méinéng

52. ____找别人帮忙，____我们俩是不能完成这个任务的。

(A) 若 …… 就
(B) 既然 …… 就
(C) 除非 …… 否则
(D) 宁可 …… 也不

52. ____zhǎo biérén bāngmáng, ____ wǒmenliǎ shì bùnéng wánchéng zhè ge rènwù de.

(A) Ruò …… jiù
(B) Jìrán …… jiù
(C) Chúfēi …… fǒuzé
(D) Nìngkě …… yěbù

53. 弟弟的脸红得____红苹果似的。

(A) 像
(B) 似
(C) 是
(D) 又

53. Dìdi de liǎn hóng de ____ hóng píngguǒ shì de.

(A) xiàng
(B) sì
(C) shì
(D) yòu

51. 昨天玩得太累了，他今天__C__起不了床。

(A) 差很多
(B) 幾乎不
(C) 差點兒
(D) 沒能

51. ㄗㄨㄛˊ ㄊㄧㄢ ㄨㄢˊ ˙ㄉㄜ ㄊㄞˋ ㄌㄟˋ ˙ㄌㄜ，ㄊㄚ ㄐㄧㄣ ㄊㄧㄢ __C__ ㄑㄧˇ ㄅㄨˋ ㄌㄧㄠˇ ㄔㄨㄤˊ。

(A) ㄔㄚˋ ㄏㄣˇ ㄉㄨㄛ
(B) ㄐㄧˋ ㄏㄨ ㄅㄨˋ
(C) ㄔㄚˋ ㄉㄧㄢˇ ㄦˊ
(D) ㄇㄟˊ ㄋㄥˊ

52. __C__找別人幫忙，____我們倆是不能完成這個任務的。

(A) 若 …… 就
(B) 既然 …… 就
(C) 除非 …… 否則
(D) 寧可 …… 也不

52. __C__ ㄓㄠˇ ㄅㄧㄝˊ ㄖㄣˊ ㄅㄤ ㄇㄤˊ，____ ㄨㄛˇ ˙ㄇㄣ ㄌㄧㄚˇ ㄕˋ ㄅㄨˋ ㄋㄥˊ ㄨㄢˊ ㄔㄥˊ ㄓㄜˋ ˙ㄍㄜ ㄖㄣˋ ㄨˋ ˙ㄉㄜ。

(A) ㄖㄨㄛˋ …… ㄐㄧㄡˋ
(B) ㄐㄧˋ ㄖㄢˊ …… ㄐㄧㄡˋ
(C) ㄔㄨˊ ㄈㄟ …… ㄈㄡˇ ㄗㄜˊ
(D) ㄋㄧㄥˊ ㄎㄜˇ …… ㄧㄝˇ ㄅㄨˋ

53. 弟弟的臉紅得__A__紅蘋果似的。

(A) 像
(B) 似
(C) 是
(D) 又

53. ㄉㄧˋ ˙ㄉㄧ ˙ㄉㄜ ㄌㄧㄢˇ ㄏㄨㄥˊ ˙ㄉㄜ __A__ ㄏㄨㄥˊ ㄆㄧㄥˊ ㄍㄨㄛˇ ㄕˋ ˙ㄉㄜ。

(A) ㄒㄧㄤˋ
(B) ㄙˋ
(C) ㄕˋ
(D) ㄧㄡˋ

54. 这个办法听____不错，就是不知道可不可行。

(A) 上来
(B) 下来
(C) 过来
(D) 起来

54. Zhè ge bànfǎ tīng____bú cuò, jiùshì bù zhīdào kě bù kě xíng.

(A) shàng lai
(B) xià lai
(C) guò lai
(D) qǐ lai

55. 最近几天____。你要注意身体，别感冒了。

(A) 连冷带热
(B) 又冷又热
(C) 忽冷忽热
(D) 似冷非热

55. Zuìjìn jǐtiān____. Nǐ yào zhùyì shēntǐ, bié gǎnmào le.

(A) lián lěng dài rè
(B) yòu lěng yòu rè
(C) hū lěng hū rè
(D) sì lěng fēi rè

54. 這個辦法聽____不錯，就是不知道可不可行。

(A) 上來
(B) 下來
(C) 過來
(D) 起來

54. ㄓㄜˋ ㄍㄜ˙ ㄅㄢˋ ㄈㄚˇ ㄊㄧㄥ ____ ㄅㄨˊ ㄘㄨㄛˋ，ㄐㄧㄡˋ ㄕˋ ㄅㄨˋ ㄓ ㄉㄠˋ ㄎㄜˇ ㄅㄨˋ ㄎㄜˇ ㄒㄧㄥˊ。

(A) ㄕㄤˋ ㄌㄞˊ
(B) ㄒㄧㄚˋ ㄌㄞˊ
(C) ㄍㄨㄛˋ ㄌㄞˊ
(D) ㄑㄧˇ ㄌㄞˊ

55. 最近幾天____。你要注意身體，別感冒了。

(A) 連冷帶熱
(B) 又冷又熱
(C) 忽冷忽熱
(D) 似冷非熱

55. ㄗㄨㄟˋ ㄐㄧㄣˋ ㄐㄧˇ ㄊㄧㄢ ____。ㄋㄧˇ ㄧㄠˋ ㄓㄨˋ ㄧˋ ㄕㄣ ㄊㄧˇ，ㄅㄧㄝˊ ㄍㄢˇ ㄇㄠˋ ㄌㄜ˙。

(A) ㄌㄧㄢˊ ㄌㄥˇ ㄉㄞˋ ㄖㄜˋ
(B) ㄧㄡˋ ㄌㄥˇ ㄧㄡˋ ㄖㄜˋ
(C) ㄏㄨ ㄌㄥˇ ㄏㄨ ㄖㄜˋ
(D) ㄙˋ ㄌㄥˇ ㄈㄟ ㄖㄜˋ

SECTION III
READING COMPREHENSION

Suggested time — 25 minutes
Questions 56 - 85

WHEN YOU BEGIN THIS SECTION, MAKE SURE THAT YOU MARK YOUR ANSWER TO THE FIRST QUESTION BY FILLING IN ONE OF THE CIRCLES NEXT TO NUMBER 56 ON YOUR ANSWER SHEET.

Directions:

Read the following texts carefully for comprehension. Each one is followed by one or more questions or incomplete statements. Select the answer or completion that is best according to the text and fill in the corresponding circle on your answer sheet.

This section of the test is presented in two writing systems: traditional characters and simplified characters. IT IS RECOMMEMD THAT YOU CHOOSE THE WRITING SYSTEM WITH WHICH YOU ARE MORE FAMILIAR WITH AND **ONLY READ THAT VERSION** AS YOU WORK THROUGH THIS SECTION OF THE TEST.

Questions 56-57

说话的礼仪

说话要自然，亲切。有时可做些手势，但动作不要太大，不要用手指人。与人谈话时，不能和对方离得太远，但也不要靠得过近。如果谈话时有急事需要离开，要向对方打招呼，表示歉意。

說話的禮儀

說話要自然，親切。有時可做些手勢，但動作不要太大，不要用手指人。與人談話時，不能和對方離得太遠，但也不要靠得過近。如果談話時有急事需要離開，要向對方打招呼，表示歉意。

56. This passage is mainly about
    (A) presentation skills
    (B) emergency situations
    (C) lecturing skills
    (D) conversation manners

57. Which of the following is NOT mentioned?
    (A) No big movements
    (B) Maintain an appropriate distance
    (C) No hand gestures allowed
    (D) Make an apology

Question 58

新片上映 《美丽人生》 放映时间： 每周二、四晚七点至十点	新片上映 《美麗人生》 放映時間： 每週二、四晚七點至十點

58. What is this advertisement about?
    (A) A new book
    (B) A new magazine
    (C) A new movie
    (D) A new comic

Questions 59-61

教育中心诚聘 中文导师 要求：硕士学位，成绩优异 联系电话：1234567	教育中心誠聘 中文導師 要求：碩士學位，成績優異 聯繫電話：1234567

59. This is a recruitment advertisement of
    (A) a radio station
    (B) a Chinese publisher
    (C) a learning center
    (D) a telephone company

60. What position is being advertised?
   (A) Chinese tutor
   (B) Translator
   (C) Education consultant
   (D) General manager

61. Which of the following is required of the applicant?
   (A) Good telephone skills
   (B) A doctoral degree
   (C) Good English skills
   (D) A master's degree

Questions 62-63

著名学者李强访谈

时间：二零零九年十二月五日
晚七点

地点：北京大学图书馆

欢迎全体同学参加

著名學者李強訪談

時間：二零零九年十二月五日
晚七點

地點：北京大學圖書館

歡迎全體同學參加

62. Where will the talk be held?
   (A) In the library
   (B) In a classroom
   (C) In the concert hall
   (D) In the sports stadium

63. Who can attend the talk?
   (A) Anyone
   (B) All students
   (C) Teachers only
   (D) All students and their parents

Question 64

请勿泊车	請勿泊車

64. What does this sign say?
    (A) No parking
    (B) No pets allowed
    (C) No visitors
    (D) No smoking

Question 65

牛奶十二元一瓶，买二赠一	牛奶十二元一瓶，買二贈一

65. How many bottles of milk can you get for $24?
    (A) Two
    (B) Three
    (C) Four
    (D) Five

Question 66

北京动物园欢迎你

门票价格：
成人：十二元/人
十二岁以上儿童：六元/人
十二岁以下儿童：三元/人

北京動物園歡迎你

門票價格：
成人：十二元/人
十二歲以上兒童：六元/人
十二歲以下兒童：三元/人

66. If two children aged 14 and 10 go to the zoo, how much are the tickets altogether?

(A) $6
(B) $12
(C) $18
(D) $9

Questions 67-68

我叫李明，是一年级二班的学生，我今年十一岁。我有一个哥哥，他叫李光，我们在同一个学校，同一个年级，不过他是三班的学生。

我叫李明，是一年級二班的學生，我今年十一歲。我有一個哥哥，他叫李光，我們在同一個學校，同一個年級，不過他是三班的學生。

67. Li Guang is Li Ming's ____ .

(A) brother
(B) sister
(C) good friend
(D) cousin

68. Which of the following is true about Li Guang and Li Ming?

(A) They are in different grades.
(B) They are in different classes.
(C) They go to different schools.
(D) They are both in 11th grade.

Questions 69-70

本店营业时间

周一至周四：
上午九点至下午五点
周五：
下午一点至三点
周六、日及公众假期休息

本店營業時間

週一至週四：
上午九點至下午五點
週五：
下午一點至三點
週六、日及公眾假期休息

69. On which days is this shop closed?

(A) Saturdays
(B) Sundays
(C) Saturdays and Sundays
(D) Saturdays, Sundays and public holidays

70. What are the opening hours on Fridays?

(A) 9 A.M. to 1 P.M.
(B) 1 P.M. to 3 P.M.
(C) 9 A.M. to 5 P.M.
(D) 9 A.M. to 3 P.M.

Question 71

员工专用	員工專用

71. What does this sign say?

(A) Staff only
(B) Handicapped only
(C) Adults only
(D) Students only

Question 72

参观注意事项	參觀注意事項
请勿拍照	請勿拍照
请勿大声喧哗	請勿大聲喧嘩
请勿乱扔垃圾	請勿亂扔垃圾

72. Which of the following is NOT mentioned?

(A) Taking photos
(B) Eating and drinking
(C) Shouting
(D) Littering

Questions 73-74

小华：
　　后天早上九点记得去火车站接阿姨。她中等个子，有点胖，头发是黑色的卷发。她会戴白色的帽子，提绿色的手袋。
妈妈

小華：
　　後天早上九點記得去火車站接阿姨。她中等個子，有點胖，頭髮是黑色的捲髮。她會戴白色的帽子，提綠色的手袋。
媽媽

73. When should Xiao Hua go to pick her aunt up?
    (A) 9 A.M. today
    (B) 9 P.M. today
    (C) 9 A.M. tomorrow
    (D) 9 A.M. the day after tomorrow

74. Her aunt will
    (A) carry a green handbag
    (B) carry a white handbag
    (C) wear a black dress
    (D) wear sunglasses

Questions 75-76

这是我的房间。在窗户旁边有一张桌子，桌上放着书、尺子、笔，还有一个大花瓶。在靠近桌子的墙上，贴着一张图画，那是我自己画的小猫。坐在窗前，我可以看到外面的大树和远处的铁路。

這是我的房間。在窗戶旁邊有一張桌子，桌上放著書、尺子、筆，還有一個大花瓶。在靠近桌子的牆上，貼著一張圖畫，那是我自己畫的小貓。坐在窗前，我可以看到外面的大樹和遠處的鐵路。

75. Which of the following is NOT placed on the desk?
    (A) Books
    (B) A vase
    (C) Photographs
    (D) Pens

76. The drawing on the wall depicts a
    (A) tree
    (B) vase
    (C) cat
    (D) railway line

Questions 77-78

京剧是中国最著名的地方戏曲，它在中国北方最为流行。以前，京剧在街上或是寺庙的广场上表演，现在，京剧大多是在高级剧院里表演的，是一种独特的表演艺术。

京劇是中國最著名的地方戲曲，它在中國北方最為流行。以前，京劇在街上或是寺廟的廣場上表演，現在，京劇大多是在高級劇院裏表演的，是一種獨特的表演藝術。

77. Which of the following statements about Peking opera is NOT true?
    (A) Peking opera is a unique type of performing arts.
    (B) Peking opera used to be performed in streets.
    (C) Peking opera can only be performed in temples.
    (D) Peking opera is performed mostly in theatres nowadays.

78. Peking opera is most popular in which part of China?
    (A) In northern China
    (B) In eastern China
    (C) In southern China
    (D) In western China

Questions 79-80

城市新闻 本期： 二零零九年九月一日出版	双周刊

城市新聞 本期： 二零零九年九月一日出版	雙週刊

79. What kind of magazine is this?

    (A) Children's magazine
    (B) News magazine
    (C) Sports magazine
    (D) Cooking magazine

80. How often is this magazine published?

    (A) Weekly
    (B) Bi-weekly
    (C) Monthly
    (D) Quarterly

Questions 81-82

香港ABC制药公司

王强 经理

电话：12345678

香港ABC製藥公司

王強 經理

電話：12345678

81. What is the occupation of Wang Qiang?

    (A) Secretary
    (B) Doctor
    (C) Manager
    (D) Consultant

82. What does this company manufacture?

(A) Toys
(B) Medicines
(C) Clothing
(D) Computers

Question 83

恭贺新禧	恭賀新禧

83. What does this phrase mean?

(A) Happy New Year
(B) Merry Christmas
(C) Happy birthday
(D) Welcome

Questions 84-85

今日天气

北京	多云	十五至二十度
上海	小雨	二十三至三十度
香港	晴	二十八至三十二度

今日天氣

北京	多雲	十五至二十度
上海	小雨	二十三至三十度
香港	晴	二十八至三十二度

84. What is today's weather forecast for Beijing?

(A) Sunny
(B) Rainy
(C) Cloudy
(D) Thunderstorms

85. What is the maximum temperature forecast for Hong Kong?

(A) 32 degrees
(B) 20 degrees
(C) 30 degrees
(D) 23 degrees

SAT Chinese Practice Test — One
SAT 中文模拟试题 — 第一套
SAT 中文模擬試題 — 第一套

听力材料
聽力材料
LISTENING TEST MATERIAL

Part A

Simplified Characters

Question 1

A：这么早出去啊？

B：是啊，儿子今天从美国回来，我得早点去机场接他。

(A) 你会英文吗？
(B) 你真是一个好父亲。
(C) 你儿子要去美国吗？

Question 2

A：这个暑假你打工赚了多少钱？

(A) 我去当售货员。
(B) 我在百货公司工作。
(C) 我赚了八千块。

Question 3

A：真难得，你竟然也参加舞会来了？

(A) 我想多认识些朋友。
(B) 我们一起参加比赛吧！
(C) 你也来看书吗？

Question 4

A：这个位子有人吗？

(A) 有，他去洗手间了，马上回来。
(B) 你回家吃饭吗？
(C) 我要买椅子。

Question 5

A： 昨天我又赶作业，很晚才去睡。

B： 你要注意多休息啊。

(A) 我们一起做作业吧！
(B) 你生病了。
(C) 我知道了。

Question 6

A： 周末我请你看电影吧？

(A) 好啊，我想吃西餐。
(B) 不好意思，我已经约了别人了。
(C) 我不喜欢唱歌。

Question 7

A： 昨天的考试怎么样？

B： 别提了，考得不好。

(A) 别难过，我这次也没考好。
(B) 没关系，我来帮你拿。
(C) 恭喜你，这样的机会很难得。

Question 8

A： 请问还有什么需要帮助的吗？

(A) 谢谢你的帮忙。
(B) 暂时没有了，谢谢你。
(C) 不用客气，我很乐意帮助你。

Question 9

A： 早点休息吧，明天还要上课。

(A) 时间还早，我现在还不想睡觉。
(B) 明天有英文课。
(C) 我已经休息了十分钟了。

Question 10

A： 你想吃点什么？

(A) 这里的东西不好吃。
(B) 我已经吃了很多了。
(C) 随便吧，你决定。

Question 11

A： 请问你知道这附近的邮局怎么走吗？
B： 附近没有，得坐车去。

(A) 要坐几路车呢？
(B) 我跟你去油站。
(C) 你坐在这里干嘛？

Question 12

A： 这件衣服多少钱？
B： 原价一百二十元，现在可以打九折，所以是一百零八元。

(A) 没有裤子了。
(B) 你吃亏了。
(C) 太便宜了！

Question 13

A： 你喜欢吃中国菜吗？

(A) 中国菜很难做。
(B) 中国菜很贵。
(C) 嗯，我最喜欢的是四川菜。

Question 14

A： 你来中国几年了？

(A) 到下个月正好三年。
(B) 中国很好玩。
(C) 中文很难学。

Question 15

A： 你今年又拿到比赛冠军了，真厉害！

(A) 哪里，哪里，您过奖了。
(B) 我说得一点也不好。
(C) 我喜欢学中文。

Part B

Questions 16-17

男：小王，听说你生病了，好点了吗？

女：好多了，不过医生说，还得在家休息一段时间。

男：你是不是这个星期都不能来公司了？

女：是啊，工作上的事情，还得麻烦您多操心了。

Questions 18-20

男：昨天的美国队对中国队的篮球比赛看了吗？很精彩！

女：昨天我加班，错过了。结果怎么样？

男：虽然最后美国队以八十六比七十八赢了，但是中国队的表现还挺让人满意的。

Questions 21-22

男：明天早上九点在图书馆门口见，然后我们一起去听讲座。

女：我听说明天的讲座要先报名，我们今天下午先去报名吧。

Questions 23-24

男：你好，请问王玲在家吗？

女：哦，真不巧，她刚刚出去，有什么事吗？我可以转告她。

男：谢谢，她托我买的书，我已经买到了，麻烦您让她有空的时候来我家拿。

女：好的，请留一下你的联系方式。

Questions 25-26

男：请问还有空房间吗？我想订一个单人间。

女：有洗手间的是二百元一天，没有洗手间的一百五十元一天。请问您要哪一种？

男：我要有洗手间的。

女：好，请把身份证给我，麻烦您先登记一下。

Questions 27-28

男：时间过得可真快，今天都二十号了，再过两天就是春节了。

女：是啊，春节你有什么打算吗？

男：我准备带家人去新加坡旅游。

Questions 29-30

男：我要一杯柠檬汁。

女：对不起，柠檬汁已经卖完了，这是我们新出的苹果汁，您要不要试一下？

男：好吧，那我要一杯。

Part A

Traditional Characters

Question 1

A：這麼早出去啊？

B：是啊，兒子今天從美國回來，我得早點去機場接他。

(A) 你會英文嗎？
(B) 你真是一個好父親。
(C) 你兒子要去美國嗎？

Question 2

A：這個暑假你打工賺了多少錢？

(A) 我去當售貨員。
(B) 我在百貨公司工作。
(C) 我賺了八千塊。

Question 3

A：真難得，你竟然也參加舞會來了？

(A) 我想多認識些朋友。
(B) 我們一起參加比賽吧！
(C) 你也來看書嗎？

Question 4

A：這個位子有人嗎？

(A) 有，他去洗手間了，馬上回來。
(B) 你回家吃飯嗎？
(C) 我要買椅子。

Question 5

A： 昨天我又趕作業，很晚才去睡。

B： 你要注意多休息啊。

(A) 我們一起做作業吧！
(B) 你生病了。
(C) 我知道了。

Question 6

A： 週末我請你看電影吧？

(A) 好啊，我想吃西餐。
(B) 不好意思，我已經約了別人了。
(C) 我不喜歡唱歌。

Question 7

A： 昨天的考試怎麼樣？

B： 別提了，考得不好。

(A) 別難過，我這次也沒考好。
(B) 沒關係，我來幫你拿。
(C) 恭喜你，這樣的機會很難得。

Question 8

A： 請問還有什麼需要幫助的嗎？

(A) 謝謝你的幫忙。
(B) 暫時沒有了，謝謝你。
(C) 不用客氣，我很樂意幫助你。

Question 9

A： 早點休息吧，明天還要上課。

(A) 時間還早，我現在還不想睡覺。
(B) 明天有英文課。
(C) 我已經休息了十分鐘了。

Question 10

A： 你想吃點什麼？

(A) 這裏的東西不好吃。
(B) 我已經吃了很多了。
(C) 隨便吧，你決定。

Question 11

A： 請問你知道這附近的郵局怎麼走嗎？
B： 附近沒有，得坐車去。

(A) 要坐幾路車呢？
(B) 我跟你去油站。
(C) 你坐在這裏幹嘛？

Question 12

A： 這件衣服多少錢？
B： 原價一百二十元，現在可以打九折，所以是一百零八元。

(A) 沒有褲子了。
(B) 你吃虧了。
(C) 太便宜了！

Question 13

A： 你喜歡吃中國菜嗎？

(A) 中國菜很難做。
(B) 中國菜很貴。
(C) 嗯，我最喜歡的是四川菜。

Question 14

A： 你來中國幾年了？

(A) 到下個月正好三年。
(B) 中國很好玩。
(C) 中文很難學。

Question 15

A： 你今年又拿到比賽冠軍了，真厲害！

(A) 哪裏，哪裏，您過獎了。
(B) 我說得一點也不好。
(C) 我喜歡學中文。

Part B

Questions 16-17

男：小王，聽說你生病了，好點了嗎？

女：好多了，不過醫生說，還得在家休息一段時間。

男：你是不是這個星期都不能來公司了？

女：是啊，工作上的事情，還得麻煩您多操心了。

Questions 18-20

男：昨天的美國隊對中國隊的籃球比賽看了嗎？很精彩！

女：昨天我加班，錯過了。結果怎麼樣？

男：雖然最後美國隊以八十六比七十八贏了，但是中國隊的表現還挺讓人滿意的。

Questions 21-22

男：明天早上九點在圖書館門口見，然後我們一起去聽講座。

女：我聽說明天的講座要先報名，我們今天下午先去報名吧。

Questions 23-24

男：你好，請問王玲在家嗎？

女：哦，真不巧，她剛剛出去，有什麼事嗎？我可以轉告她。

男：謝謝，她托我買的書，我已經買到了，麻煩您讓她有空的時候來我家拿。

女：好的，請留一下你的聯繫方式。

Questions 25-26

男：請問還有空房間嗎？我想訂一個單人間。

女：有洗手間的是二百元一天，沒有洗手間的一百五十元一天。請問您要哪一種？

男：我要有洗手間的。

女：好，請把身份證給我，麻煩您先登記一下。

Questions 27-28

男：時間過得可真快，今天都二十號了，再過兩天就是春節了。

女：是啊，春節你有什麼打算嗎？

男：我準備帶家人去新加坡旅遊。

Questions 29-30

男：我要一杯檸檬汁。

女：對不起，檸檬汁已經賣完了，這是我們新出的蘋果汁，您要不要試一下？

男：好吧，那我要一杯。

Part A

Pinyin Romanization

Question 1

A : Zhème zǎo chūqù a ?

B : Shì a, érzi jīntiān cóng Měiguó huílai, wǒ děi zǎodiǎn qù jīchǎng jiē tā.

(A) Nǐ huì yīngwén ma ?

(B) Nǐ zhēnshì yí ge hǎo fùqīn.

(C) Nǐ érzi yào qù Měiguó ma ?

Question 2

A : Zhè ge shǔjià nǐ dǎgōng zhuàn le duōshǎo qián ?

(A) Wǒ qù dāng shòuhuòyuán.

(B) Wǒ zài bǎihuògōngsī gōngzuò.

(C) Wǒ zhuàn le bā qiān kuài.

Question 3

A : Zhēn nándé, nǐ jìngrán yě cānjiā wǔhuì lái le ?

(A) Wǒ xiǎng duō rènshi xiē péngyou.

(B) Wǒmen yìqǐ cānjiā bǐsài ba !

(C) Nǐ yě lái kànshū ma ?

Question 4

A : Zhè ge wèizi yǒu rén ma ?

(A) Yǒu, tā qù xǐshǒujiān le, mǎshàng huílai.

(B) Nǐ huíjiā chīfàn ma ?

(C) Wǒ yào mǎi yǐzi.

Question 5

A：Zuótiān wǒ yòu gǎn zuòyè, hěn wǎn cái qù shuì.

B：Nǐ yào zhùyì duō xiūxi a.

(A) Wǒmen yìqǐ zuò zuòyè ba！
(B) Nǐ shēngbìng le.
(C) Wǒ zhīdào le.

Question 6

A：Zhōumò wǒ qǐng nǐ kàn diànyǐng ba？

(A) Hǎo a, wǒ xiǎng chī xīcān.
(B) Bù hǎoyìsi, wǒ yǐjīng yuē le biérén le.
(C) Wǒ bù xǐhuan chànggē.

Question 7

A：Zuótiān de kǎoshì zěnme yàng？

B：Bié tí le, kǎo dé bù hǎo.

(A) Bié nánguò, wǒ zhè cì yě méi kǎo hǎo.
(B) Méi guānxi, wǒ lái bāng nǐ ná.
(C) Gōngxǐ nǐ, zhèyàng de jīhuì hěn nándé.

Question 8

A：Qǐngwèn háiyǒu shénme xūyào bāngzhù de ma？

(A) Xièxie nǐ de bāngmáng.
(B) Zànshí méiyǒu le, xièxie nǐ.
(C) Búyòng kèqi, wǒ hěn lèyì bāngzhù nǐ.

Question 9

A: Zǎodiǎn xiūxi ba, míngtiān hái yào shàngkè.

(A) Shíjiān hái zǎo, wǒ xiànzài hái bù xiǎng shuìjiào.
(B) Míngtiān yǒu Yīngwénkè.
(C) Wǒ yǐjīng xiūxi le shí fēnzhōng le.

Question 10

A: Nǐ xiǎng chī diǎn shénme?

(A) Zhèlǐ de dōngxi bù hǎochī.
(B) Wǒ yǐjīng chī le hěnduō le.
(C) Suíbiàn ba, nǐ juédìng.

Question 11

A: Qǐngwèn nǐ zhīdào zhè fùjìn de yóujú zěnme zǒu ma?
B: Fùjìn méiyǒu, děi zuòchē qù.

(A) Yào zuò jǐ lù chē ne?
(B) Wǒ gēn nǐ qù yóuzhàn.
(C) Nǐ zuò zài zhèli gànma?

Question 12

A: Zhè jiàn yīfu duōshǎo qián?
B: Yuánjià yìbǎi èrshí yuán, xiànzài kěyǐ dǎ jiǔ zhé, suǒyǐ shì yìbǎi líng bā yuán.

(A) Méiyǒu kùzi le.
(B) Nǐ chīkuī le.
(C) Tài piányi le!

Question 13

A：Nǐ xǐhuan chī Zhōngguócài ma？

(A) Zhōngguócài hěn nán zuò.
(B) Zhōngguócài hěn guì.
(C) Ēn, wǒ zuì xǐhuan de shì Sìchuāncài.

Question 14

A：Nǐ lái Zhōngguó jǐ nián le？

(A) Dào xià ge yuè zhènghǎo sān nián.
(B) Zhōngguó hěn hǎowán.
(C) Zhōngwén hěn nán xué.

Question 15

A：Nǐ jīnnián yòu nádào bǐsài guànjūn le, zhēn lìhai！

(A) Nǎlǐ, nǎlǐ, nín guòjiǎng le.
(B) Wǒ shuō dé yìdiǎn yě bù hǎo.
(C) Wǒ xǐhuan xué Zhōngwén.

Part B

Questions 16-17

Nán：Xiǎo Wáng, tīngshuō nǐ shēngbìng le, hǎo diǎn le ma？
Nǚ：Hǎo duō le, búguò yīshēng shuō, hái děi zàijiā xiūxi yí duàn shíjiān.
Nán：Nǐ shì bu shì zhè ge xīngqī dōu bùnéng lái gōngsī le？
Nǚ：Shì a, gōngzuò shàng de shìqing, hái děi máfan nín duō cāoxīn le.

Questions 18-20

Nán：Zuótiān de Měiguóduì duì Zhōngguóduì de lánqiú bǐsài kàn le ma？ Hěn jīngcǎi！
Nǚ：Zuótiān wǒ jiābān, cuòguò le. Jiēguǒ zěnmeyàng？
Nán：Suīrán zuìhòu Měiguóduì yǐ bāshí liù bǐ qīshí bā yíng le, dànshì Zhōngguóduì de biǎoxiàn hái tǐng ràngrén mǎnyì de.

Questions 21-22

Nán : Míngtiān zǎoshàng jiǔ diǎn zài túshūguǎn ménkǒu jiàn, ránhòu wǒmen yìqǐ qù tīng jiǎngzuò.

Nǚ : Wǒ tīngshuō míngtiān de jiǎngzuò yào xiān bàomíng, wǒmen jīntiān xiàwǔ xiān qù bàomíng ba.

Questions 23-24

Nán : Nǐ hǎo, qǐngwèn Wáng Líng zài jiā ma?

Nǚ : Ò, zhēn bùqiǎo, tā gānggāng chūqù, yǒu shénme shì ma? Wǒ kěyǐ zhuǎngào tā.

Nán : Xièxie, tā tuō wǒ mǎi de shū, wǒ yǐjīng mǎidàole, máfan nín ràng tā yǒu kòng de shíhou lái wǒ jiā ná.

Nǚ : Hǎo de, qǐng liú yíxià nǐ de liánxì fāngshì.

Questions 25-26

Nán : Qǐngwèn háiyǒu kōng fángjiān ma? Wǒ xiǎng dìng yí ge dānrénjiān.

Nǚ : Yǒu xǐshǒujiān de shì èrbǎi yuán yì tiān, méiyǒu xǐshǒujiān de yìbǎi wǔshí yuán yìtiān. Qǐngwèn nín yào nǎ yì zhǒng?

Nán : Wǒ yào yǒu xǐshǒujiān de.

Nǚ : Hǎo, qǐng bǎ shēnfènzhèng gěi wǒ, máfan nín xiān dēngjì yí xià.

Questions 27-28

Nán : Shíjiān guò dé kě zhēn kuài, jīntiān dōu èrshí hào le, zài guò liǎng tiān jiùshì Chūn Jié le.

Nǚ : Shì a, Chūn Jié nǐ yǒu shénme dǎsuan ma?

Nán : Wǒ zhǔnbèi dài jiārén qù Xīnjiāpō lǚyóu.

Questions 29-30

Nán : Wǒ yào yì bēi níngméngzhī.

Nǚ : Duì bu qǐ, níngméngzhī yǐjīng mài wán le, zhèshì wǒmen xīn chū de píngguǒzhī, nín yào bu yào shì yí xià?

Nán : Hǎo ba, nà wǒ yào yì bēi.

Practice Test One

1	Ⓐ	Ⓑ	Ⓒ	Ⓓ	31	Ⓐ	Ⓑ	Ⓒ	Ⓓ	56	Ⓐ	Ⓑ	Ⓒ	Ⓓ
2	Ⓐ	Ⓑ	Ⓒ	Ⓓ	32	Ⓐ	Ⓑ	Ⓒ	Ⓓ	57	Ⓐ	Ⓑ	Ⓒ	Ⓓ
3	Ⓐ	Ⓑ	Ⓒ	Ⓓ	33	Ⓐ	Ⓑ	Ⓒ	Ⓓ	58	Ⓐ	Ⓑ	Ⓒ	Ⓓ
4	Ⓐ	Ⓑ	Ⓒ	Ⓓ	34	Ⓐ	Ⓑ	Ⓒ	Ⓓ	59	Ⓐ	Ⓑ	Ⓒ	Ⓓ
5	Ⓐ	Ⓑ	Ⓒ	Ⓓ	35	Ⓐ	Ⓑ	Ⓒ	Ⓓ	60	Ⓐ	Ⓑ	Ⓒ	Ⓓ
6	Ⓐ	Ⓑ	Ⓒ	Ⓓ	36	Ⓐ	Ⓑ	Ⓒ	Ⓓ	61	Ⓐ	Ⓑ	Ⓒ	Ⓓ
7	Ⓐ	Ⓑ	Ⓒ	Ⓓ	37	Ⓐ	Ⓑ	Ⓒ	Ⓓ	62	Ⓐ	Ⓑ	Ⓒ	Ⓓ
8	Ⓐ	Ⓑ	Ⓒ	Ⓓ	38	Ⓐ	Ⓑ	Ⓒ	Ⓓ	63	Ⓐ	Ⓑ	Ⓒ	Ⓓ
9	Ⓐ	Ⓑ	Ⓒ	Ⓓ	39	Ⓐ	Ⓑ	Ⓒ	Ⓓ	64	Ⓐ	Ⓑ	Ⓒ	Ⓓ
10	Ⓐ	Ⓑ	Ⓒ	Ⓓ	40	Ⓐ	Ⓑ	Ⓒ	Ⓓ	65	Ⓐ	Ⓑ	Ⓒ	Ⓓ
11	Ⓐ	Ⓑ	Ⓒ	Ⓓ	41	Ⓐ	Ⓑ	Ⓒ	Ⓓ	66	Ⓐ	Ⓑ	Ⓒ	Ⓓ
12	Ⓐ	Ⓑ	Ⓒ	Ⓓ	42	Ⓐ	Ⓑ	Ⓒ	Ⓓ	67	Ⓐ	Ⓑ	Ⓒ	Ⓓ
13	Ⓐ	Ⓑ	Ⓒ	Ⓓ	43	Ⓐ	Ⓑ	Ⓒ	Ⓓ	68	Ⓐ	Ⓑ	Ⓒ	Ⓓ
14	Ⓐ	Ⓑ	Ⓒ	Ⓓ	44	Ⓐ	Ⓑ	Ⓒ	Ⓓ	69	Ⓐ	Ⓑ	Ⓒ	Ⓓ
15	Ⓐ	Ⓑ	Ⓒ	Ⓓ	45	Ⓐ	Ⓑ	Ⓒ	Ⓓ	70	Ⓐ	Ⓑ	Ⓒ	Ⓓ
16	Ⓐ	Ⓑ	Ⓒ	Ⓓ	46	Ⓐ	Ⓑ	Ⓒ	Ⓓ	71	Ⓐ	Ⓑ	Ⓒ	Ⓓ
17	Ⓐ	Ⓑ	Ⓒ	Ⓓ	47	Ⓐ	Ⓑ	Ⓒ	Ⓓ	72	Ⓐ	Ⓑ	Ⓒ	Ⓓ
18	Ⓐ	Ⓑ	Ⓒ	Ⓓ	48	Ⓐ	Ⓑ	Ⓒ	Ⓓ	73	Ⓐ	Ⓑ	Ⓒ	Ⓓ
19	Ⓐ	Ⓑ	Ⓒ	Ⓓ	49	Ⓐ	Ⓑ	Ⓒ	Ⓓ	74	Ⓐ	Ⓑ	Ⓒ	Ⓓ
20	Ⓐ	Ⓑ	Ⓒ	Ⓓ	50	Ⓐ	Ⓑ	Ⓒ	Ⓓ	75	Ⓐ	Ⓑ	Ⓒ	Ⓓ
21	Ⓐ	Ⓑ	Ⓒ	Ⓓ	51	Ⓐ	Ⓑ	Ⓒ	Ⓓ	76	Ⓐ	Ⓑ	Ⓒ	Ⓓ
22	Ⓐ	Ⓑ	Ⓒ	Ⓓ	52	Ⓐ	Ⓑ	Ⓒ	Ⓓ	77	Ⓐ	Ⓑ	Ⓒ	Ⓓ
23	Ⓐ	Ⓑ	Ⓒ	Ⓓ	53	Ⓐ	Ⓑ	Ⓒ	Ⓓ	78	Ⓐ	Ⓑ	Ⓒ	Ⓓ
24	Ⓐ	Ⓑ	Ⓒ	Ⓓ	54	Ⓐ	Ⓑ	Ⓒ	Ⓓ	79	Ⓐ	Ⓑ	Ⓒ	Ⓓ
25	Ⓐ	Ⓑ	Ⓒ	Ⓓ	55	Ⓐ	Ⓑ	Ⓒ	Ⓓ	80	Ⓐ	Ⓑ	Ⓒ	Ⓓ
26	Ⓐ	Ⓑ	Ⓒ	Ⓓ						81	Ⓐ	Ⓑ	Ⓒ	Ⓓ
27	Ⓐ	Ⓑ	Ⓒ	Ⓓ						82	Ⓐ	Ⓑ	Ⓒ	Ⓓ
28	Ⓐ	Ⓑ	Ⓒ	Ⓓ						83	Ⓐ	Ⓑ	Ⓒ	Ⓓ
29	Ⓐ	Ⓑ	Ⓒ	Ⓓ						84	Ⓐ	Ⓑ	Ⓒ	Ⓓ
30	Ⓐ	Ⓑ	Ⓒ	Ⓓ						85	Ⓐ	Ⓑ	Ⓒ	Ⓓ

SAT Chinese Practice Test — Two
SAT 中文模拟试题 — 第二套
SAT 中文模擬試題 — 第二套

Time — 1 hour
Questions 1 - 85

PLEASE NOTE THAT YOUR ANSWER SHEET HAS FOUR ANSWER POSITIONS, MARKED A, B, C, AND D, WHILE THE QUESTIONS THROUGHOUT THIS TEST CONTAIN EITHER THREE OR FOUR ANSWER CHOICES. BE SURE NOT TO MARK YOUR ANSWERS IN COLUMN D IF THERE ARE ONLY THREE CHOICES GIVEN.

SECTION I
LISTENING

Approximate time — 20 minutes
Questions 1 - 30

Part A

Directions:

In this part of the test, you will hear short questions, statements, or commands in Mandarin Chinese, followed by three responses in Mandarin Chinese, designated (A), (B), and (C). You will hear the questions or statements, as well as the responses, only once, and they are not printed in your test booklet. Therefore, you must listen very carefully. Select the best response and fill in the corresponding circle on your answer sheet.

Question 1 Mark your answer on your answer sheet.

Question 2 Mark your answer on your answer sheet.

Question 3 Mark your answer on your answer sheet.

Question 4 Mark your answer on your answer sheet.

Question 5 Mark your answer on your answer sheet.

Question 6 Mark your answer on your answer sheet.

Question 7 Mark your answer on your answer sheet.

Question 8 Mark your answer on your answer sheet.

Question 9 Mark your answer on your answer sheet.

Question 10 Mark your answer on your answer sheet.

Question 11 Mark your answer on your answer sheet.

Question 12 Mark your answer on your answer sheet.

Question 13 Mark your answer on your answer sheet.

Question 14 Mark your answer on your answer sheet.

Question 15 Mark your answer on your answer sheet.

Part B

Directions:

You will now hear a series of dialogues. You will hear them only once, and they are not printed in your test booklet. After each selection, you will be asked to answer one or more questions about what you have just heard. These questions, each with four possible answers, are printed in your test booklet. Select the best answer to each question from among the four choices printed and fill in the corresponding circle on your answer sheet.

Questions 16-17

16. What is the weather forecast for tomorrow?
    - (A) Rain
    - (B) Snow
    - (C) Windy
    - (D) Sunny

17. What did the woman plan to do originally?
    - (A) Have a barbecue
    - (B) Go swimming
    - (C) Visit the Great Wall
    - (D) Go hiking

Question 18

18. Where does the man want to go?
    - (A) Hospital
    - (B) Library
    - (C) Market
    - (D) Cinema

Questions 19-20

19. What does the man ask the woman to do?
    (A) Serve as an interpreter
    (B) Contact two clients
    (C) Arrange a meeting with two clients in Germany
    (D) Teach him German

20. How does the woman respond?
    (A) She has been learning German for a long time.
    (B) She needs to see her teacher tomorrow.
    (C) She wants to return the German book to her teacher.
    (D) She only learnt German at university.

Questions 21-22

21. Why does the man want to dine out?
    (A) He prefers the food served in restaurants.
    (B) There is no food left at home.
    (C) Cooking takes too much time.
    (D) He wants to invite the woman out for dinner.

22. What is the woman's response?
    (A) She will go home and cook.
    (B) She will dine at her mother's house.
    (C) She refuses to dine out with the man.
    (D) She recommends a Chinese restaurant.

Questions 23-24

23. How much does one catty of imported apples cost?

(A) $3
(B) $5
(C) $10
(D) $15

24. What does the man buy in the end?

(A) Two catties of local apples
(B) Two catties of imported apples
(C) One catty of local apples and two catties of imported apples
(D) Two catties of local apples and one catty of imported apples

Questions 25-26

25. Why does the woman thank the man?

(A) He invited her out for dinner.
(B) He took her to the hospital.
(C) He bought her a present.
(D) He helped her organize an activity.

26. What is the relationship between the two people?

(A) Colleagues
(B) Husband and wife
(C) Schoolmates
(D) Doctor and patient

Question 27

27. The woman suggests they should leave at

(A) 8:00
(B) 9:00
(C) 9:10
(D) 9:15

Questions 28-29

28. Which form of transport does the woman suggest?
    (A) Ferry
    (B) Bus
    (C) Subway
    (D) Taxi

29. Where is Nanjing Road?
    (A) Near the sports stadium
    (B) Near the hotel
    (C) Near the hospital
    (D) Near the school

Question 30

30. What does the woman plan to do after graduation?
    (A) Travel
    (B) Go to university
    (C) Find a job
    (D) Get married

SECTION II USAGE

Suggested time — 15 minutes
Questions 31 - 55

Part A

Directions:

This section consists of a number of incomplete statements, each of which has four possible completions. Select the word or phrase that best completes the sentence structurally and logically and fill in the corresponding circle on your answer sheet.

This section of the test is presented in four different ways of representing Chinese: traditional characters, simplified characters, pinyin romanization, and the Chinese phonetic alphabet. IT IS RECOMMEMD THAT YOU CHOOSE THE WRITING SYSTEM WITH WHICH YOU ARE MORE FAMILIAR WITH AND <u>**ONLY READ THAT VERSION**</u> AS YOU WORK THROUGH THIS SECTION OF THE TEST.

31. 他连书都没有看过，这次考试____能通过，真是太幸运了。
    (A) 自然
    (B) 突然
    (C) 当然
    (D) 竟然

31. 他連書都沒有看過，這次考試____能通過，真是太幸運了。
    (A) 自然
    (B) 突然
    (C) 當然
    (D) 竟然

31. Tā lián shū dōu méiyǒu kàn guo, zhè cì kǎoshì____néng tōngguò, zhēn shì tài xìngyùn le.
    (A) zìrán
    (B) tūrán
    (C) dāngrán
    (D) jìngrán

31. ㄊㄚ ㄌㄧㄢˊ ㄕㄨ ㄉㄡ ㄇㄟˊ ㄧㄡˇ ㄎㄢˋ ㄍㄨㄛˋ，ㄓㄜˋ ㄘˋ ㄎㄠˇ ㄕˋ ____ ㄋㄥˊ ㄊㄨㄥ ㄍㄨㄛˋ，ㄓㄣ ㄕˋ ㄊㄞˋ ㄒㄧㄥˋ ㄩㄣˋ ˙ㄌㄜ。
    (A) ㄗˋ ㄖㄢˊ
    (B) ㄊㄨˊ ㄖㄢˊ
    (C) ㄉㄤ ㄖㄢˊ
    (D) ㄐㄧㄥˋ ㄖㄢˊ

32. 他给我寄来了一____图片。
    (A) 张
    (B) 个
    (C) 封
    (D) 篇

32. 他給我寄來了一____圖片。
    (A) 張
    (B) 個
    (C) 封
    (D) 篇

32. Tā gěi wǒ jì lái le yī____túpiàn.
    (A) zhāng
    (B) ge
    (C) fēng
    (D) piān

32. ㄊㄚ ㄍㄟˇ ㄨㄛˇ ㄐㄧˋ ㄌㄞˊ ˙ㄌㄜ ㄧ ____ ㄊㄨˊ ㄆㄧㄢˋ。
    (A) ㄓㄤ
    (B) ˙ㄍㄜ
    (C) ㄈㄥ
    (D) ㄆㄧㄢ

33. 衣服____旧了点儿，____穿在身上很舒服。

(A) 无论 …… 都
(B) 不但 …… 反而
(C) 因为 …… 所以
(D) 虽然 …… 但是

33. Yīfu ____ jiù le diǎnr, ____ chuān zài shēn shang hěn shūfu.

(A) wúlùn …… dōu
(B) búdàn …… fǎn'ér
(C) yīnwèi …… suǒyǐ
(D) suīrán …… dànshì

34. 这孩子不听话，____他在家，____不得安宁。

(A) 只要 …… 就
(B) 只有 …… 那
(C) 虽然 …… 却
(D) 无论 …… 都

34. Zhè háizi bù tīnghuà, ____ tā zài jiā, ____ bù dé ānníng.

(A) zhǐyào …… jiù
(B) zhǐyǒu …… nà
(C) suīrán …… què
(D) wúlùn …… dōu

35. 你必须承认错误，____大家都不会原谅你。

(A) 就
(B) 那么
(C) 要么
(D) 否则

35. Nǐ bìxū chéngrèn cuòwù, ____ dàjiā dōu bú huì yuánliàng nǐ.

(A) jiù
(B) nàme
(C) yàome
(D) fǒuzé

33. 衣服____舊了點兒，____穿在身上很舒服。

(A) 無論 …… 都
(B) 不但 …… 反而
(C) 因爲 …… 所以
(D) 雖然 …… 但是

33. ㄧ ㄈㄨˊ ____ ㄐㄧㄡˋ ˙ㄌㄜ ㄉㄧㄢˇ ˙ㄦ，____ ㄔㄨㄢ ㄗㄞˋ ㄕㄣ ㄕㄤˋ ㄏㄣˇ ㄕㄨ ㄈㄨˊ。

(A) ㄨˊ ㄌㄨㄣˋ …… ㄉㄡ
(B) ㄅㄨˊ ㄉㄢˋ …… ㄈㄢˇ ㄦˊ
(C) ㄧㄣ ㄨㄟˋ …… ㄙㄨㄛˇ ㄧˇ
(D) ㄙㄨㄟ ㄖㄢˊ …… ㄉㄢˋ ㄕˊ

34. 這孩子不聽話，____他在家，____不得安寧。

(A) 只要 …… 就
(B) 只有 …… 那
(C) 雖然 …… 卻
(D) 無論 …… 都

34. ㄓㄜˋ ㄏㄞˊ ˙ㄗ ㄅㄨˋ ㄊㄧㄥ ㄏㄨㄚˋ，____ ㄊㄚ ㄗㄞˋ ㄐㄧㄚ，____ ㄅㄨˋ ㄉㄜˊ ㄢ ㄋㄧㄥˊ。

(A) ㄓ ㄧㄠˋ …… ㄐㄧㄡˋ
(B) ㄓˇ ㄧㄡˇ …… ㄋㄚˋ
(C) ㄙㄨㄟ ㄖㄢˊ …… ㄑㄩㄝˋ
(D) ㄨˊ ㄌㄨㄣˋ …… ㄉㄡ

35. 你必須承認錯誤，____大家都不會原諒你。

(A) 就
(B) 那麼
(C) 要麼
(D) 否則

35. ㄋㄧˇ ㄅㄧˋ ㄒㄩ ㄔㄥˊ ㄖㄣˋ ㄘㄨㄛˋ ㄨˋ，____ ㄉㄚˋ ㄐㄧㄚ ㄉㄡ ㄅㄨˊ ㄏㄨㄟˋ ㄩㄢˊ ㄌㄧㄤˋ ㄋㄧˇ。

(A) ㄐㄧㄡˋ
(B) ㄋㄚˋ ˙ㄇㄜ
(C) ㄧㄠˋ ˙ㄇㄜ
(D) ㄈㄡˇ ㄗㄜˊ

36. ____明天刮大风下大雨，我就不去了。

(A) 即使

(B) 尽管

(C) 就算

(D) 要是

36. ____míngtiān guā dà fēng xià dà yǔ, wǒ jiù bú qù le.

(A) jíshǐ

(B) jǐnguǎn

(C) jiùsuàn

(D) yàoshì

37. 他____还是一个孩子，不能要求他什么都懂。

(A) 根据

(B) 毕竟

(C) 甚至

(D) 如何

37. Tā ____háishì yí ge háizi, bù néng yāoqiú tā shénme dōu dǒng.

(A) gēnjù

(B) bìjìng

(C) shènzhì

(D) rúhé

38. 请替我____你的家人问好。

(A) 往

(B) 向

(C) 让

(D) 叫

38. Qǐng tì wǒ____nǐ de jiārén wènhǎo.

(A) wǎng

(B) xiàng

(C) ràng

(D) jiào

36. ____明天刮大風下大雨，我就不去了。

(A) 即使

(B) 儘管

(C) 就算

(D) 要是

36. ____ㄇㄧㄥˊ ㄊㄧㄢ ㄍㄨㄚ ㄉㄚˋ ㄈㄥ ㄒㄧㄚˋ ㄉㄚˋ ㄩˇ，ㄨㄛˇ ㄐㄧㄡˋ ㄅㄨˊ ㄑㄩˋ ㄌㄜ˙。

(A) ㄐㄧˊ ㄕˇ

(B) ㄐㄧㄣˇ ㄍㄨㄢˇ

(C) ㄐㄧㄡˋ ㄙㄨㄢˋ

(D) ㄧㄠˋ ㄕˋ

37. 他____還是一個孩子，不能要求他什麼都懂。

(A) 根據

(B) 畢竟

(C) 甚至

(D) 如何

37. ㄊㄚ ____ ㄏㄞˊ ㄕˋ ㄧˊ ㄍㄜ˙ ㄏㄞˊ ㄗ˙，ㄅㄨˋ ㄋㄥˊ ㄧㄠ ㄑㄧㄡˊ ㄊㄚ ㄕㄣˊ ㄇㄜ˙ ㄉㄡ ㄉㄨㄥˇ。

(A) ㄍㄣ ㄐㄩˋ

(B) ㄅㄧˋ ㄐㄧㄥˋ

(C) ㄕㄣˋ ㄓˋ

(D) ㄖㄨˊ ㄏㄜˊ

38. 請替我____你的家人問好。

(A) 往

(B) 向

(C) 讓

(D) 叫

38. ㄑㄧㄥˇ ㄊㄧˋ ㄨㄛˇ ____ ㄋㄧˇ ㄉㄜ˙ ㄐㄧㄚ ㄖㄣˊ ㄨㄣˋ ㄏㄠˇ。

(A) ㄨㄤˇ

(B) ㄒㄧㄤˋ

(C) ㄖㄤˋ

(D) ㄐㄧㄠˋ

39. 过马路时你____要小心，别让车撞到。

(A) 十分
(B) 千万
(C) 百万
(D) 多半

39. Guò mǎlù shí nǐ____yào xiǎoxīn, bié ràng chē zhuàng dào.

(A) shífēn
(B) qiānwàn
(C) bǎiwàn
(D) duōbàn

40. 在这个问题____，我们的看法有一致的地方。

(A) 前
(B) 中
(C) 上
(D) 右

40. Zài zhè ge wèntí ____, wǒmen de kànfǎ yǒu yízhì de dìfang.

(A) qián
(B) zhōng
(C) shàng
(D) yòu

41. 我的生日蛋糕____掉了。

(A) 吃弟弟叫给
(B) 给叫弟弟吃
(C) 叫弟弟给吃
(D) 弟弟叫给吃

41. Wǒ de shēngrì dàngāo____diào le.

(A) chī dìdi jiào gěi
(B) gěi jiào dìdi chī
(C) jiào dìdi gěi chī
(D) dìdi jiào gěi chī

39. 過馬路時你____要小心，別讓車撞到。

(A) 十分
(B) 千萬
(C) 百萬
(D) 多半

39. ㄍㄨㄛˋ ㄇㄚˇ ㄌㄨˋ ㄕˊ ㄋㄧˇ ____ ㄧㄠˋ ㄒㄧㄠˇ ㄒㄧㄣ，ㄅㄧㄝˊ ㄖㄤˋ ㄔㄜ ㄓㄨㄤˋ ㄉㄠˋ。

(A) ㄕˊ ㄈㄣ
(B) ㄑㄧㄢ ㄨㄢˋ
(C) ㄅㄞˇ ㄨㄢˋ
(D) ㄉㄨㄛ ㄅㄢˋ

40. 在這個問題____，我們的看法有一致的地方。

(A) 前
(B) 中
(C) 上
(D) 右

40. ㄗㄞˋ ㄓㄜˋ ˙ㄍㄜ ㄨㄣˋ ㄊㄧˊ ____，ㄨㄛˇ ˙ㄇㄣ ˙ㄉㄜ ㄎㄢˋ ㄈㄚˇ ㄧㄡˇ ㄧˊ ㄓˋ ˙ㄉㄜ ㄉㄧˋ ˙ㄈㄤ。

(A) ㄑㄧㄢˊ
(B) ㄓㄨㄥ
(C) ㄕㄤˋ
(D) ㄧㄡˋ

41. 我的生日蛋糕____掉了。

(A) 吃弟弟叫給
(B) 給叫弟弟吃
(C) 叫弟弟給吃
(D) 弟弟叫給吃

41. ㄨㄛˇ ˙ㄉㄜ ㄕㄥ ㄖˋ ㄉㄢˋ ㄍㄠ ____ ㄉㄧㄠˋ ˙ㄌㄜ。

(A) ㄔ ㄉㄧˋ ˙ㄉㄧ ㄐㄧㄠˋ ㄍㄟˇ
(B) ㄍㄟˇ ㄐㄧㄠˋ ㄉㄧˋ ˙ㄉㄧ ㄔ
(C) ㄐㄧㄠˋ ㄉㄧˋ ˙ㄉㄧ ㄍㄟˇ ㄔ
(D) ㄉㄧˋ ˙ㄉㄧ ㄐㄧㄠˋ ㄍㄟˇ ㄔ

42. 事情哪儿____你说的这么容易?

(A) 像
(B) 和
(C) 与
(D) 要

42. Shìqing nǎr____nǐ shuō de zhème róngyì?

(A) xiàng
(B) hé
(C) yǔ
(D) yào

43. 那个戴____帽子的女孩是谁?

(A) 不
(B) 着
(C) 过
(D) 的

43. Nà ge dài____màozi de nǚhái shì shéi?

(A) bú
(B) zhe
(C) guo
(D) de

44. 原来外面在下大雪，____天气这么冷。

(A) 怪不得
(B) 恨不得
(C) 好容易
(D) 看不惯

44. Yuánlái wàimiàn zài xià dàxuě, ____tiānqì zhème lěng.

(A) guàibude
(B) hènbude
(C) hǎoróngyi
(D) kànbuguàn

42. 事情哪兒____你說的這麼容易?

(A) 像
(B) 和
(C) 與
(D) 要

42. ㄕˋ ㄑㄧㄥˊ ㄋㄚˇ ˙ㄦ ____ ㄋㄧˇ ㄕㄨㄛ ˙ㄉㄜ ㄓㄜˋ ˙ㄇㄜ ㄖㄨㄥˊ ㄧˋ?

(A) ㄒㄧㄤˋ
(B) ㄏㄢˋ
(C) ㄩˇ
(D) ㄧㄠˋ

43. 那個戴____帽子的女孩是誰？

(A) 不
(B) 著
(C) 過
(D) 的

43. ㄋㄚˋ ˙ㄍㄜ ㄉㄞˋ ____ ㄇㄠˋ ˙ㄗ ˙ㄉㄜ ㄋㄩˇ ㄏㄞˊ ㄕˋ ㄕㄟˊ？

(A) ㄅㄨˊ
(B) ˙ㄓㄜ
(C) ㄍㄨㄛˋ
(D) ˙ㄉㄜ

44. 原來外面在下大雪，____天氣這麼冷。

(A) 怪不得
(B) 恨不得
(C) 好容易
(D) 看不慣

44. ㄩㄢˊ ㄌㄞˊ ㄨㄞˋ ㄇㄧㄢˋ ㄗㄞˋ ㄒㄧㄚˋ ㄉㄚˋ ㄒㄩㄝˇ， ____ ㄊㄧㄢ ㄑㄧˋ ㄓㄜˋ ˙ㄇㄜ ㄌㄥˇ。

(A) ㄍㄨㄞˋ ㄅㄨˋ ˙ㄉㄜ
(B) ㄏㄣˋ ㄅㄨˋ ˙ㄉㄜ
(C) ㄏㄠˇ ㄖㄨㄥˊ ˙ㄧ
(D) ㄎㄢˋ ㄅㄨˊ ㄍㄨㄢˋ

45. 我____爸爸去电影院看电影。
(A) 从
(B) 跟
(C) 对
(D) 以

45. wǒ____bàba qù diànyǐngyuàn kàn diànyǐng.
(A) cóng
(B) gēn
(C) duì
(D) yǐ

46. ____这个问题，我们还没有想出办法来。
(A) 对于
(B) 自从
(C) 还是
(D) 接着

46. ____zhè ge wèntí, wǒmen hái méiyǒu xiǎng chū bànfǎ lái.
(A) Duìyú
(B) Zìcóng
(C) Háishì
(D) Jiēzhe

47. 他的进步____使其他同学____使所有的老师都感到十分惊讶。
(A) 尽管 …… 但是
(B) 不但 …… 甚至
(C) 不但不 …… 还
(D) 不是 …… 而是

47. Tā de jìnbù____shǐ qítā tóngxué ____shǐ suǒyǒu de lǎoshī dōu gǎndào shífēn jīngyà.
(A) jǐnguǎn …… dànshì
(B) búdàn …… shènzhì
(C) búdànbù …… hái
(D) búshì …… érshì

45. 我____爸爸去電影院看電影。
(A) 從
(B) 跟
(C) 對
(D) 以

45. ㄨㄛˇ ____ ㄅㄚˋ ˙ㄅㄚ ㄑㄩˋ ㄉㄧㄢˋ ㄧㄥˇ ㄩㄢˋ ㄎㄢˋ ㄉㄧㄢˋ ㄧㄥˇ。
(A) ㄘㄨㄥˊ
(B) ㄍㄣ
(C) ㄉㄨㄟˋ
(D) ㄧˇ

46. ____這個問題，我們還沒有想出辦法來。
(A) 對於
(B) 自從
(C) 還是
(D) 接著

46. ____ ㄓㄜˋ ˙ㄍㄜ ㄨㄣˋ ㄊㄧˊ，ㄨㄛˇ ˙ㄇㄣ ㄏㄞˊ ㄇㄟˊ ㄧㄡˇ ㄒㄧㄤˇ ㄔㄨ ㄅㄢˋ ㄈㄚˇ ㄌㄞˊ。
(A) ㄉㄨㄟˋ ㄩˊ
(B) ㄗˋ ㄘㄨㄥˊ
(C) ㄏㄞˊ ㄕˋ
(D) ㄐㄧㄝ ˙ㄓㄜ

47. 他的進步____使其他同學____使所有的老師都感到十分驚訝。
(A) 儘管 …… 但是
(B) 不但 …… 甚至
(C) 不但不 …… 還
(D) 不是 …… 而是

47. ㄊㄚ ˙ㄉㄜ ㄐㄧㄣˋ ㄅㄨˋ ____ ㄕˇ ㄑㄧˊ ㄊㄚ ㄊㄨㄥˊ ㄒㄩㄝˊ ____ ㄕˇ ㄙㄨㄛˇ ㄧㄡˇ ˙ㄉㄜ ㄌㄠˇ ㄕ ㄉㄡ ㄍㄢˇ ㄉㄠˋ ㄕˊ ㄈㄣ ㄐㄧㄥ ㄧㄚˋ。
(A) ㄐㄧㄣˇ ㄍㄨㄢˇ …… ㄉㄢˋ ㄕˋ
(B) ㄅㄨˋ ㄉㄢˋ …… ㄕㄣˋ ㄓˋ
(C) ㄅㄨˊ ㄉㄢˋ ㄅㄨˋ …… ㄏㄞˊ
(D) ㄅㄨˋ ㄕˋ …… ㄦˊ ㄕˋ

48. 他最近特别忙，经常____吃饭____看书。
(A) 又 …… 又
(B) 也 …… 也
(C) 一边 …… 一边
(D) 一时 …… 一时

48. Tā zuìjìn tèbié máng, jīngcháng ____ chīfàn ____ kànshū.
(A) yòu …… yòu
(B) yě …… yě
(C) yìbiān …… yìbiān
(D) yìshí …… yìshí

49. 出门前记得____门关好！
(A) 开
(B) 被
(C) 把
(D) 拿

49. Chū mén qián jìde ____ mén guān hǎo!
(A) kāi
(B) bèi
(C) bǎ
(D) ná

50. 桌子是今天____运来的。
(A) 才
(B) 却
(C) 而
(D) 但

50. Zhuōzi shì jīntiān ____ yùn lái de.
(A) cái
(B) què
(C) ér
(D) dàn

48. 他最近特別忙，經常____吃飯____看書。
(A) 又 …… 又
(B) 也 …… 也
(C) 一邊 …… 一邊
(D) 一時 …… 一時

48. ㄊㄚ ㄗㄨㄟˋ ㄐㄧㄣˋ ㄊㄜˋ ㄅㄧㄝˊ ㄇㄤˊ，ㄐㄧㄥ ㄔㄤˊ ____ ㄔ ㄈㄢˋ ____ ㄎㄢˋ ㄕㄨ。
(A) ㄧㄡˋ …… ㄧㄡˋ
(B) ㄧㄝˇ …… ㄧㄝˇ
(C) ㄧˋ ㄅㄧㄢ …… ㄧˋ ㄅㄧㄢ
(D) ㄧˋ ㄕˊ …… ㄧˋ ㄕˊ

49. 出門前記得____門關好！
(A) 開
(B) 被
(C) 把
(D) 拿

49. ㄔㄨ ㄇㄣˊ ㄑㄧㄢˊ ㄐㄧˋ ˙ㄉㄜ ____ ㄇㄣˊ ㄍㄨㄢ ㄏㄠˇ！
(A) ㄎㄞ
(B) ㄅㄟˋ
(C) ㄅㄚˇ
(D) ㄋㄚˊ

50. 桌子是今天____運來的。
(A) 才
(B) 卻
(C) 而
(D) 但

50. ㄓㄨㄛ ˙ㄗ ㄕˋ ㄐㄧㄣ ㄊㄧㄢ ____ ㄩㄣˋ ㄌㄞˊ ˙ㄉㄜ。
(A) ㄘㄞˊ
(B) ㄑㄩㄝˋ
(C) ㄦˊ
(D) ㄉㄢˋ

51. 上午的考试只进行了____就结束了。
(A) 一个半小时
(B) 一半个小时
(C) 半一个小时
(D) 一个小时半

51. Shàngwǔ de kǎoshì zhǐ jìnxíng le ____ jiù jiéshù le.
(A) yí ge bàn xiǎoshí
(B) yí bàn ge xiǎoshí
(C) bàn yí ge xiǎoshí
(D) yí ge xiǎoshí bàn

52. 我那天在路上____遇到了他。
(A) 顺便
(B) 偶然
(C) 因而
(D) 或者

52. Wǒ nàtiān zài lùshang ____ yùdàole tā.
(A) shùnbiàn
(B) ǒurán
(C) yīn'ér
(D) huòzhě

53. 我希望大家____行动帮助有需要的人。
(A) 而
(B) 为
(C) 以
(D) 就

53. Wǒ xīwàng dàjiā ____ xíngdòng bāngzhù yǒu xūyào de rén.
(A) ér
(B) wèi
(C) yǐ
(D) jiù

51. 上午的考試只進行了____就結束了。
(A) 一個半小時
(B) 一半個小時
(C) 半一個小時
(D) 一個小時半

51. ㄕㄤˋ ㄨˇ ˙ㄉㄜ ㄎㄠˇ ㄕˋ ㄓˇ ㄐㄧㄣˋ ㄒㄧㄥˊ ˙ㄌㄜ ____ ㄐㄧㄡˋ ㄐㄧㄝˊ ㄕㄨˋ ˙ㄌㄜ 。
(A) ㄧˊ ˙ㄍㄜ ㄅㄢˋ ㄒㄧㄠˇ ㄕˊ
(B) ㄧˊ ㄅㄢˋ ˙ㄍㄜ ㄒㄧㄠˇ ㄕˊ
(C) ㄅㄢˋ ㄧˊ ˙ㄍㄜ ㄒㄧㄠˇ ㄕˊ
(D) ㄧˊ ˙ㄍㄜ ㄒㄧㄠˇ ㄕˊ ㄅㄢˋ

52. 我那天在路上____遇到了他。
(A) 順便
(B) 偶然
(C) 因而
(D) 或者

52. ㄨㄛˇ ㄋㄚˋ ㄊㄧㄢ ㄗㄞˋ ㄌㄨˋ ˙ㄕㄤ ____ ㄩˋ ㄉㄠˋ ˙ㄌㄜ ㄊㄚ 。
(A) ㄕㄨㄣˋ ㄅㄧㄢˋ
(B) ㄡˇ ㄖㄢˊ
(C) ㄧㄣ ㄦˊ
(D) ㄏㄨㄛˋ ㄓㄜˇ

53. 我希望大家____行動幫助有需要的人。
(A) 而
(B) 爲
(C) 以
(D) 就

53. ㄨㄛˇ ㄒㄧ ㄨㄤˋ ㄉㄚˋ ㄐㄧㄚ ____ ㄒㄧㄥˊ ㄉㄨㄥˋ ㄅㄤ ㄓㄨˋ ㄧㄡˇ ㄒㄩ ㄧㄠˋ ˙ㄉㄜ ㄖㄣˊ 。
(A) ㄦˊ
(B) ㄨㄟˋ
(C) ㄧˇ
(D) ㄐㄧㄡˋ

54. 这本书我看了好多____了，甚至都可以背下来了。

(A) 顿
(B) 件
(C) 遍
(D) 节

54. 這本書我看了好多____了，甚至都可以背下來了。

(A) 頓
(B) 件
(C) 遍
(D) 節

54. Zhè běn shū wǒ kàn le hǎoduō____ le, shènzhì dōu kěyǐ bèi xiàlai le.

(A) dùn
(B) jiàn
(C) biàn
(D) jié

54. ㄓㄜˋ ㄅㄣˇ ㄕㄨ ㄨㄛˇ ㄎㄢˋ ˙ㄌㄜ ㄏㄠˇ ㄉㄨㄛ ____ ˙ㄌㄜ ，ㄕㄣˋ ㄓˋ ㄉㄡ ㄎㄜˇ ㄧˇ ㄅㄟˋ ㄒㄧㄚˋ ㄌㄞˊ ˙ㄌㄜ 。

(A) ㄉㄨㄣˋ
(B) ㄐㄧㄢˋ
(C) ㄅㄧㄢˋ
(D) ㄐㄧㄝˊ

55. 你上班____很累，她做家务____不轻松啊！

(A) 与其 …… 不如
(B) 如果 …… 就
(C) 不管 …… 都
(D) 固然 …… 也

55. 你上班____很累，她做家務____不輕鬆啊！

(A) 與其 …… 不如
(B) 如果 …… 就
(C) 不管 …… 都
(D) 固然 …… 也

55. Nǐ shàngbān ____ hěn lèi, tā zuò jiāwù ____ bù qīngsōng a!

(A) yǔqí …… bùrú
(B) rúguǒ …… jiù
(C) bùguǎn …… dōu
(D) gùrán …… yě

55. ㄋㄧˇ ㄕㄤˋ ㄅㄢ ____ ㄏㄣˇ ㄌㄟˋ ，ㄊㄚ ㄗㄨㄛˋ ㄐㄧㄚ ㄨˋ ____ ㄅㄨˋ ㄑㄧㄥ ㄙㄨㄥ ㄚ ！

(A) ㄩˇ ㄑㄧˊ …… ㄅㄨˋ ㄖㄨˊ
(B) ㄖㄨˊ ㄍㄨㄛˇ …… ㄐㄧㄡˋ
(C) ㄅㄨˋ ㄍㄨㄢˇ …… ㄉㄡ
(D) ㄍㄨˋ ㄖㄢˊ …… ㄧㄝˇ

SECTION III
READING COMPREHENSION

Suggested time — 25 minutes
Questions 56 - 85

WHEN YOU BEGIN THIS SECTION, MAKE SURE THAT YOU MARK YOUR ANSWER TO THE FIRST QUESTION BY FILLING IN ONE OF THE CIRCLES NEXT TO NUMBER 56 ON YOUR ANSWER SHEET.

Directions:

Read the following texts carefully for comprehension. Each one is followed by one or more questions or incomplete statements. Select the answer or completion that is best according to the text and fill in the corresponding circle on your answer sheet.

This section of the test is presented in two writing systems: traditional characters and simplified characters. IT IS RECOMMEMD THAT YOU CHOOSE THE WRITING SYSTEM WITH WHICH YOU ARE MORE FAMILIAR WITH AND **ONLY READ THAT VERSION** AS YOU WORK THROUGH THIS SECTION OF THE TEST.

Question 56

一日两次，一次三片 孕妇及小孩，依照医生吩咐。	一日兩次，一次三片 孕婦及小孩，依照醫生吩咐。

56. Where would this message most likely be found?

(A) In a newspaper
(B) On a medicine label
(C) In a manual
(D) In a cookbook

Questions 57-58

家具大减价	傢俱大減價
沙发..... 七折	沙發..... 七折
椅子..... 八折	椅子..... 八折
书桌..... 送椅子	書桌..... 送椅子
单人床... 七折	單人床... 七折
衣柜..... 六折	衣櫃..... 六折
台灯..... 买一送一	檯燈..... 買一送一
减价日期:	減價日期:
一月十二日到一月二十八日	一月十二日到一月二十八日
地址：纽约市东七街二十二号	地址：紐約市東七街二十二號
电话：33382459	電話：33382459

57. Which item is offered with a 20% discount?
    (A) Chair
    (B) Desk lamp
    (C) Sofa
    (D) Cupboard

58. Which of the following items is NOT mentioned?
    (A) Desk
    (B) Double bed
    (C) Single bed
    (D) Sofa

Question 59

请勿打扰	請勿打擾

59. What does this notice say?
    (A) No smoking
    (B) Do not disturb
    (C) No visitors
    (D) Staff only

Question 60

单行道	單行道

60. What does this sign say?
    (A) No parking
    (B) One way street
    (C) Right turn
    (D) Left turn

Questions 61-62

长期以来，英文是世界上最通用的语言，但随着中国的经济快速发展，现在越来越多人开始学习中文。至今，全世界已有三千多万外籍人士在学习中文了，而且，这个数字还在不断增长。据估计，学习中文的外国人会在五年内达到一亿。许多外国人学中文是因为他们相信只要学好中文，对他们将来的就业和发展事业有很大的帮助。有些学生甚至认为中文有机会取代英文成为最通用的语言。

長期以來，英文是世界上最通用的語言，但隨著中國的經濟快速發展，現在越來越多人開始學習中文。至今，全世界已有三千多萬外籍人士在學習中文了，而且，這個數字還在不斷增長。據估計，學習中文的外國人會在五年內達到一億。許多外國人學中文是因為他們相信只要學好中文，對他們將來的就業和發展事業有很大的幫助。有些學生甚至認為中文有機會取代英文成為最通用的語言。

61. How many foreigners learning Chinese will there be in five years' time?
    (A) 10 million
    (B) 30 million
    (C) 100 million
    (D) 300 million

62. Why do foreigners want to learn Chinese?
    (A) They like Chinese culture.
    (B) They like to travel to China.
    (C) They believe Chinese is very useful in their careers.
    (D) They like to watch Chinese movies.

Questions 63-65

出发日期	一月二十一日	起飞时间	七时三十分	到达时间	九时三十分
航班号	CA1949	机型	波音747	航空公司	中国国际航空公司
出发地	北京	目的地	上海	原价	一千零二十元
				特价	七百二十元

出發日期	一月二十一日	起飛時間	七時三十分	到達時間	九時三十分
航班號	CA1949	機型	波音747	航空公司	中國國際航空公司
出發地	北京	目的地	上海	原價	一千零二十元
				特價	七百二十元

63. What time does the flight depart?

(A) 9:30 A.M.
(B) 10:20 A.M.
(C) 7:30 A.M.
(D) 5:30 P.M.

64. What is its destination?

(A) Beijing
(B) Shanghai
(C) Hangzhou
(D) Guangzhou

65. What is the discounted air fare?

(A) $1020
(B) $1740
(C) $300
(D) $720

Questions 66-67

十月份 移动电话月结单

本地通话	二十二元
长途	十五元
信息费	八元
本月应缴	四十二元

十月份 移動電話月結單

本地通話	二十二元
長途	十五元
信息費	八元
本月應繳	四十二元

66. This is
    (A) a home phone bill
    (B) an office phone bill
    (C) a cell phone bill
    (D) a hotel phone bill

67. How much should be paid in total?
    (A) $15
    (B) $22
    (C) $48
    (D) $42

Question 68

现在越来越多人喜欢到商场买东西，因为大商场有各式各样的货品，什么都可以买到。虽然大商场货品的价钱比较贵，但是质量大都比较好。而且，如果你不满意你所买的商品，还可以拿回去换别的东西，甚至可以退钱。在大商场付款也非常方便，可以使用现金、支票和信用卡。

現在越來越多人喜歡到商場買東西，因為大商場有各式各樣的貨品，什麼都可以買到。雖然大商場貨品的價錢比較貴，但是質量大都比較好。而且，如果你不滿意你所買的商品，還可以拿回去換別的東西，甚至可以退錢。在大商場付款也非常方便，可以使用現金、支票和信用卡。

68. Which of the following statements is true?
    (A) Not many people like to shop at shopping malls.
    (B) Goods are cheaper in large shopping malls.
    (C) Refunds and exchanges are available in large shopping malls.
    (D) Goods sold in large shopping malls are of poor quality.

Question 69

森林防火，人人有责

森林防火，人人有責

69. What is this message about?
    (A) Swimming safety
    (B) Drunk driving
    (C) Fire prevention
    (D) Pickpockets

Question 70

请勿践踏草地

請勿踐踏草地

70. What does this sign say?
    (A) No cycling
    (B) Do not feed the birds
    (C) Do not pick flowers
    (D) Do not step on the grass

Questions 71-72

哥哥：

我和姐姐一起去看电影，看完电影以后我们一起去北京饭店吃中餐，所以晚饭不在家吃，请你不要等我们了。吃过饭我们还要去逛商店，晚上十点半打的回家。

小强

哥哥：

我和姐姐一起去看電影，看完電影以後我們一起去北京飯店吃中餐，所以晚飯不在家吃，請你不要等我們了。吃過飯我們還要去逛商店，晚上十點半打的回家。

小強

71. Who is this note addressed to?
    (A) Elder brother
    (B) Elder sister
    (C) Mother
    (D) Father

72. Which of the following is NOT true about Xiao Qiang?
    (A) He will dine at a Chinese restaurant.
    (B) He will have dinner at home.
    (C) He will go shopping after dinner.
    (D) He will watch a movie with his sister.

Question 73

日记　　　九月一日　天晴

今天我的钟坏了，所以我晚了起床。因为太赶时间了，所以我没有吃早餐，可还是来不及赶上校车。为了不迟到，我只好乘坐出租车回学校，我刚坐下来就打铃了，还好赶得及，没有被老师罚。

日記　　　九月一日　天晴

今天我的鐘壞了，所以我晚了起床。因爲太趕時間了，所以我沒有吃早餐，可還是來不及趕上校車。爲了不遲到，我只好乘坐出租車回學校，我剛坐下來就打鈴了，還好趕得及，沒有被老師罰。

73. Which of the following statements about the writer of this diary entry is true?
    (A) He was late for school.
    (B) He took a taxi to school.
    (C) He had breakfast at home.
    (D) He was punished by his teacher.

Question 74

只接受现金

只接受現金

74. Which method of payment is mentioned?
   (A) Check
   (B) Cash
   (C) Credit card
   (D) Travelers' checks

Question 75

电视节目精选
星期一至五

12:30pm–1:00pm	新闻报道
1:00pm–2:30pm	旅游看世界
2:30pm–4:00pm	动画片
4:00pm–5:30pm	财经动态
5:30pm–7:30pm	连续剧：我的母亲

星期六

12:30pm–2:00pm	动物世界
2:00pm–3:30pm	动画片
3:30pm–5:00pm	专题报道—环境与科技
5:00pm–6:30 pm	一周新闻回顾
6:30pm–7:30 pm	日剧：白色富士山
7:30pm–8:30pm	本周最流行歌曲

星期日

3:00pm–5:00pm	民以食为天
4:00pm–6:00pm	进修时间：如何提高竞争力
6:00pm–7:00pm	动画片
7:00pm–8:30pm	科技资讯

電視節目精選
星期一至五

12:30pm–1:00pm	新聞報道
1:00pm–2:30pm	旅遊看世界
2:30pm–4:00pm	動畫片
4:00pm–5:30pm	財經動態
5:30pm–7:30pm	連續劇：我的母親

星期六

12:30pm–2:00pm	動物世界
2:00pm–3:30pm	動畫片
3:30pm–5:00pm	專題報道—環境與科技
5:00pm–6:30 pm	一週新聞回顧
6:30pm–7:30 pm	日劇：白色富士山
7:30pm–8:30pm	本週最流行歌曲

星期日

3:00pm–5:00pm	民以食爲天
4:00pm–6:00pm	進修時間：如何提高競爭力
6:00pm–7:00pm	動畫片
7:00pm–8:30pm	科技資訊

75. What program is shown at 7:45 P.M. on Saturdays?
   (A) Soap opera
   (B) Cartoons
   (C) Pop music
   (D) Cooking

Question 76

今天特餐	
羊排饭	35元
炸鱼饭	40元
白菜牛肉饭	45元
虾仁蛋炒饭	40元
红烧牛肉饭	55元
附餐：红茶/咖啡	

今天特餐	
羊排飯	35元
炸魚飯	40元
白菜牛肉飯	45元
蝦仁蛋炒飯	40元
紅燒牛肉飯	55元
附餐：紅茶/咖啡	

76. How much is one order of beef and vegetables with rice?

(A) $35
(B) $40
(C) $45
(D) $55

Questions 77-78

据《东南快报》六月二十一日的报道，上海市将在未来五年内为七十岁以上老人看病提供优惠。这是上海市针对老人看病难的问题提出的一个解决办法。

據《東南快報》六月二十一日的報導，上海市將在未來五年內為七十歲以上老人看病提供優惠。這是上海市針對老人看病難的問題提出的一個解決辦法。

77. This report is targeted at

(A) children
(B) adults
(C) the elderly
(D) students

78. How long would it take the to implement the project?

(A) Five years
(B) Six years
(C) Seven years
(D) 10 years

Question 79

大特卖	大特賣

79. What does this sign say?
    (A) Keep clear
    (B) Sold out
    (C) Special offer
    (D) New arrivals

Question 80

租房信息

南园	两室一厅	六百五十元/月	简单装修
北园	两室一厅	两千五百元/月	好装修
西园A座	两室一厅	八百五十元/月	豪华装修
西园B座	三室两厅	一千八百元/月	好装修

租房信息

南園	兩室一廳	六百五十元/月	簡單裝修
北園	兩室一廳	兩千五百元/月	好裝修
西園A座	兩室一廳	八百五十元/月	豪華裝修
西園B座	三室兩廳	一千八百元/月	好裝修

80. Where is the cheapest apartment located?
    (A) South Garden
    (B) North Garden
    (C) Block A, West Garden
    (D) Block B, West Garden

Question 81

中文大学医学院在零八至零九年，為三百五十九名教师做身体检查，结果发现超过百分之五十的小学教师出现喉咙痛、头痛和头晕等情况，但只有百分之十的患者会求医。

中文大学医学院主管建议教育界為老师定期进行身体检查，令老师有更健康的身体。

中文大學醫學院在零八至零九年，為三百五十九名教師做身體檢查，結果發現超過百分之五十的小學教師出現喉嚨痛、頭痛和頭暈等情況，但只有百分之十的患者會求醫。

中文大學醫學院主管建議教育界為老師定期進行身體檢查，令老師有更健康的身體。

81. Which of the following symptoms is not mentioned?
   (A) Toothache
   (B) Sore throat
   (C) Headache
   (D) Dizziness

Questions 82-83

［本报专讯］由于今年春节前后出入火车站的旅客特别多，市政府建议市民尽量不要开车，改为坐公共汽车到体育馆，然后在体育馆乘地铁前往火车站。

［本報專訊］由於今年春節前後出入火車站的旅客特別多，市政府建議市民儘量不要開車，改為坐公共汽車到體育館，然後在體育館乘地鐵前往火車站。

82. Citizens are reminded that they should avoid driving to the
   (A) sports stadium
   (B) government office
   (C) train station
   (D) airport

83. Which form of transport should citizens use to reach the sports stadium?

(A) Car
(B) Bus
(C) Train
(D) Subway

Question 84

真诚旅行社

我们是有七年导游经验的旅行社，专办上海一日游。相信我们的导游服务一定会使您的上海之旅开心难忘。

联络电话：13974489663

電郵：123455@hotmail.com

真誠旅行社

我們是有七年導遊經驗的旅行社，專辦上海一日遊。相信我們的導遊服務一定會使您的上海之旅開心難忘。

聯絡電話：13974489663

電郵：123455@hotmail.com

84. This is an advertisement for

(A) a car rental company
(B) a tourism college
(C) a travel agency
(D) a hotel reservation agent

Question 85

此座已预订

此座已預訂

85. Where would this sign most likely appear?

(A) In a restaurant
(B) In a school
(C) In an office
(D) In a hospital

SAT Chinese Practice Test — Two
SAT 中文模拟试题 — 第二套
SAT 中文模擬試題 — 第二套

听力材料
聽力材料
LISTENING TEST MATERIAL

Part A

Simplified Characters

Question 1

A： 今天的天气怎么样？

(A) 还不错，就是有点冷。
(B) 昨天下雨了。
(C) 天气预报说明天会下雨。

Question 2

A： 小王，吃过饭了吗？

(A) 今天的菜很好吃。
(B) 我已经很饱了。
(C) 吃过了。

Question 3

A： 你穿的衣服真漂亮，在哪里买的？

(A) 不是买的，是我姐姐送我的。
(B) 谢谢你的大衣。
(C) 漂亮的衣服越来越贵了。

Question 4

A： 晚上早点回来，别玩得太晚了，不安全。

B： 放心吧，我跟小张说好了，十点之前他会开车送我回来的。

(A) 小刘可靠吗？
(B) 十点之前别回来。
(C) 那我就安心了。

Question 5

A： 你会做中国菜吗？

(A) 会一点点。
(B) 我喜欢中国菜。
(C) 我昨天吃了中国菜。

Question 6

A： 我不太会画画，你教我好吗？

(A) 没问题。
(B) 这些题太难了。
(C) 天气太热了。

Question 7

A： 我考试又失败了！

(A) 这位是我的老师。
(B) 我相信你会喜欢这件毛衣的。
(C) 别灰心，你下次一定会成功的。

Question 8

A： 今天幸好有你帮忙，不然，这么多东西我肯定拿不回来。

B： 那么客气干吗？反正我也是顺便。

(A) 我自己拿吧。
(B) 还是很感谢你的。
(C) 你今天太幸运了。

Question 9

A： 最近小明家的电话总是打不通。

(A) 我不知道他家的电话号码。
(B) 他的电话坏了。
(C) 太晚了，不方便打电话。

Question 10

A： 最近老是加班，真累。

(A) 你累不累？
(B) 你得注意休息。
(C) 你上班可以吃东西吗？

Question 11

A： 你这学期上过什么课？

(A) 除了中文课之外，我还修了法文课。
(B) 我学法文学了三年多了。
(C) 法文比中文难学多了。

Question 12

A： 这本书你看过吗？

(A) 我不大喜欢看电影。
(B) 看过了，写得非常精彩。
(C) 西南图书馆很大。

Question 13

A： 你买到火车票了吗？

B： 买不到，春节火车票不好买。

(A) 你真幸运。
(B) 音乐会的票都卖完了。
(C) 我也买不到。

Question 14

A： 你周末看的房子怎么样？打算买吗？

B： 买什么呀！跟广告上说的完全不一样。

(A) 我也打算买房。
(B) 远是远了点，坐车还是挺方便的。
(C) 是啊，现在的广告真的不能相信。

Question 15

A： 恭喜你取得了这么好的成绩。

(A) 谢谢，你太客气了。
(B) 谢谢，我会继续努力的。
(C) 衣服已经洗好了。

Part B

Questions 16-17

男：天气预报说明天会下雨。

女：唉，真可惜，看来又不能去爬山了。

Question 18

男：你知道菜市场怎样走吗？

女：一直往前走就是了！

Questions 19-20

男：小张，听说你学过德语，明天公司要来两位德国客人，你帮忙翻译翻译？

女：唉，我那点德语还是大学时候学的，早忘记了。

Questions 21-22

男：今天晚上我们出去吃吧？

女：又出去吃？每个月得花多少钱啊？

男：自己做饭多费时间，在外面吃比在家做饭快。

女：随你怎么说，要去你自己去，反正我不去！

Questions 23-24

男：请问苹果怎么卖？

女：本地的三块一斤，外国的十五块一斤。

男：我想要本地的，能便宜点不？

女：这样吧，两斤五块吧。

男：好，就要两斤。

Questions 25-26

男：那天的活动怎么样？

女：很成功，谢谢你的帮忙。

男：客气什么？我们是同学，这是应该的嘛。

Question 27

男：我们八点走吧，早点到，免得让别人等。

女：走路十分钟就到了，不用这麼早。九点再走吧，一定来得及。

Questions 28-29

男：你知道南京路怎么走吗?

女：从这坐公共汽车，在体育馆下车就是了。

男：那大概要多长时间？

女：一个小时左右吧。

Question 30

男：你毕业后打算做什么？

女：我暂时不打算升学，我计划去国外旅游一年。

Part A

Traditional Characters

Question 1

A： 今天的天氣怎麼樣？

(A) 還不錯，就是有點冷。
(B) 昨天下雨了。
(C) 天氣預報說明天會下雨。

Question 2

A： 小王，吃過飯了嗎？

(A) 今天的菜很好吃。
(B) 我已經很飽了。
(C) 吃過了。

Question 3

A： 你穿的衣服真漂亮，在哪裏買的？

(A) 不是買的，是我姐姐送我的。
(B) 謝謝你的大衣。
(C) 漂亮的衣服越來越貴了。

Question 4

A： 晚上早點回來，別玩得太晚了，不安全。

B： 放心吧，我跟小張說好了，十點之前他會開車送我回來的。

(A) 小劉可靠嗎？
(B) 十點之前別回來。
(C) 那我就安心了。

Question 5

A： 你會做中國菜嗎？

(A) 會一點點。
(B) 我喜歡中國菜。
(C) 我昨天吃了中國菜。

Question 6

A： 我不太會畫畫，你教我好嗎？

(A) 沒問題。
(B) 這些題太難了。
(C) 天氣太熱了。

Question 7

A： 我考試又失敗了！

(A) 這位是我的老師。
(B) 我相信你會喜歡這件毛衣的。
(C) 別灰心，你下次一定會成功的。

Question 8

A： 今天幸好有你幫忙，不然，這麼多東西我肯定拿不回來。
B： 那麼客氣幹嗎？反正我也是順便。

(A) 我自己拿吧。
(B) 還是很感謝你的。
(C) 你今天太幸運了。

Question 9

A： 最近小明家的電話總是打不通。

(A) 我不知道他家的電話號碼。
(B) 他的電話壞了。
(C) 太晚了，不方便打電話。

Question 10

A： 最近老是加班，真累。

(A) 你累不累？
(B) 你得注意休息。
(C) 你上班可以吃東西嗎？

Question 11

A： 你這學期上過什麼課？

(A) 除了中文課之外，我還修了法文課。
(B) 我學法文學了三年多了。
(C) 法文比中文難學多了。

Question 12

A： 這本書你看過嗎？

(A) 我不大喜歡看電影。
(B) 看過了，寫得非常精彩。
(C) 西南圖書館很大。

Question 13

A： 你買到火車票了嗎？

B： 買不到，春節火車票不好買。

(A) 你真幸運。
(B) 音樂會的票都賣完了。
(C) 我也買不到。

Question 14

A： 你週末看的房子怎麼樣？打算買嗎？

B： 買什麼呀！跟廣告上說的完全不一樣。

(A) 我也打算買房。
(B) 遠是遠了點，坐車還是挺方便的。
(C) 是啊，現在的廣告真的不能相信。

Question 15

A： 恭喜你取得了這麼好的成績。

(A) 謝謝，你太客氣了。
(B) 謝謝，我會繼續努力的。
(C) 衣服已經洗好了。

Part B

Questions 16-17

男：天氣預報說明天會下雨。

女：唉，真可惜，看來又不能去爬山了。

Question 18

男：你知道菜市場怎樣走嗎？

女：一直往前走就是了！

Questions 19-20

男：小張，聽說你學過德語，明天公司要來兩位德國客人，你幫忙翻譯翻譯？

女：唉，我那點德語還是大學時候學的，早忘記了。

Questions 21-22

男：今天晚上我們出去吃吧？

女：又出去吃？每個月得花多少錢啊？

男：自己做飯多費時間，在外面吃比在家做飯快。

女：隨你怎麼說，要去你自己去，反正我不去！

Questions 23-24

男：請問蘋果怎麼賣？

女：本地的三塊一斤，外國的十五塊一斤。

男：我想要本地的，能便宜點不？

女：這樣吧，兩斤五塊吧。

男：好，就要兩斤。

Questions 25-26

男：那天的活動怎麼樣？

女：很成功，謝謝你的幫忙。

男：客氣什麼？我們是同學，這是應該的嘛。

Question 27

男：我們八點走吧，早點到，免得讓別人等。

女：走路十分鐘就到了，不用這麼早。九點再走吧，一定來得及。

Questions 28-29

男：你知道南京路怎麼走嗎?

女：從這坐公共汽車，在體育館下車就是了。

男：那大概要多長時間？

女：一個小時左右吧。

Question 30

男：你畢業後打算做什麼？

女：我暫時不打算升學，我計劃去國外旅遊一年。

Part A

Pinyin Romanization

Question 1

A： Jīntiān de tiānqì zěnme yàng?

(A) Hái bú cuò, jiùshì yǒudiǎn lěng.
(B) Zuótiān xiàyǔ le.
(C) Tiānqì yùbào shuō míngtiān huì xiàyǔ.

Question 2

A： Xiǎo Wáng, chī guo fàn le ma?

(A) Jīntiān de cài hěn hǎochī.
(B) Wǒ yǐjīng hěn bǎo le.
(C) Chīguo le.

Question 3

A： Nǐ chuān de yīfu zhēn piàoliang, zài nǎli mǎi de?

(A) Bú shì mǎi de, shì wǒ jiějie sòng wǒ de.
(B) Xièxie nǐ de dàyī.
(C) Piàoliang de yīfu yuè lái yuè guì le.

Question 4

A： Wǎnshang zǎodiǎn huílai, bié wán de tài wǎn le, bù'ānquán.

B： Fàngxīn ba, wǒ gēn Xiǎo Zhāng shuō hǎo le, shí diǎn zhī qián tā huì kāichē sòng wǒ huílai de.

(A) Xiǎo Liú kěkào ma?
(B) Shí diǎn zhīqián bié huílai.
(C) Nà wǒ jiù ānxīn le.

Question 5

A： Nǐ huì zuò Zhōngguócài ma?

(A) Huì yìdiǎn dian.

(B) Wǒ xǐhuan Zhōngguócài.

(C) Wǒ zuótiān chīle Zhōngguócài.

Question 6

A： Wǒ bú tài huì huàhuà, nǐ jiào wǒ hǎo ma?

(A) Méi wèntí.

(B) Zhè xiē tí tài nán le.

(C) Tiānqì tài rè le.

Question 7

A： Wǒ kǎoshì yòu shībài le!

(A) Zhè wèi shì wǒ de lǎoshī.

(B) Wǒ xiāngxìn nǐ huì xǐhuan zhè jiàn máoyī de.

(C) Bié huīxīn, nǐ xiàcì yídìng huì chénggōng de.

Question 8

A： Jīntiān xìnghǎo yǒu nǐ bāngmáng, bùrán, zhème duō dōngxi wǒ kěndìng ná bù huílai.

B： Nàme kèqi gànmá? Fǎnzhèng wǒ yě shì shùnbiàn.

(A) Wǒ zìjǐ ná ba.

(B) Háishì hěn gǎnxiè nǐ de.

(C) Nǐ jīntiān tài xìngyùn le.

Question 9

A：Zuìjìn Xiǎo Míng jiā de diànhuà zǒngshì dǎ bù tōng.

(A) Wǒ bù zhīdào tā jiā de diànhuà hàomǎ.
(B) Tā de diànhuà huàile.
(C) Tài wǎn le, bù fāngbiàn dǎ diànhuà.

Question 10

A：Zuìjìn lǎoshì jiābān, zhēn lèi.

(A) Nǐ lèi bu lèi?
(B) Nǐ děi zhùyì xiūxi.
(C) Nǐ shàngbān kěyǐ chī dōngxi ma?

Question 11

A：Nǐ zhè xuéqī shàng guo shénme kè?

(A) Chú le Zhōngwénkè zhī wài, wǒ hái xiū le Fǎwénkè.
(B) Wǒ xué Fǎwén xué le sān nián duō le.
(C) Fǎwén bǐ Zhōngwén nán xué duō le.

Question 12

A：Zhè běn shū nǐ kàn guo ma?

(A) Wǒ bú dà xǐhuan kàn diànyǐng.
(B) Kàn guo le, xiě de fēicháng jīngcǎi.
(C) Xīnán túshūguǎn hěn dà.

Question 13

A：Nǐ mǎi dào huǒchēpiào le ma?

B：Mǎi bu dào, Chūnjié huǒchēpiào bù hǎo mǎi.

(A) Nǐ zhēn xìngyùn.
(B) Yīnyuèhuì de piào dōu mài wán le.
(C) Wǒ yě mǎi bu dào.

Question 14

A：Nǐ zhōumò kàn de fángzi zěnme yàng? Dǎsuan mǎi ma?

B：Mǎi shénme ya! Gēn guǎnggào shàng shuō de wánquán bù yíyàng.

(A) Wǒ yě dǎsuan mǎi fang.
(B) Yuǎn shì yuǎn le diǎn, zuòchē háishì tǐng fāngbiàn de.
(C) Shì a, xiànzài de guǎnggào zhēn de bù néng xiāngxìn.

Question 15

A：Gōngxǐ nǐ qǔdéle zhème hǎo de chéngjì.

(A) Xièxie, nǐ tài kèqi le.
(B) Xièxie, wǒ huì jìxù nǔlì de.
(C) Yīfu yǐjīng xǐ hǎo le.

Part B

Questions 16-17

Nán：Tiānqì yùbào shuō míngtiān huì xiàyǔ.

Nǚ ：Āi, zhēn kěxī, kàn lái yòu bù néng qù páshān le.

Questions 18

Nán：Nǐ zhīdào càishìchǎng zěnyàng zǒu ma?
Nǚ ：Yìzhí wǎngqián zǒu jiùshì le!

Questions 19-20

Nán：Xiǎo Zhāng, tīng shuō nǐ xué guo Déyǔ, míngtiān gōngsī yào lái liǎng wèi Déguó kèren, nǐ bāngmáng fānyifānyi?
Nǚ ：Āi, wǒ nà diǎn Déyǔ háishì dàxué shíhou xué de, zǎo wàngjìle.

Questions 21-22

Nán : Jīntiān wǎnshang wǒmen chūqu chī ba?

Nǚ : Yòu chūqu chī? Měi ge yuè děi huā duōshǎo qián a?

Nán : Zìjǐ zuòfàn duō fèi shíjiān, zài wàimiàn chī bǐ zàijiā zuòfàn kuài.

Nǚ : Suí nǐ zěnme shuō, yào qù nǐ zìjǐ qù, fǎnzhèng wǒ bú qù!

Questions 23-24

Nán : Qǐngwèn píngguǒ zěnme mài?

Nǚ : Běndì de sān kuài yì jīn, wài guó de shí wǔ kuài yì jīn.

Nán : Wǒ xiǎng yào běndì de, néng piányi diǎn bù?

Nǚ : Zhèyàng ba, liǎng jīn wǔ kuài ba.

Nán : Hǎo, jiù yào liǎng jīn.

Questions 25-26

Nán : Nà tiān de huódòng zěnme yàng?

Nǚ : Hěn chénggōng, xièxie nǐ de bāngmáng.

Nán : Kèqi shénme? Wǒmen shì tóngxué, zhè shì yīnggāi de ma.

Question 27

Nán : Wǒmen bā diǎn zǒu ba, zǎodiǎn dào, miǎnde ràng biérén děng.

Nǚ : Zǒulù shí fēnzhōng jiù dào le, bú yòng zhème zǎo. Jiǔ diǎn zài zǒu ba, yídìng láidejí.

Questions 28-29

Nán : Nǐ zhīdào Nánjīnglù zěnme zǒu ma?

Nǚ : Cóng zhè zuò gōnggòngqìchē, zài tǐyùguǎn xià chē jiù shì le.

Nán : Nà dàgài yào duō cháng shíjiān?

Nǚ : Yí ge xiǎoshí zuǒyòu ba.

Question 30

Nán : Nǐ bìyè hòu dǎsuan zuò shénme?

Nǚ : Wǒ zànshí bù dǎsuan shēngxué, wǒ jìhuà qù guówài lǚyóu yì nián.

Practice Test Two

1	Ⓐ	Ⓑ	Ⓒ	Ⓓ	31	Ⓐ	Ⓑ	Ⓒ	Ⓓ	56	Ⓐ	Ⓑ	Ⓒ	Ⓓ
2	Ⓐ	Ⓑ	Ⓒ	Ⓓ	32	Ⓐ	Ⓑ	Ⓒ	Ⓓ	57	Ⓐ	Ⓑ	Ⓒ	Ⓓ
3	Ⓐ	Ⓑ	Ⓒ	Ⓓ	33	Ⓐ	Ⓑ	Ⓒ	Ⓓ	58	Ⓐ	Ⓑ	Ⓒ	Ⓓ
4	Ⓐ	Ⓑ	Ⓒ	Ⓓ	34	Ⓐ	Ⓑ	Ⓒ	Ⓓ	59	Ⓐ	Ⓑ	Ⓒ	Ⓓ
5	Ⓐ	Ⓑ	Ⓒ	Ⓓ	35	Ⓐ	Ⓑ	Ⓒ	Ⓓ	60	Ⓐ	Ⓑ	Ⓒ	Ⓓ
6	Ⓐ	Ⓑ	Ⓒ	Ⓓ	36	Ⓐ	Ⓑ	Ⓒ	Ⓓ	61	Ⓐ	Ⓑ	Ⓒ	Ⓓ
7	Ⓐ	Ⓑ	Ⓒ	Ⓓ	37	Ⓐ	Ⓑ	Ⓒ	Ⓓ	62	Ⓐ	Ⓑ	Ⓒ	Ⓓ
8	Ⓐ	Ⓑ	Ⓒ	Ⓓ	38	Ⓐ	Ⓑ	Ⓒ	Ⓓ	63	Ⓐ	Ⓑ	Ⓒ	Ⓓ
9	Ⓐ	Ⓑ	Ⓒ	Ⓓ	39	Ⓐ	Ⓑ	Ⓒ	Ⓓ	64	Ⓐ	Ⓑ	Ⓒ	Ⓓ
10	Ⓐ	Ⓑ	Ⓒ	Ⓓ	40	Ⓐ	Ⓑ	Ⓒ	Ⓓ	65	Ⓐ	Ⓑ	Ⓒ	Ⓓ
11	Ⓐ	Ⓑ	Ⓒ	Ⓓ	41	Ⓐ	Ⓑ	Ⓒ	Ⓓ	66	Ⓐ	Ⓑ	Ⓒ	Ⓓ
12	Ⓐ	Ⓑ	Ⓒ	Ⓓ	42	Ⓐ	Ⓑ	Ⓒ	Ⓓ	67	Ⓐ	Ⓑ	Ⓒ	Ⓓ
13	Ⓐ	Ⓑ	Ⓒ	Ⓓ	43	Ⓐ	Ⓑ	Ⓒ	Ⓓ	68	Ⓐ	Ⓑ	Ⓒ	Ⓓ
14	Ⓐ	Ⓑ	Ⓒ	Ⓓ	44	Ⓐ	Ⓑ	Ⓒ	Ⓓ	69	Ⓐ	Ⓑ	Ⓒ	Ⓓ
15	Ⓐ	Ⓑ	Ⓒ	Ⓓ	45	Ⓐ	Ⓑ	Ⓒ	Ⓓ	70	Ⓐ	Ⓑ	Ⓒ	Ⓓ
16	Ⓐ	Ⓑ	Ⓒ	Ⓓ	46	Ⓐ	Ⓑ	Ⓒ	Ⓓ	71	Ⓐ	Ⓑ	Ⓒ	Ⓓ
17	Ⓐ	Ⓑ	Ⓒ	Ⓓ	47	Ⓐ	Ⓑ	Ⓒ	Ⓓ	72	Ⓐ	Ⓑ	Ⓒ	Ⓓ
18	Ⓐ	Ⓑ	Ⓒ	Ⓓ	48	Ⓐ	Ⓑ	Ⓒ	Ⓓ	73	Ⓐ	Ⓑ	Ⓒ	Ⓓ
19	Ⓐ	Ⓑ	Ⓒ	Ⓓ	49	Ⓐ	Ⓑ	Ⓒ	Ⓓ	74	Ⓐ	Ⓑ	Ⓒ	Ⓓ
20	Ⓐ	Ⓑ	Ⓒ	Ⓓ	50	Ⓐ	Ⓑ	Ⓒ	Ⓓ	75	Ⓐ	Ⓑ	Ⓒ	Ⓓ
21	Ⓐ	Ⓑ	Ⓒ	Ⓓ	51	Ⓐ	Ⓑ	Ⓒ	Ⓓ	76	Ⓐ	Ⓑ	Ⓒ	Ⓓ
22	Ⓐ	Ⓑ	Ⓒ	Ⓓ	52	Ⓐ	Ⓑ	Ⓒ	Ⓓ	77	Ⓐ	Ⓑ	Ⓒ	Ⓓ
23	Ⓐ	Ⓑ	Ⓒ	Ⓓ	53	Ⓐ	Ⓑ	Ⓒ	Ⓓ	78	Ⓐ	Ⓑ	Ⓒ	Ⓓ
24	Ⓐ	Ⓑ	Ⓒ	Ⓓ	54	Ⓐ	Ⓑ	Ⓒ	Ⓓ	79	Ⓐ	Ⓑ	Ⓒ	Ⓓ
25	Ⓐ	Ⓑ	Ⓒ	Ⓓ	55	Ⓐ	Ⓑ	Ⓒ	Ⓓ	80	Ⓐ	Ⓑ	Ⓒ	Ⓓ
26	Ⓐ	Ⓑ	Ⓒ	Ⓓ						81	Ⓐ	Ⓑ	Ⓒ	Ⓓ
27	Ⓐ	Ⓑ	Ⓒ	Ⓓ						82	Ⓐ	Ⓑ	Ⓒ	Ⓓ
28	Ⓐ	Ⓑ	Ⓒ	Ⓓ						83	Ⓐ	Ⓑ	Ⓒ	Ⓓ
29	Ⓐ	Ⓑ	Ⓒ	Ⓓ						84	Ⓐ	Ⓑ	Ⓒ	Ⓓ
30	Ⓐ	Ⓑ	Ⓒ	Ⓓ						85	Ⓐ	Ⓑ	Ⓒ	Ⓓ

SAT Chinese Practice Test — Three

SAT 中文模拟试题 — 第三套

SAT 中文模擬試題 — 第三套

Time — 1 hour

Questions 1 - 85

PLEASE NOTE THAT YOUR ANSWER SHEET HAS FOUR ANSWER POSITIONS, MARKED A, B, C, AND D, WHILE THE QUESTIONS THROUGHOUT THIS TEST CONTAIN EITHER THREE OR FOUR ANSWER CHOICES. BE SURE NOT TO MARK YOUR ANSWERS IN COLUMN D IF THERE ARE ONLY THREE CHOICES GIVEN.

SECTION I
LISTENING

Approximate time — 20 minutes
Questions 1 - 30

Part A

Directions:

In this part of the test, you will hear short questions, statements, or commands in Mandarin Chinese, followed by three responses in Mandarin Chinese, designated (A), (B), and (C). You will hear the questions or statements, as well as the responses, only once, and they are not printed in your test booklet. Therefore, you must listen very carefully. Select the best response and fill in the corresponding circle on your answer sheet.

Question 1 Mark your answer on your answer sheet.

Question 2 Mark your answer on your answer sheet.

Question 3 Mark your answer on your answer sheet.

Question 4 Mark your answer on your answer sheet.

Question 5 Mark your answer on your answer sheet.

Question 6 Mark your answer on your answer sheet.

Question 7 Mark your answer on your answer sheet.

Question 8 Mark your answer on your answer sheet.

Question 9 Mark your answer on your answer sheet.

Question 10 Mark your answer on your answer sheet.

Question 11 Mark your answer on your answer sheet.

Question 12 Mark your answer on your answer sheet.

Question 13 Mark your answer on your answer sheet.

Question 14 Mark your answer on your answer sheet.

Question 15 Mark your answer on your answer sheet.

Part B

Directions:

You will now hear a series of dialogues. You will hear them only once, and they are not printed in your test booklet. After each selection, you will be asked to answer one or more questions about what you have just heard. These questions, each with four possible answers, are printed in your test booklet. Select the best answer to each question from among the four choices printed and fill in the corresponding circle on your answer sheet.

Question 16

16. What does the woman want to buy?
    (A) A watch
    (B) A movie ticket
    (C) An air ticket
    (D) Travelers' checks

Questions 17-18

17. What does the man want to do during the summer?
    (A) Travel
    (B) Get a job
    (C) Learn Japanese
    (D) Take a break

18. Which of the following statements about the woman is true?
    (A) She will travel to France and Japan.
    (B) She is a nurse.
    (C) She graduated three years ago.
    (D) She wants to be an air hostess.

Questions 19-20

19. What is on offer for breakfast today?
    (A) Milk and eggs
    (B) Salad and bread
    (C) Congee and milk
    (D) Bread and dumplings

20. What does the man order in the end?
    (A) Milk and eggs
    (B) Congee and dumplings
    (C) Sandwich and salad
    (D) Milk and sandwich

Questions 21-22

21. What does the man want to buy?
    (A) A phone card
    (B) Some noodles
    (C) A magazine
    (D) A greeting card

22. How much does the man need to pay?
    (A) $20
    (B) $25
    (C) $50
    (D) $52

Questions 23-24

23. What is wrong with the woman?
    (A) Headache
    (B) Cough
    (C) Stomachache
    (D) Diarrhea

24. When did she start feeling ill?
    (A) Yesterday morning
    (B) Last night
    (C) This morning
    (D) Tonight

Question 25

25. For how long has the woman been studying Chinese?
    (A) Six months
    (B) One year
    (C) Two years
    (D) Two and a half years

Questions 26-27

26. What are the two people going to do?
    (A) Watch a movie
    (B) Go shopping
    (C) Go to a concert
    (D) Go to a restaurant

27. When are they going to meet?
    (A) 8:00
    (B) 8:40
    (C) 9:00
    (D) 9:40

Questions 28-29

28. What time does the train leave?
    (A) 9:40
    (B) 9:50
    (C) 10:00
    (D) 10:10

29. Where does the man invite the woman to visit?
    (A) Beijing
    (B) Shanghai
    (C) Hong Kong
    (D) Tokyo

Question 30

30. Which subject does the woman want to study?
    (A) Politics
    (B) Economics
    (C) Law
    (D) Art

SECTION II
USAGE

Suggested time — 15 minutes

Questions 31 - 55

Part A

Directions:

This section consists of a number of incomplete statements, each of which has four possible completions. Select the word or phrase that best completes the sentence structurally and logically and fill in the corresponding circle on your answer sheet.

This section of the test is presented in four different ways of representing Chinese: traditional characters, simplified characters, pinyin romanization, and the Chinese phonetic alphabet. IT IS RECOMMEMD THAT YOU CHOOSE THE WRITING SYSTEM WITH WHICH YOU ARE MORE FAMILIAR WITH AND **ONLY READ THAT VERSION** AS YOU WORK THROUGH THIS SECTION OF THE TEST.

31. 这个问题____科学家都不懂，小孩子就更不用说了。
    (A) 才
    (B) 连
    (C) 就
    (D) 跟

31. 這個問題____科學家都不懂，小孩子就更不用說了。
    (A) 才
    (B) 連
    (C) 就
    (D) 跟

31. Zhè ge wèntí____kēxuéjiā dōu bù dǒng, xiǎoháizi jiù gèng bú yòng shuō le.
    (A) cái
    (B) lián
    (C) jiù
    (D) gēn

31. ㄓㄜˋ ˙ㄍㄜ ㄨㄣˋ ㄊㄧˊ ____ ㄎㄜ ㄒㄩㄝˊ ㄐㄧㄚ ㄉㄡ ㄅㄨˋ ㄉㄨㄥˇ，ㄒㄧㄠˇ ㄏㄞˊ ˙ㄗ ㄐㄧㄡˋ ㄍㄥˋ ㄅㄨˊ ㄩㄥˋ ㄕㄨㄛ ˙ㄌㄜ 。
    (A) ㄘㄞˊ
    (B) ㄌㄧㄢˊ
    (C) ㄐㄧㄡˋ
    (D) ㄍㄣ

32. 最近天气十分寒冷，你可____不能着凉了。
    (A) 万一
    (B) 一万
    (C) 千万
    (D) 百万

32. 最近天氣十分寒冷，你可____不能著涼了。
    (A) 萬一
    (B) 一萬
    (C) 千萬
    (D) 百萬

32. Zuìjìn tiānqì shífēn hánlěng, nǐ kě____bù néng zháoliáng le.
    (A) wànyī
    (B) yíwàn
    (C) qiānwàn
    (D) bǎiwàn

32. ㄗㄨㄟˋ ㄐㄧㄣˋ ㄊㄧㄢ ㄑㄧˋ ㄕˊ ㄈㄣ ㄏㄢˊ ㄌㄥˇ，ㄋㄧˇ ㄎㄜˇ ____ ㄅㄨˋ ㄋㄥˊ ㄓㄠˊ ㄌㄧㄤˊ ˙ㄌㄜ 。
    (A) ㄨㄢˋ ㄧ
    (B) ㄧ ㄨㄢˋ
    (C) ㄑㄧㄢ ㄨㄢˋ
    (D) ㄅㄞˇ ㄨㄢˋ

33. 这个问题讲完了，____ 他又讲了另一个问题。
(A) 接着
(B) 就
(C) 然而
(D) 可能

33. 這個問題講完了，____ 他又講了另一個問題。
(A) 接著
(B) 就
(C) 然而
(D) 可能

33. Zhè ge wèntí jiǎng wán le, ____ tā yòu jiǎngle lìng yí ge wèntí.
(A) jiēzhe
(B) jiù
(C) rán'ér
(D) kěnéng

33. ㄓㄜˋ ˙ㄍㄜ ㄨㄣˋ ㄊㄧˊ ㄐㄧㄤˇ ㄨㄢˊ ˙ㄌㄜ ， ____ ㄊㄚ ㄧㄡˋ ㄐㄧㄤˇ ˙ㄌㄜ ㄌㄧㄥˋ ㄧˊ ˙ㄍㄜ ㄨㄣˋ ㄊㄧˊ 。
(A) ㄐㄧㄝ ˙ㄓㄜ
(B) ㄐㄧㄡˋ
(C) ㄖㄢˊ ㄦˊ
(D) ㄎㄜˇ ㄋㄥˊ

34. 你____学法语，____学英语，总之，一定要学一门外语。
(A) 要么 …… 要么
(B) 一边 …… 一边
(C) 不仅 …… 也
(D) 与其 …… 不如

34. 你____學法語，____學英語，總之，一定要學一門外語。
(A) 要麼 …… 要麼
(B) 一邊 …… 一邊
(C) 不僅 …… 也
(D) 與其 …… 不如

34. Nǐ ____ xué Fǎyǔ, ____ xué Yīngyǔ, zǒngzhī, yídìng yào xué yìmén wàiyǔ.
(A) yàome …… yàome
(B) yìbiān …… yìbiān
(C) bùjǐn …… yě
(D) yǔqí …… bùrú

34. ㄋㄧˇ ____ ㄒㄩㄝˊ ㄈㄚˇ ㄩˇ ， ____ ㄒㄩㄝˊ ㄧㄥ ㄩˇ ， ㄗㄨㄥˇ ㄓ ， ㄧˊ ㄉㄧㄥˋ ㄧㄠˋ ㄒㄩㄝˊ ㄧˋ ㄇㄣˊ ㄨㄞˋ ㄩˇ 。
(A) ㄧㄠˋ ˙ㄇㄜ …… ㄧㄠˋ ˙ㄇㄜ
(B) ㄧˋ ㄅㄧㄢ …… ㄧˋ ㄅㄧㄢ
(C) ㄅㄨˋ ㄐㄧㄣˇ …… ㄧㄝˇ
(D) ㄩˇ ㄑㄧˊ …… ㄅㄨˋ ㄖㄨˊ

35. 这个代表团____十五名专家教授组成。
(A) 因
(B) 以
(C) 由
(D) 让

35. 這個代表團____十五名專家教授組成。
(A) 因
(B) 以
(C) 由
(D) 讓

35. Zhè ge dàibiǎotuán ____ shíwǔ míng zhuānjiā jiàoshòu zǔchéng.
(A) yīn
(B) yǐ
(C) yóu
(D) ràng

35. ㄓㄜˋ ˙ㄍㄜ ㄉㄞˋ ㄅㄧㄠˇ ㄊㄨㄢˊ ____ ㄕˊ ㄨˇ ㄇㄧㄥˊ ㄓㄨㄢ ㄐㄧㄚ ㄐㄧㄠˋ ㄕㄡˋ ㄗㄨˇ ㄔㄥˊ 。
(A) ㄧㄣ
(B) ㄧˇ
(C) ㄧㄡˊ
(D) ㄖㄤˋ

36. 他____所有功课都做完了。
(A) 为
(B) 把
(C) 用
(D) 以

36. Tā ____ suǒyǒu gōngkè dōu zuò wán le.
(A) wèi
(B) bǎ
(C) yòng
(D) yǐ

37. 只要一直努力____，就一定能成功。
(A) 出来
(B) 上去
(C) 上来
(D) 下去

37. Zhǐyào yìzhí nǔlì____, jiù yídìng néng chénggōng.
(A) chūlai
(B) shàngqu
(C) shànglai
(D) xiàqu

38. ____就要考试了，大家都在认真地复习。
(A) 马上
(B) 竟然
(C) 虽然
(D) 于是

38. ____jiù yào kǎoshì le, dàjiā dōu zài rènzhēn de fùxí.
(A) Mǎshàng
(B) Jìngrán
(C) Suīrán
(D) Yúshì

36. 他____所有功課都做完了。
(A) 爲
(B) 把
(C) 用
(D) 以

36. ㄊㄚ ____ ㄙㄨㄛˇ ㄧㄡˇ ㄍㄨㄥ ㄎㄜˋ ㄉㄡ ㄗㄨㄛˋ ㄨㄢˊ ˙ㄌㄜ 。
(A) ㄨㄟˋ
(B) ㄅㄚˇ
(C) ㄩㄥˋ
(D) ㄧˇ

37. 只要一直努力____，就一定能成功。
(A) 出來
(B) 上去
(C) 上來
(D) 下去

37. ㄓˇ ㄧㄠˋ ㄧˋ ㄓˊ ㄋㄨˇ ㄌㄧˋ ____ ，ㄐㄧㄡˋ ㄧˊ ㄉㄧㄥˋ ㄋㄥˊ ㄔㄥˊ ㄍㄨㄥ 。
(A) ㄔㄨ ˙ㄌㄞ
(B) ㄕㄤˋ ㄑㄩˋ
(C) ㄕㄤˋ ㄌㄞˊ
(D) ㄒㄧㄚˋ ˙ㄑㄩ

38. ____就要考試了，大家都在認真地複習。
(A) 馬上
(B) 竟然
(C) 雖然
(D) 於是

38. ____ ㄐㄧㄡˋ ㄧㄠˋ ㄎㄠˇ ㄕˋ ˙ㄌㄜ ，ㄉㄚˋ ㄐㄧㄚ ㄉㄡ ㄗㄞˋ ㄖㄣˋ ㄓㄣ ˙ㄉㄜ ㄈㄨˋ ㄒㄧˊ 。
(A) ㄇㄚˇ ㄕㄤˋ
(B) ㄐㄧㄥˋ ㄖㄢˊ
(C) ㄙㄨㄟ ㄖㄢˊ
(D) ㄩˊ ㄕˋ

39. 明天是妈妈的生日，我给她买了一____衣服。

(A) 道
(B) 本
(C) 件
(D) 条

39. 明天是媽媽的生日，我給她買了一____衣服。

(A) 道
(B) 本
(C) 件
(D) 條

39. Míngtiān shì māma de shēngrì, wǒ gěi tā mǎile yī____yīfu.

(A) dào
(B) běn
(C) jiàn
(D) tiáo

39. ㄇㄧㄥˊ ㄊㄧㄢ ㄕˋ ㄇㄚ ˙ㄇㄚ ˙ㄉㄜ ㄕㄥ ㄖˋ，ㄨㄛˇ ㄍㄟˇ ㄊㄚ ㄇㄞˇ ˙ㄌㄜ ㄧ ____ ㄧ ˙ㄈㄨ。

(A) ㄉㄠˋ
(B) ㄅㄣˇ
(C) ㄐㄧㄢˋ
(D) ㄊㄧㄠˊ

40. 我的成绩不太好，要加倍努力____能赶上其他同学。

(A) 才
(B) 就
(C) 有
(D) 还

40. 我的成績不太好，要加倍努力____能趕上其他同學。

(A) 才
(B) 就
(C) 有
(D) 還

40. Wǒ de chéngjì bú tài hǎo, yào jiābèi nǔlì____néng gǎn shàng qítā tóngxué.

(A) cái
(B) jiù
(C) yǒu
(D) hái

40. ㄨㄛˇ ˙ㄉㄜ ㄔㄥˊ ㄐㄧˋ ㄅㄨˊ ㄊㄞˋ ㄏㄠˇ，ㄧㄠˋ ㄐㄧㄚ ㄅㄟˋ ㄋㄨˇ ㄌㄧˋ ____ ㄋㄥˊ ㄍㄢˇ ㄕㄤˋ ㄑㄧˊ ㄊㄚ ㄊㄨㄥˊ ㄒㄩㄝˊ。

(A) ㄘㄞˊ
(B) ㄐㄧㄡˋ
(C) ㄧㄡˇ
(D) ㄏㄞˊ

41. ____学了弹琴，她每天都会练习几个小时。

(A) 从此
(B) 自从
(C) 从
(D) 于

41. ____學了彈琴，她每天都會練習幾個小時。

(A) 從此
(B) 自從
(C) 從
(D) 於

41. ____xuéle tánqín, tā měitiān dōuhuì liànxí jǐ gè xiǎoshí.

(A) Cóngcǐ
(B) Zìcóng
(C) Cóng
(D) Yú

41. ____ ㄒㄩㄝˊ ˙ㄌㄜ ㄊㄢˊ ㄑㄧㄣˊ，ㄊㄚ ㄇㄟˇ ㄊㄧㄢ ㄉㄡ ㄏㄨㄟˋ ㄌㄧㄢˋ ㄒㄧˊ ㄐㄧˇ ˙ㄍㄜ ㄒㄧㄠˇ ㄕˊ。

(A) ㄘㄨㄥˊ ㄘˇ
(B) ㄗˋ ㄘㄨㄥˊ
(C) ㄘㄨㄥˊ
(D) ㄩˊ

42. 他上学的地方，____ 。
(A) 离医院不太远
(B) 不远离医院太
(C) 太不远医院离
(D) 医院离不太远

42. Tā shàngxué de dìfang, ____ .
(A) lí yīyuàn bú tài yuǎn
(B) bù yuǎn lí yīyuàn tài
(C) tài bù yuǎn yīyuàn lí
(D) yīyuàn lí bú tài yuǎn

43. ____ ，他的成绩有了很大的进步。
(A) 训练一年经过的
(B) 经过一年的训练
(C) 一年训练经过的
(D) 经过训练的一年

43. ____ , tā de chéngjì yǒule hěn dà de jìnbù.
(A) Xùnliàn yì nián jīngguò de
(B) Jīngguò yì nián de xùnliàn
(C) Yì nián xùnliàn jīngguò de
(D) Jīngguò xùnliàn de yì nián

44. 他____有时间____看书，所以知识很丰富。
(A) 又 …… 又
(B) 带 …… 又
(C) 既 …… 也
(D) 一 …… 就

44. Tā ____ yǒu shíjiān ____ kànshū, suǒyǐ zhīshi hěn fēngfù.
(A) yòu …… yòu
(B) dài …… yòu
(C) jì …… yě
(D) yī …… jiù

42. 他上學的地方，____ 。
(A) 離醫院不太遠
(B) 不遠離醫院太
(C) 太不遠醫院離
(D) 醫院離不太遠

42. ㄊㄚ ㄕㄤˋ ㄒㄩㄝˊ ㄉㄜ˙ ㄉㄧˋ ㄈㄤ˙ ， ____ 。
(A) ㄌㄧˊ ㄧ ㄩㄢˋ ㄅㄨˊ ㄊㄞˋ ㄩㄢˇ
(B) ㄅㄨˋ ㄩㄢˇ ㄌㄧˊ ㄧ ㄩㄢˋ ㄊㄞˋ
(C) ㄊㄞˋ ㄅㄨˋ ㄩㄢˇ ㄧ ㄩㄢˋ ㄌㄧˊ
(D) ㄧ ㄩㄢˋ ㄌㄧˊ ㄅㄨˊ ㄊㄞˋ ㄩㄢˇ

43. ____ ，他的成績有了很大的進步。
(A) 訓練一年經過的
(B) 經過一年的訓練
(C) 一年訓練經過的
(D) 經過訓練的一年

43. ____ ，ㄊㄚ ㄉㄜ˙ ㄔㄥˊ ㄐㄧ ㄧㄡˇ ㄌㄜ˙ ㄏㄣˇ ㄉㄚˋ ㄉㄜ˙ ㄐㄧㄣˋ ㄅㄨˋ。
(A) ㄒㄩㄣˋ ㄌㄧㄢˋ ㄧˋ ㄋㄧㄢˊ ㄐㄧㄥ ㄍㄨㄛˋ ㄉㄜ˙
(B) ㄐㄧㄥ ㄍㄨㄛˋ ㄧˋ ㄋㄧㄢˊ ㄉㄜ˙ ㄒㄩㄣˋ ㄌㄧㄢˋ
(C) ㄧˋ ㄋㄧㄢˊ ㄒㄩㄣˋ ㄌㄧㄢˋ ㄐㄧㄥ ㄍㄨㄛˋ ㄉㄜ˙
(D) ㄐㄧㄥ ㄍㄨㄛˋ ㄒㄩㄣˋ ㄌㄧㄢˋ ㄉㄜ˙ ㄧˋ ㄋㄧㄢˊ

44. 他____有時間____看書，所以知識很豐富。
(A) 又 …… 又
(B) 帶 …… 又
(C) 既 …… 也
(D) 一 ……就

44. ㄊㄚ ____ ㄧㄡˇ ㄕˊ ㄐㄧㄢ ____ ㄎㄢˋ ㄕㄨ ，ㄙㄨㄛˇ ㄧˇ ㄓ ㄕˋ ㄏㄣˇ ㄈㄥ ㄈㄨˋ。
(A) ㄧㄡˋ …… ㄧㄡˋ
(B) ㄉㄞˋ …… ㄧㄡˋ
(C) ㄐㄧˋ …… ㄧㄝˇ
(D) ㄧ …… ㄐㄧㄡˋ

45. 上了一天的课，小王觉得____了。
(A) 累一点
(B) 一点累
(C) 有点累
(D) 累有点

45. Shàngle yì tiān de kè, Xiǎo Wáng juédé____ le.
(A) lèi yì diǎn
(B) yìdiǎn lèi
(C) yǒudiǎn lèi
(D) lèi yǒudiǎn

46. ____我怎么说，他____不同意。
(A) 无论 …… 都
(B) 虽然 …… 都
(C) 即使 …… 但
(D) 宁可 …… 但

46. ____wǒ zěnme shuō, tā____bù tóngyì.
(A) Wúlùn …… dōu
(B) Suīrán …… dōu
(C) Jíshǐ …… dàn
(D) Nìngkě …… dàn

47. 别着急，慢慢來，____我们还有很多时间。
(A) 可是
(B) 无论
(C) 反正
(D) 只得

47. Bié zháojí, mànmàn lái, ____ wǒmen háiyǒu hěnduō shíjiān.
(A) kěshì
(B) wúlùn
(C) fǎnzhèng
(D) zhǐděi

45. 上了一天的課，小王覺得____了。
(A) 累一點
(B) 一點累
(C) 有點累
(D) 累有點

45. ㄕㄤˋ ㄌㄜ˙ ㄧˋ ㄊㄧㄢ ㄉㄜ˙ ㄎㄜˋ，ㄒㄧㄠˇ ㄨㄤˊ ㄐㄩㄝˊ ㄉㄜˊ ____ ㄌㄜ˙。
(A) ㄌㄟˋ ㄧˋ ㄉㄧㄢˇ
(B) ㄧˋ ㄉㄧㄢˇ ㄌㄟˋ
(C) ㄧㄡˇ ㄉㄧㄢˇ ㄌㄟˋ
(D) ㄌㄟˋ ㄧㄡˇ ㄉㄧㄢˇ

46. ____我怎麼說，他____不同意。
(A) 無論 …… 都
(B) 雖然 …… 都
(C) 即使 …… 但
(D) 寧可 …… 但

46. ____ ㄨㄛˇ ㄗㄣˇ ㄇㄜ˙ ㄕㄨㄛ，ㄊㄚ ____ ㄅㄨˋ ㄊㄨㄥˊ ㄧˋ。
(A) ㄨˊ ㄌㄨㄣˋ …… ㄉㄡ
(B) ㄙㄨㄟ ㄖㄢˊ …… ㄉㄡ
(C) ㄐㄧˊ ㄕˇ …… ㄉㄢˋ
(D) ㄋㄧㄥˋ ㄎㄜˇ …… ㄉㄢˋ

47. 別著急，慢慢來，____我們還有很多時間。
(A) 可是
(B) 無論
(C) 反正
(D) 只得

47. ㄅㄧㄝˊ ㄓㄠˊ ㄐㄧˊ，ㄇㄢˋ ㄇㄢˋ ㄌㄞˊ，____ ㄨㄛˇ ㄇㄣ˙ ㄏㄞˊ ㄧㄡˇ ㄏㄣˇ ㄉㄨㄛ ㄕˊ ㄐㄧㄢ。
(A) ㄎㄜˇ ㄕˋ
(B) ㄨˊ ㄌㄨㄣˋ
(C) ㄈㄢˇ ㄓㄥˋ
(D) ㄓˇ ㄉㄟˇ

48. 中国人喜欢吃米饭和面，美国人____喜欢吃汉堡包。
(A) 则
(B) 不
(C) 可
(D) 而

48. Zhōngguórén xǐhuan chī mǐfàn hé miàn, Měiguórén ____ xǐhuan chī hànbǎobāo.
(A) zé
(B) bù
(C) kě
(D) ér

49. 我____中国历史一直很有兴趣。
(A) 在
(B) 关于
(C) 对
(D) 由于

49. Wǒ ____ Zhōngguó lìshǐ yìzhí hěn yǒu xìngqù.
(A) zài
(B) guānyú
(C) duì
(D) yóuyú

50. 你看他一直在____，一定是有什么心事。
(A) 走走去来
(B) 走走来去
(C) 来走来去
(D) 走来走去

50. Nǐ kàn tā yìzhí zài____, yídìng shì yǒu shénme xīnshì.
(A) zǒu zou qù lái
(B) zǒu zou lái qù
(C) lái zǒu lái qù
(D) zǒu lái zǒu qù

48. 中國人喜歡吃米飯和麵，美國人____喜歡吃漢堡包。
(A) 則
(B) 不
(C) 可
(D) 而

48. ㄓㄨㄥ ㄍㄨㄛˊ ㄖㄣˊ ㄒㄧˇ ㄏㄨㄢ ㄔ ㄇㄧˇ ㄈㄢˋ ㄏㄜˊ ㄇㄧㄢˋ，ㄇㄟˇ ㄍㄨㄛˊ ㄖㄣˊ ____ ㄒㄧˇ ㄏㄨㄢ ㄔ ㄏㄢˋ ㄅㄠˇ ㄅㄠ。
(A) ㄗㄜˊ
(B) ㄅㄨˋ
(C) ㄎㄜˇ
(D) ㄦˊ

49. 我____中國歷史一直很有興趣。
(A) 在
(B) 關於
(C) 對
(D) 由於

49. ㄨㄛˇ ____ ㄓㄨㄥ ㄍㄨㄛˊ ㄌㄧˋ ㄕˇ ㄧˋ ㄓˊ ㄏㄣˇ ㄧㄡˇ ㄒㄧㄥˋ ㄑㄩˋ。
(A) ㄗㄞˋ
(B) ㄍㄨㄢ ㄩˊ
(C) ㄉㄨㄟˋ
(D) ㄧㄡˊ ㄩˊ

50. 你看他一直在____，一定是有什麼心事。
(A) 走走去來
(B) 走走來去
(C) 來走來去
(D) 走來走去

50. ㄋㄧˇ ㄎㄢˋ ㄊㄚ ㄧˋ ㄓˊ ㄗㄞˋ ____，ㄧˊ ㄉㄧㄥˋ ㄕˋ ㄧㄡˇ ㄕㄣˊ ㄇㄜ˙ ㄒㄧㄣ ㄕˋ。
(A) ㄗㄡˇ ㄗㄡˇ ㄑㄩˋ ㄌㄞˊ
(B) ㄗㄡˇ ㄗㄡˇ ㄌㄞˊ ㄑㄩˋ
(C) ㄌㄞˊ ㄗㄡˇ ㄌㄞˊ ㄑㄩˋ
(D) ㄗㄡˇ ㄌㄞˊ ㄗㄡˇ ㄑㄩˋ

51. 他说两天之内一定到，____今天到，____明天到。
(A) 不仅 …… 而且
(B) 不是 …… 就是
(C) 不但 …… 而且
(D) 是 …… 还是

51. 他說兩天之內一定到，____今天到，____明天到。
(A) 不僅 …… 而且
(B) 不是 …… 就是
(C) 不但 …… 而且
(D) 是 …… 還是

51. Tā shuō liǎngtiān zhī nèi yídìng dào, ____ jīntiān dào, ____ míngtiān dào.
(A) bùjǐn …… érqiě
(B) búshì …… jiùshì
(C) búdàn …… érqiě
(D) shì …… háishì

51. ㄊㄚ ㄕㄨㄛ ㄌㄧㄤˇ ㄊㄧㄢ ㄓ ㄋㄟˋ ㄧˊ ㄉㄧㄥˋ ㄉㄠˋ，____ ㄐㄧㄣ ㄊㄧㄢ ㄉㄠˋ，____ ㄇㄧㄥˊ ㄊㄧㄢ ㄉㄠˋ。
(A) ㄅㄨˊ ㄐㄧㄣˇ …… ㄦˊ ㄑㄧㄝˇ
(B) ㄅㄨˊ ㄕˋ …… ㄐㄧㄡˋ ㄕˋ
(C) ㄅㄨˊ ㄉㄢˋ …… ㄦˊ ㄑㄧㄝˇ
(D) ㄕˋ …… ㄏㄞˊ ㄕˋ

52. ____你不喜欢爬山，我们____去看电影吧。
(A) 与其 …… 不如
(B) 不但 …… 而且
(C) 既然 …… 就
(D) 之所以 …… 是因为

52. ____你不喜歡爬山，我們____去看電影吧。
(A) 與其 …… 不如
(B) 不但 …… 而且
(C) 既然 …… 就
(D) 之所以 …… 是因爲

52. ____ nǐ bù xǐhuan páshān, wǒmen ____ qù kàn diànyǐng ba.
(A) Yǔqí …… bùrú
(B) Búdàn …… érqiě
(C) Jìrán …… jiù
(D) Zhīsuǒyǐ …… shì yīnwèi

52. ____ ㄋㄧˇ ㄅㄨˋ ㄒㄧˇ ˙ㄏㄨㄢ ㄆㄚˊ ㄕㄢ，ㄨㄛˇ ˙ㄇㄣ ____ ㄑㄩˋ ㄎㄢˋ ㄉㄧㄢˋ ㄧㄥˇ ˙ㄅㄚ。
(A) ㄩˇ ㄑㄧˊ …… ㄅㄨˋ ㄖㄨˊ
(B) ㄅㄨˊ ㄉㄢˋ …… ㄦˊ ㄑㄧㄝˇ
(C) ㄐㄧˋ ㄖㄢˊ …… ㄐㄧㄡˋ
(D) ㄓ ㄙㄨㄛˇ ㄧˇ …… ㄕˋ ㄧㄣ ㄨㄟˋ

53. 玻璃窗____弟弟打破了。
(A) 为
(B) 把
(C) 被
(D) 受

53. 玻璃窗____弟弟打破了。
(A) 爲
(B) 把
(C) 被
(D) 受

53. Bōlichuāng ____ dìdi dǎ pò le.
(A) wèi
(B) bǎ
(C) bèi
(D) shòu

53. ㄅㄛ ㄌㄧˊ ㄔㄨㄤ ____ ㄉㄧˋ ˙ㄉㄧ ㄉㄚˇ ㄆㄛˋ ˙ㄌㄜ。
(A) ㄨㄟˋ
(B) ㄅㄚˇ
(C) ㄅㄟˋ
(D) ㄕㄡˋ

54. 太晚了，公交车都没有了，我____打车回家。

(A) 只好
(B) 为了
(C) 反而
(D) 顺便

54. Tài wǎn le, gōngjiāochē dōu méiyǒu le, wǒ ____ dǎchē huíjiā.

(A) zhǐhǎo
(B) wèile
(C) fǎn'ér
(D) shùnbiàn

55. 这件衣服 ____ 很便宜，____ 很好看。

(A) 除非 …… 否则
(B) 不但 …… 而且
(C) 既 …… 也
(D) 因为 …… 所以

55. Zhè jiàn yīfu ____ hěn piányi, ____ hěn hǎokàn.

(A) chúfēi …… fǒuzé
(B) búdàn …… érqiě
(C) jì …… yě
(D) yīnwèi …… suǒyǐ

54. 太晚了，公交車都沒有了，我____打車回家。

(A) 只好
(B) 爲了
(C) 反而
(D) 順便

54. ㄊㄞˋ ㄨㄢˇ ˙ㄌㄜ，ㄍㄨㄥ ㄐㄧㄠ ㄔㄜ ㄉㄡ ㄇㄟˊ ㄧㄡˇ ˙ㄌㄜ，ㄨㄛˇ ____ ㄉㄚˇ ㄔㄜ ㄏㄨㄟˊ ㄐㄧㄚ。

(A) ㄓˇ ㄏㄠˇ
(B) ㄨㄟˋ ˙ㄌㄜ
(C) ㄈㄢˇ ㄦˊ
(D) ㄕㄨㄣˋ ㄅㄧㄢˋ

55. 這件衣服 ____ 很便宜，____ 很好看。

(A) 除非 …… 否則
(B) 不但 …… 而且
(C) 既 …… 也
(D) 因爲 …… 所以

55. ㄓㄜˋ ㄐㄧㄢˋ ㄧ ˙ㄈㄨ ____ ㄏㄣˇ ㄆㄧㄢˊ ˙ㄧ，____ ㄏㄣˇ ㄏㄠˇ ㄎㄢˋ。

(A) ㄔㄨˊ ㄈㄟ …… ㄈㄡˇ ㄗㄜˊ
(B) ㄅㄨˊ ㄉㄢˋ …… ㄦˊ ㄑㄧㄝˇ
(C) ㄐㄧˋ …… ㄧㄝˇ
(D) ㄧㄣ ㄨㄟˋ …… ㄙㄨㄛˇ ㄧˇ

SECTION III
READING COMPREHENSION

Suggested time — 25 minutes
Questions 56 - 85

WHEN YOU BEGIN THIS SECTION, MAKE SURE THAT YOU MARK YOUR ANSWER TO THE FIRST QUESTION BY FILLING IN ONE OF THE CIRCLES NEXT TO NUMBER 56 ON YOUR ANSWER SHEET.

Directions:

Read the following texts carefully for comprehension. Each one is followed by one or more questions or incomplete statements. Select the answer or completion that is best according to the text and fill in the corresponding circle on your answer sheet.

This section of the test is presented in two writing systems: traditional characters and simplified characters. IT IS RECOMMEMD THAT YOU CHOOSE THE WRITING SYSTEM WITH WHICH YOU ARE MORE FAMILIAR WITH AND **ONLY READ THAT VERSION** AS YOU WORK THROUGH THIS SECTION OF THE TEST.

Question 56

请勿靠近车门	請勿靠近車門

56. What does this sign say?
    (A) No smoking
    (B) Please do not litter
    (C) Please keep quiet
    (D) Please mind the door

Question 57

电量不足，请立即充电	電量不足，請立即充電

57. What does this message say?

(A) Switch off immediately

(B) Insert disc

(C) Recharge immediately

(D) Insufficient credit remaining

Question 58

乐韵钢琴班招生
联络电话：1234567

樂韻鋼琴班招生
聯絡電話：1234567

58. This advertisement is about

(A) piano classes

(B) violin classes

(C) painting classes

(D) calligraphy classes

Questions 59-60

我的朋友马克是美国人，今年十七岁。他长得不太高，但眼睛很大。他特别喜欢中国菜，尤其喜欢吃年糕和饺子。他每天六点就起床，坚持早上读中文已经有两年多了，所以他的中文成绩很好。

我的朋友馬克是美國人，今年十七歲。他長得不太高，但眼睛很大。他特別喜歡中國菜，尤其喜歡吃年糕和餃子。他每天六點就起床，堅持早上讀中文已經有兩年多了，所以他的中文成績很好。

59. Which of the following is Mark's favorite food?

(A) Noodles

(B) French fries

(C) Hamburger

(D) Dumplings

60. Why is Mark doing so well in Chinese?

(A) He got up at 6 A.M. yesterday.
(B) He has many Chinese friends.
(C) He has been studying Chinese every morning for two years.
(D) He is very interested in Chinese culture.

Question 61

请小心看管自己的财物	請小心看管自己的財物

61. What does this sign say?

(A) Look after your children
(B) Look after your personal belongings
(C) No pets allowed
(D) Beware of traffic

Question 62

博物馆开放时间 自七月一日起周六 延长开放时间至晚上八时	博物館開放時間 自七月一日起週六 延長開放時間至晚上八時

62. What is this notice about?

(A) Rules and regulations
(B) Permanent closure from July 1st
(C) Free entry
(D) Extended opening times

Questions 63-64

小张昨天晚上从纽约给我打来电话，说他今天下午四点三刻到香港，让我去机场接他。

但是很不巧，今天早上我的车子坏了，我只好坐地铁去机场。飞机延误了一个小时，小张一下飞机就赶忙向我道歉。

然后我打的送小张去了他住的酒店，老朋友见面，我们都很高兴。

小張昨天晚上從紐約給我打來電話，說他今天下午四點三刻到香港，讓我去機場接他。

但是很不巧，今天早上我的車子壞了，我只好坐地鐵去機場。飛機延誤了一個小時，小張一下飛機就趕忙向我道歉。

然後我打的送小張去了他住的酒店，老朋友見面，我們都很高興。

63. What time did Xiao Zhang arrive in Hong Kong?
    (A) 4:15 P.M.
    (B) 4:45 P.M.
    (C) 5:15 P.M.
    (D) 5:45 P.M.

64. Why did Xiao Zhang apologize?
    (A) His car has broken down.
    (B) He has a lot of luggage.
    (C) His flight was delayed.
    (D) He did not book a hotel room.

Questions 65-66

儿童感冒药

[一] 用于小儿，治疗咳嗽、发烧。

[二] 一日三次，每次一粒，温开水送服。

兒童感冒藥

[一] 用於小兒，治療咳嗽、發燒。

[二] 一日三次，每次一粒，溫開水送服。

65. Which group of people is this medicine prescribed for?
    (A) Children
    (B) The elderly
    (C) Men
    (D) Women

66. How should this medicine be taken?
    (A) With cold milk
    (B) With warm milk
    (C) With cold water
    (D) With warm water

Question 67

意大利餐厅	意大利餐廳
诚征经验丰富的营业经理 逢周日休假，提供宿舍 有意者请电：98765432	誠徵經驗豐富的營業經理 逢週日休假，提供宿舍 有意者請電：98765432

67. This restaurant is looking to employ
    (A) a waiter
    (B) a cleaner
    (C) a manager
    (D) a chef

Question 68

收 银 台	收 銀 台

68. What does this sign say?
    (A) Cashier
    (B) Information desk
    (C) Customer service center
    (D) Recycling station

Questions 69-70

招　　租

住房条件：三室一厅，家具齐全。睡房有床、床头柜、书桌和衣柜。厨房有冰箱、微波炉和餐桌。
交　　通：近地铁站和巴士站。
房　　租：大房间一千元/月
小房间九百元/月
水电网费均摊
电　　话：96501898

招　　租

住房條件：三室一廳，傢俱齊全。睡房有床、床頭櫃、書桌和衣櫃。廚房有冰箱、微波爐和餐桌。
交　　通：近地鐵站和巴士站。
房　　租：大房間一千元/月
小房間九百元/月
水電網費均攤
電　　話：96501898

69. Which of the following is true of the apartment advertised?

(A) It has three bedrooms.
(B) It includes a telephone and a computer.
(C) There is no kitchen.
(D) There is a taxi stand nearby.

70. How much is the monthly rent for a large room?

(A) $900
(B) $1000
(C) $1900
(D) $2000

Question 71

切洋葱不流眼泪的方法

切洋葱前，把刀在冷水中浸一会儿，或者将洋葱浸入热水中三分钟，再切洋葱。

切洋蔥不流眼淚的方法

切洋蔥前，把刀在冷水中浸一會兒，或者將洋蔥浸入熱水中三分鐘，再切洋蔥。

71. Which of the following can help avoid tears when chopping an onion?

(A) Put the onion in cold water for three minutes
(B) Put the knife in hot water for three minutes
(C) Put the onion in hot water for three minutes
(D) Put the knife in hot water for a few moments

Question 72

小明：

我去图书馆了，大概下午四点会回来，如果有人打电话给我，你就叫他去图书馆找我吧。

姐姐

小明：

我去圖書館了，大概下午四點會回來，如果有人打電話給我，你就叫他去圖書館找我吧。

姐姐

72. Where did Xiao Ming's sister go?

(A) Library
(B) Shops
(C) Museum
(D) School

Questions 73-74

通　知

学校将于二月二十三日晚上七点至十点在我校学生活动中心播放电影《人生》。

售票时间和地点：

二月十九日至二月二十二日
上午九点至十一点　图书馆508室
下午一点至六点　化学楼105室

价格：

五十元，二十五元（学生票）

通　知

學校將於二月二十三日晚上七點至十點在我校學生活動中心播放電影《人生》。

售票時間和地點：

二月十九日至二月二十二日
上午九點至十一點　圖書館508室
下午一點至六點　化學樓105室

價格：

五十元，二十五元（學生票）

73. How long is the movie?

(A) One hour
(B) Two hours
(C) Three hours
(D) Four hours

74. Which of the following statements about the movie is true?

(A) Tickets are only available from the library.
(B) Tickets are available for sale on February 21st.
(C) The movie will be shown daily from February 19th thru February 22nd.
(D) The movie starts at 1:00 P.M.

Question 75

100011
北京市新街口外大街15号
北京语言大学汉语水平考试中心

李　刚　收

上海复旦大学光华楼A403室
李明寄
200043

100011
北京市新街口外大街15號
北京語言大學漢語水平考試中心

李　剛　收

上海復旦大學光華樓A403室
李明寄
200043

75. What is this?

(A) An envelope
(B) A business card
(C) An advertisement
(D) A resume

Questions 76-77

李美出生於北京，自六岁起跟黄江教授学习钢琴。她在小学时就开始在德国公开演出，之后她还去过加拿大、澳大利亚进行公开演出。她在十四岁那年到德国做交换学生，十五岁那年又独自到美国学习，在她十八岁的时候出版了第一张唱片，受到了许多好评。她平时努力练习，放假的时候也会看书、看电影，她最喜欢看美国电影。她对科学、演出也很感兴趣，将来如果不做钢琴家，她也希望自己能做一个科学家或者是演员。

李美出生於北京，自六歲起跟黃江教授學習鋼琴。她在小學時就開始在德國公開演出，之後她還去過加拿大、澳大利亞進行公開演出。她在十四歲那年到德國做交換學生，十五歲那年又獨自到美國學習，在她十八歲的時候出版了第一張唱片，受到了許多好評。她平時努力練習，放假的時候也會看書、看電影，她最喜歡看美國電影。她對科學、演出也很感興趣，將來如果不做鋼琴家，她也希望自己能做一個科學家或者是演員。

76. What did Li Mei do when she was 15 years old?

(A) Released an album
(B) Went to Germany as an exchange student
(C) Studied in the USA
(D) Learnt to play the piano

77. What does Li Mei want to do if she does not become a pianist?

(A) Singer
(B) Teacher
(C) Writer
(D) Scientist

Question 78

小孩请由大人陪同搭乘电梯

小孩請由大人陪同搭乘電梯

78. What does this sign say?
   (A) Children should be accompanied by adults when using the escalator
   (B) Adults should look after their children
   (C) Keep away from children
   (D) No entry for children

Question 79

尊敬的顾客：	尊敬的顧客：
即日起至十二月二十五日于本商场购物满四百元，可获二十元的现金折扣；购物满一千元，可获二百元现金折扣及玩具公仔一只。	即日起至十二月二十五日於本商場購物滿四百元，可獲二十元的現金折扣；購物滿一千元，可獲二百元現金折扣及玩具公仔一隻。
万邦购物中心	萬邦購物中心
十二月一日	十二月一日

79. What special offer is available for spending \$600 in this shopping mall on December 12th?
   (A) 20% off
   (B) \$20 off
   (C) \$200 off
   (D) A free soft toy

Question 80

独家发售	獨家發售

80. Where would this sign mostly likely appear?
   (A) In a shopping mall
   (B) In a factory
   (C) In a hospital
   (D) In a school

Question 81

我刚开始学习英文，现在还看不懂英文报纸，不过只要我努力学习英文，将来一定能看懂的。	我剛開始學習英文，現在還看不懂英文報紙，不過只要我努力學習英文，將來一定能看懂的。

81. Which of the following statements about the writer is true?
    (A) He speaks very good English.
    (B) He has just started learning English.
    (C) He can read an English newspaper.
    (D) He is an English teacher.

Question 82

有些人为了方便，也有些人为了好看，把冰箱放进了卧室。 据研究，冰箱放在房间里会产生三种污染：一是声音污染；二是电子污染；三是化学污染。因此，最好把冰箱请出卧室。	有些人為了方便，也有些人為了好看，把冰箱放進了臥室。 據研究，冰箱放在房間裏會產生三種污染：一是聲音污染；二是電子污染；三是化學污染。因此，最好把冰箱請出臥室。

82. What is this passage mainly about?
    (A) Problems caused by using refrigerators
    (B) The functions of refrigerators
    (C) How to maintain refrigerators
    (D) How to improve the quality of sleep

Question 83

目前，全世界大约有八十个国家、占全球百分之四十的人口正面临着严重的水资源短缺问题。发展中国家有十三亿人口缺乏干净的饮用水，二十亿人没有足够的卫生设施。	目前，全世界大約有八十個國家、佔全球百分之四十的人口正面臨著嚴重的水資源短缺問題。發展中國家有十三億人口缺乏乾淨的飲用水，二十億人沒有足夠的衛生設施。

83. What percentage of the world population faces the problems of water resource shortages?

(A) 80%
(B) 40%
(C) 20%
(D) 13%

Questions 84-85

《自然世界》是许多中国人喜欢的一个电视节目，它开播至今已有二十年了，通过向观众介绍动物在自然界的生活，告诉观众应该如何保护动物，保护自然环境。这个节目逢星期四晚上八点播出，是大人和小孩都喜欢的节目。负责制作这个节目的工作人员经常亲自到中国偏远的森林去拍摄被保护的、稀有的各种野生动物，他们的努力工作使得这个节目多次获得国内和国外电视节目的奖项。

《自然世界》是許多中國人喜歡的一個電視節目，它開播至今已有二十年了，通過向觀眾介紹動物在自然界的生活，告訴觀眾應該如何保護動物，保護自然環境。這個節目逢星期四晚上八點播出，是大人和小孩都喜歡的節目。負責製作這個節目的工作人員經常親自到中國偏遠的森林去拍攝被保護的、稀有的各種野生動物，他們的努力工作使得這個節目多次獲得國內和國外電視節目的獎項。

84. This program is about

(A) nature
(B) movies
(C) books
(D) music

85. Which of the following statements about the program is NOT true?

(A) It was first shown 20 years ago.
(B) It is shown twice a week.
(C) It is shown in the evening.
(D) It has won numerous awards.

SAT Chinese Practice Test — Three
SAT 中文模拟试题 — 第三套
SAT 中文模擬試題 — 第三套

听力材料
聽力材料
LISTENING TEST MATERIAL

Part A

Simplified Characters

Question 1

A： 你的汉语说得真标准，你一定花了很多时间学习。

(A) 是的，我每天都花一个小时温习。
(B) 是的，我最喜欢看花了。
(C) 不是，你看错了。

Question 2

A： 你怎么去故宫？

(A) 故宫很远。
(B) 我坐公共汽车去的。
(C) 我去过故宫。

Question 3

A： 明天去看电影吗？听说新上映的电影很好看。

(A) 不用客气。
(B) 明天好像会下雨。
(C) 好啊，我正想找人跟我一起去呢。

Question 4

A： 我昨天在网上买了一本书，今天就到了，现在网上购物可真方便。

B： 网上购物好是好，不过也有很多风险，你可要小心啊。

(A) 谢谢你的提醒，我下次一定会注意的。
(B) 你怎么能这么不小心？
(C) 下次我帮你买吧。

Question 5

A： 你妈妈是做什么的？

(A) 她是坐地铁来的。
(B) 她是教师。
(C) 我最爱做菜。

Question 6

A： 最近不知怎么了，牙齿很疼，都吃不下东西了。

(A) 别生气，气坏了身子可不好。
(B) 你去看看医生吧。
(C) 我这里有点感冒药，你拿去试试。

Question 7

A： 你好，请问有没有空房间？

(A) 谢谢，你暂时不用预订。
(B) 对不起，房间都预订了。
(C) 昨天一位姓王的先生订了。

Question 8

A： 一共是六百二十元，请问是付现金还是刷卡？

(A) 有电话卡卖吗？
(B) 对不起，我的现金不够。
(C) 刷卡吧。

Question 9

A： 请问中央公园怎么走？

B： 往前面第二个十字路口左拐，就是中央公园。

(A) 请慢用。
(B) 你太客气了！
(C) 我明白了，谢谢你！

Question 10

A： 你昨天去哪儿了？

(A) 那里真不错。
(B) 我去了动物园。
(C) 昨天下雨了。

Question 11

A： 你想吃什么水果？

(A) 我想吃面条。
(B) 苹果吧。
(C) 给我来一瓶可乐。

Question 12

A： 你平均一天花多少时间玩电脑游戏？

(A) 大概八十块吧。
(B) 超过三个小时。
(C) 三十公里左右。

Question 13

A： 这是我新买的手提电话。
B： 真漂亮，多少钱？

(A) 在英国买的。
(B) 黑色和粉红色。
(C) 三百五十元。

Question 14

A： 快要放假了，你有什么打算？
B： 我打算去日本旅行。

(A) 你算术真好。
(B) 我最喜欢吃日本料理了。
(C) 那么远的地方，你要带很多行李吧？

Question 15

A： 我是来跟你道别的，我要离开上海了。
B： 你要回国了？

(A) 不是的，我要去北京，我在那里找到了新的工作。
(B) 欢迎你到我家来。
(C) 是的，我要回上海了。

Part B

Question 16

女：我想订一张去美国的机票。

男：你要单程票还是双程票？

女：单程票，下个星期三出发。

男：费用是美金八百元。

Questions 17-18

男：我今年暑假想去打工，你呢？

女：我不想去打工，打工太累了，我想去旅行。

男：你想去哪里旅行？

女：我打算先去法国，再去日本。

Questions 19-20

男：今天的早餐有什么？

女：牛奶、面包和稀饭。

男：有没有三明治？

女：哦，有的，你要什么？

男：我要一个三明治，一杯牛奶。

Questions 21-22

男：小姐，我要买张电话卡。

女：你要多少钱面值的？

男：五十的，给你钱。

女：你得给我五十二，还有两块钱的手续费。

Questions 23-24

男：你哪儿不舒服？

女：我肚子疼。

男：什么时候开始的？

女：昨天晚上就有点疼，今天早上更疼了。

Question 25

男：你学了几年汉语？

女：原来在美国的时候学过六个月，然后来中国学了两年。

Questions 26-27

男：我们一起去听音乐会好吗？

女：好啊，几点钟？

男：音乐会九点开始，我们八点四十分在音乐厅门口见吧。

Questions 28-29

男：现在都九点四十了，还有十分钟就要开车了，该上车了。谢谢你们来送我。

女：不客气，祝你一路顺风。

男：再见，有空欢迎你来上海找我玩。

Question 30

男：你想在大学主修什么课？

女：我想主修法律。

男：为什么不学经济呀？

女：我没兴趣。

Part A

Traditional Characters

Question 1

A： 你的漢語說得真標準，你一定花了很多時間學習。

(A) 是的，我每天都花一個小時溫習。
(B) 是的，我最喜歡看花了。
(C) 不是，你看錯了。

Question 2

A： 你怎麼去故宮？

(A) 故宮很遠。
(B) 我坐公共汽車去的。
(C) 我去過故宮。

Question 3

A： 明天去看電影嗎？聽說新上映的電影很好看。

(A) 不用客氣。
(B) 明天好像會下雨。
(C) 好啊，我正想找人跟我一起去呢。

Question 4

A： 我昨天在網上買了一本書，今天就到了，現在網上購物可真方便。
B： 網上購物好是好，不過也有很多風險，你可要小心啊。

(A) 謝謝你的提醒，我下次一定會注意的。
(B) 你怎麼能這麼不小心？
(C) 下次我幫你買吧。

Question 5

A： 你媽媽是做什麼的？

(A) 她是坐地鐵來的。
(B) 她是教師。
(C) 我最愛做菜。

Question 6

A： 最近不知怎麼了，牙齒很疼，都吃不下東西了。

(A) 別生氣，氣壞了身子可不好。
(B) 你去看看醫生吧。
(C) 我這裏有點感冒藥，你拿去試試。

Question 7

A： 你好，請問有沒有空房間？

(A) 謝謝，你暫時不用預訂。
(B) 對不起，房間都預訂了。
(C) 昨天一位姓王的先生訂了。

Question 8

A： 一共是六百二十元，請問是付現金還是刷卡？

(A) 有電話卡賣嗎？
(B) 對不起，我的現金不夠。
(C) 刷卡吧。

Question 9

A： 請問中央公園怎麼走？
B： 往前面第二個十字路口左拐，就是中央公園。

(A) 請慢用。
(B) 你太客氣了！
(C) 我明白了，謝謝你！

Question 10

A： 你昨天去哪兒了？

(A) 那裏真不錯。
(B) 我去了動物園。
(C) 昨天下雨了。

Question 11

A： 你想吃什麼水果？

(A) 我想吃麵條。
(B) 蘋果吧。
(C) 給我來一瓶可樂。

Question 12

A： 你平均一天花多少時間玩電腦遊戲？

(A) 大概八十塊吧。
(B) 超過三個小時。
(C) 三十公里左右。

Question 13

A： 這是我新買的手提電話。
B： 真漂亮，多少錢？

(A) 在英國買的。
(B) 黑色和粉紅色。
(C) 三百五十元。

Question 14

A： 快要放假了，你有什麼打算？
B： 我打算去日本旅行。

(A) 你算術真好。
(B) 我最喜歡吃日本料理了。
(C) 那麼遠的地方，你要帶很多行李吧？

Question 15

A： 我是來跟你道別的，我要離開上海了。
B： 你要回國了？

(A) 不是的，我要去北京，我在那裏找到了新的工作。
(B) 歡迎你到我家來。
(C) 是的，我要回上海了。

Part B

Question 16

女：我想訂一張去美國的機票。

男：你要單程票還是雙程票？

女：單程票，下個星期三出發。

男：費用是美金八百元。

Questions 17-18

男：我今年暑假想去打工，你呢？

女：我不想去打工，打工太累了，我想去旅行。

男：你想去哪裏旅行？

女：我打算先去法國，再去日本。

Questions 19-20

男：今天的早餐有什麼？

女：牛奶、麵包和稀飯。

男：有沒有三明治？

女：哦，有的，你要什麼？

男：我要一個三明治，一杯牛奶。

Questions 21-22

男：小姐，我要買張電話卡。

女：你要多少錢面值的？

男：五十的，給你錢。

女：你得給我五十二，還有兩塊錢的手續費。

Questions 23-24

男：你哪兒不舒服？

女：我肚子疼。

男：什麼時候開始的？

女：昨天晚上就有點疼，今天早上更疼了。

Question 25

男：你學了幾年漢語？

女：原來在美國的時候學過六個月，然後來中國學了兩年。

Questions 26-27

男：我們一起去聽音樂會好嗎？

女：好啊，幾點鐘？

男：音樂會九點開始，我們八點四十分在音樂廳門口見吧。

Questions 28-29

男：現在都九點四十了，還有十分鐘就要開車了，該上車了。謝謝你們來送我。

女：不客氣，祝你一路順風。

男：再見，有空歡迎你來上海找我玩。

Question 30

男：你想在大學主修什麼課？

女：我想主修法律。

男：爲什麼不學經濟呀？

女：我沒興趣。

Part A

Pinyin Romanization

Question 1

A： Nǐ de Hànyǔ shuō de zhēn biāozhǔn, nǐ yídìng huāle hěn duō shíjiān xuéxí.

(A) Shì de, wǒ měitiān dōu huā yí ge xiǎoshí wēnxí.
(B) Shì de, wǒ zuì xǐhuan kàn huā le.
(C) Bú shì, nǐ kàn cuò le.

Question 2

A： Nǐ zěnme qù gùgōng?

(A) Gùgōng hěn yuǎn.
(B) Wǒ zuò gōnggòngqìchē qù de.
(C) Wǒ qù guo gùgōng.

Question 3

A： Míngtiān qù kàn diànyǐng ma? Tīngshuō xīn shàngyìng de diànyǐng hěn hǎokàn.

(A) Bú yòng kèqi.
(B) Míngtiān hǎoxiàng huì xiàyǔ.
(C) Hǎo a, wǒ zhèng xiǎng zhǎo rén gēn wǒ yìqǐ qù ne.

Question 4

A： Wǒ zuótiān zài wǎng shang mǎile yì běn shū, jīntiān jiù dàole, xiànzài wǎng shang gòuwù kě zhēn fāngbiàn.

B： Wǎng shang gòuwù hǎo shì hǎo, búguò yě yǒu hěnduō fēngxiǎn, nǐ kě yào xiǎoxīn a.

(A) Xièxie nǐ de tíxǐng, wǒ xià cì yídìng huì zhùyì de.
(B) Nǐ zěnme néng zhème bù xiǎoxīn?
(C) Xià cì wǒ bāng nǐ mǎi ba.

Question 5

A： Nǐ māma shì zuò shénme de?

(A) Tā shì zuò dìtiě lái de.
(B) Tā shì jiàoshī.
(C) Wǒ zuì ài zuòcài.

Question 6

A： Zuìjìn bù zhī zěnme le, yáchǐ hěn téng, dōu chī bú xià dōngxi le.

(A) Bié shēngqì, qì huài le shēnzi kě bù hǎo.
(B) Nǐ qù kànkan yīshēng ba.
(C) Wǒ zhèli yǒu diǎn gǎnmàoyào, nǐ ná qù shìshi.

Question 7

A： Nǐ hǎo, qǐngwèn yǒu méi yǒu kōng fángjiān?

(A) Xièxie, nǐ zànshí bú yòng yùdìng.
(B) Duìbuqǐ, fángjiān dōu yùdìng le.
(C) Zuótiān yí wèi xìng Wáng de xiānsheng dìng le.

Question 8

A： Yígòng shì liù bǎi èr shí yuán, qǐngwèn shì fù xiànjīn háishì shuā kǎ?

(A) Yǒu diànhuàkǎ mài ma?
(B) Duìbuqǐ, wǒ de xiànjīn búgòu.
(C) Shuā kǎ ba.

Question 9

A： Qǐngwèn zhōngyāng gōngyuán zěnme zǒu?

B： Wǎng qiánmiàn dì èr ge shí zì lùkǒu zuǒ guǎi, jiùshì zhōngyāng gōngyuán.

(A) Qǐng mànyòng.
(B) Nǐ tài kèqi le!
(C) Wǒ míngbaile, xièxie nǐ!

Question 10

A： Nǐ zuótiān qù nǎr le?

(A) Nàli zhēn búcuò.
(B) Wǒ qùle dòngwùyuán.
(C) Zuótiān xiàyǔ le.

Question 11

A：Nǐ xiǎng chī shénme shuǐguǒ?

(A) Wǒ xiǎng chī miàntiáo.

(B) Píngguǒ ba.

(C) Gěi wǒ lái yì píng kělè.

Question 12

A：Nǐ píngjūn yì tiān huā duōshǎo shíjiān wán diànnǎo yóuxì?

(A) Dàgài bāshí kuài ba.

(B) Chāoguò sān ge xiǎoshí.

(C) Sānshí gōnglǐ zuǒyòu.

Question 13

A：Zhè shì wǒ xīn mǎi de shǒutí diànhuà.

B：Zhēn piàoliang, duōshǎo qián?

(A) Zài Yīngguó mǎi de.

(B) Hēi sè hé fěnhóng sè.

(C) Sānbǎi wǔshí yuán.

Question 14

A：Kuàiyào fàngjià le, nǐ yǒu shénme dǎsuan?

B：Wǒ dǎsuan qù Rìběn lǚxíng.

(A) Nǐ suànshù zhēn hǎo.

(B) Wǒ zuì xǐhuan chī Rìběn liàolǐ le.

(C) Nàme yuǎn de dìfang, nǐ yào dài hěnduō xíngli ba?

Question 15

A：Wǒ shì lái gēn nǐ dàobié de, wǒ yào líkāi Shànghǎi le.

B：Nǐ yào huíguó le?

(A) Búshì de, wǒ yào qù Běijīng, wǒ zài nàli zhǎodàole xīn de gōngzuò.

(B) Huānyíng nǐ dào wǒ jiā lái.

(C) Shì de, wǒ yào huí Shànghǎi le.

Part B

Question 16

Nǚ : Wǒ xiǎng dìng yì zhāng qù Měiguó de jīpiào.
Nán : Nǐ yào dānchéngpiào háishì shuāngchéngpiào?
Nǚ : Dānchéngpiào, xià ge xīngqī sān chūfā.
Nán : Fèiyòng shì měijīn bābǎi yuán.

Questions 17-18

Nán : Wǒ jīnnián shǔjià xiǎng qù dǎgōng, nǐ ne?
Nǚ : Wǒ bù xiǎng qù dǎgōng, dǎgōng tài lèi le, wǒ xiǎng qù lǚxíng.
Nán : Nǐ xiǎng qù nǎli lǚxíng?
Nǚ : Wǒ dǎsuan xiān qù Fǎguó, zài qù Rìběn.

Questions 19-20

Nán : Jīntiān de zǎocān yǒu shénme?
Nǚ : Niú nǎi, miàn bāo hé xī fàn.
Nán : Yǒu méiyǒu sānmíngzhì?
Nǚ : Ò, yǒude, nǐ yào shénme?
Nán : Wǒ yào yí ge sānmíngzhì, yì bēi niúnǎi.

Questions 21-22

Nán : Xiǎojiě, wǒ yào mǎi zhāng diànhuàkǎ.
Nǚ : Nǐ yào duōshǎo qián miànzhí de?
Nán : Wǔshí de, gěi nǐ qián.
Nǚ : Nǐ děi gěi wǒ wǔshí èr, háiyǒu liǎng kuài qián de shǒuxùfèi.

Questions 23-24

Nán : Nǐ nǎr bù shūfu?
Nǚ : Wǒ dùzi téng.
Nán : Shénme shíhou kāishǐ de?
Nǚ : Zuótiān wǎnshang jiù yǒu diǎn téng, jīntiān zǎoshang gèng téng le.

Question 25

Nán : Nǐ xuéle jǐnián Hànyǔ?

Nǚ : Yuánlái zài Měiguó de shíhòu xuéguo liù gè yuè, ránhòu lái Zhōngguó xuéle liǎng nián.

Questions 26-27

Nán : Wǒmen yìqǐ qù tīng yīnyuèhuì hǎo ma?

Nǚ : Hǎo a, jīdiǎn zhōng?

Nán : Yīnyuèhuì jiǔ diǎn kāishǐ, wǒmen bā diǎn sìshí fēn zài yīnyu tīng ménkǒu jiàn ba.

Questions 28-29

Nán : Xiànzài dōu jiǔ diǎn sìshí le, háiyǒu shí fēnzhōng jiù yào kāichē le, gāi shàngchē le. Xièxie nǐmen lái sòng wǒ.

Nǚ : Búkèqi, zhù nǐ yílùshùnfēng.

Nán : Zàijiàn, yǒu kōng huānyíng nǐ lái Shànghǎi zhǎo wǒ wán.

Question 30

Nán : Nǐ xiǎng zài dàxué zhǔxiū shénme kè?

Nǚ : Wǒ xiǎng zhǔxiū fǎlǜ.

Nán : Wéi shénme bù xué jīngjì ya?

Nǚ : Wǒ méi xìngqù.

Practice Test Three

1	Ⓐ	Ⓑ	Ⓒ	Ⓓ	31	Ⓐ	Ⓑ	Ⓒ	Ⓓ	56	Ⓐ	Ⓑ	Ⓒ	Ⓓ
2	Ⓐ	Ⓑ	Ⓒ	Ⓓ	32	Ⓐ	Ⓑ	Ⓒ	Ⓓ	57	Ⓐ	Ⓑ	Ⓒ	Ⓓ
3	Ⓐ	Ⓑ	Ⓒ	Ⓓ	33	Ⓐ	Ⓑ	Ⓒ	Ⓓ	58	Ⓐ	Ⓑ	Ⓒ	Ⓓ
4	Ⓐ	Ⓑ	Ⓒ	Ⓓ	34	Ⓐ	Ⓑ	Ⓒ	Ⓓ	59	Ⓐ	Ⓑ	Ⓒ	Ⓓ
5	Ⓐ	Ⓑ	Ⓒ	Ⓓ	35	Ⓐ	Ⓑ	Ⓒ	Ⓓ	60	Ⓐ	Ⓑ	Ⓒ	Ⓓ
6	Ⓐ	Ⓑ	Ⓒ	Ⓓ	36	Ⓐ	Ⓑ	Ⓒ	Ⓓ	61	Ⓐ	Ⓑ	Ⓒ	Ⓓ
7	Ⓐ	Ⓑ	Ⓒ	Ⓓ	37	Ⓐ	Ⓑ	Ⓒ	Ⓓ	62	Ⓐ	Ⓑ	Ⓒ	Ⓓ
8	Ⓐ	Ⓑ	Ⓒ	Ⓓ	38	Ⓐ	Ⓑ	Ⓒ	Ⓓ	63	Ⓐ	Ⓑ	Ⓒ	Ⓓ
9	Ⓐ	Ⓑ	Ⓒ	Ⓓ	39	Ⓐ	Ⓑ	Ⓒ	Ⓓ	64	Ⓐ	Ⓑ	Ⓒ	Ⓓ
10	Ⓐ	Ⓑ	Ⓒ	Ⓓ	40	Ⓐ	Ⓑ	Ⓒ	Ⓓ	65	Ⓐ	Ⓑ	Ⓒ	Ⓓ
11	Ⓐ	Ⓑ	Ⓒ	Ⓓ	41	Ⓐ	Ⓑ	Ⓒ	Ⓓ	66	Ⓐ	Ⓑ	Ⓒ	Ⓓ
12	Ⓐ	Ⓑ	Ⓒ	Ⓓ	42	Ⓐ	Ⓑ	Ⓒ	Ⓓ	67	Ⓐ	Ⓑ	Ⓒ	Ⓓ
13	Ⓐ	Ⓑ	Ⓒ	Ⓓ	43	Ⓐ	Ⓑ	Ⓒ	Ⓓ	68	Ⓐ	Ⓑ	Ⓒ	Ⓓ
14	Ⓐ	Ⓑ	Ⓒ	Ⓓ	44	Ⓐ	Ⓑ	Ⓒ	Ⓓ	69	Ⓐ	Ⓑ	Ⓒ	Ⓓ
15	Ⓐ	Ⓑ	Ⓒ	Ⓓ	45	Ⓐ	Ⓑ	Ⓒ	Ⓓ	70	Ⓐ	Ⓑ	Ⓒ	Ⓓ
16	Ⓐ	Ⓑ	Ⓒ	Ⓓ	46	Ⓐ	Ⓑ	Ⓒ	Ⓓ	71	Ⓐ	Ⓑ	Ⓒ	Ⓓ
17	Ⓐ	Ⓑ	Ⓒ	Ⓓ	47	Ⓐ	Ⓑ	Ⓒ	Ⓓ	72	Ⓐ	Ⓑ	Ⓒ	Ⓓ
18	Ⓐ	Ⓑ	Ⓒ	Ⓓ	48	Ⓐ	Ⓑ	Ⓒ	Ⓓ	73	Ⓐ	Ⓑ	Ⓒ	Ⓓ
19	Ⓐ	Ⓑ	Ⓒ	Ⓓ	49	Ⓐ	Ⓑ	Ⓒ	Ⓓ	74	Ⓐ	Ⓑ	Ⓒ	Ⓓ
20	Ⓐ	Ⓑ	Ⓒ	Ⓓ	50	Ⓐ	Ⓑ	Ⓒ	Ⓓ	75	Ⓐ	Ⓑ	Ⓒ	Ⓓ
21	Ⓐ	Ⓑ	Ⓒ	Ⓓ	51	Ⓐ	Ⓑ	Ⓒ	Ⓓ	76	Ⓐ	Ⓑ	Ⓒ	Ⓓ
22	Ⓐ	Ⓑ	Ⓒ	Ⓓ	52	Ⓐ	Ⓑ	Ⓒ	Ⓓ	77	Ⓐ	Ⓑ	Ⓒ	Ⓓ
23	Ⓐ	Ⓑ	Ⓒ	Ⓓ	53	Ⓐ	Ⓑ	Ⓒ	Ⓓ	78	Ⓐ	Ⓑ	Ⓒ	Ⓓ
24	Ⓐ	Ⓑ	Ⓒ	Ⓓ	54	Ⓐ	Ⓑ	Ⓒ	Ⓓ	79	Ⓐ	Ⓑ	Ⓒ	Ⓓ
25	Ⓐ	Ⓑ	Ⓒ	Ⓓ	55	Ⓐ	Ⓑ	Ⓒ	Ⓓ	80	Ⓐ	Ⓑ	Ⓒ	Ⓓ
26	Ⓐ	Ⓑ	Ⓒ	Ⓓ						81	Ⓐ	Ⓑ	Ⓒ	Ⓓ
27	Ⓐ	Ⓑ	Ⓒ	Ⓓ						82	Ⓐ	Ⓑ	Ⓒ	Ⓓ
28	Ⓐ	Ⓑ	Ⓒ	Ⓓ						83	Ⓐ	Ⓑ	Ⓒ	Ⓓ
29	Ⓐ	Ⓑ	Ⓒ	Ⓓ						84	Ⓐ	Ⓑ	Ⓒ	Ⓓ
30	Ⓐ	Ⓑ	Ⓒ	Ⓓ						85	Ⓐ	Ⓑ	Ⓒ	Ⓓ

SAT Chinese Practice Test — Four
SAT 中文模拟试题 — 第四套
SAT 中文模擬試題 — 第四套

Time — 1 hour
Questions 1 - 85

PLEASE NOTE THAT YOUR ANSWER SHEET HAS FOUR ANSWER POSITIONS, MARKED A, B, C, AND D, WHILE THE QUESTIONS THROUGHOUT THIS TEST CONTAIN EITHER THREE OR FOUR ANSWER CHOICES. BE SURE NOT TO MARK YOUR ANSWERS IN COLUMN D IF THERE ARE ONLY THREE CHOICES GIVEN.

SECTION I
LISTENING

Approximate time — 20 minutes
Questions 1 - 30

Part A

Directions:

In this part of the test, you will hear short questions, statements, or commands in Mandarin Chinese, followed by three responses in Mandarin Chinese, designated (A), (B), and (C). You will hear the questions or statements, as well as the responses, only once, and they are not printed in your test booklet. Therefore, you must listen very carefully. Select the best response and fill in the corresponding circle on your answer sheet.

Question 1 Mark your answer on your answer sheet.

Question 2 Mark your answer on your answer sheet.

Question 3 Mark your answer on your answer sheet.

Question 4 Mark your answer on your answer sheet.

Question 5 Mark your answer on your answer sheet.

Question 6 Mark your answer on your answer sheet.

Question 7 Mark your answer on your answer sheet.

Question 8 Mark your answer on your answer sheet.

Question 9 Mark your answer on your answer sheet.

Question 10 Mark your answer on your answer sheet.

Question 11 Mark your answer on your answer sheet.

Question 12 Mark your answer on your answer sheet.

Question 13 Mark your answer on your answer sheet.

Question 14 Mark your answer on your answer sheet.

Question 15 Mark your answer on your answer sheet.

Part B

Directions:

You will now hear a series of dialogues. You will hear them only once, and they are not printed in your test booklet. After each selection, you will be asked to answer one or more questions about what you have just heard. These questions, each with four possible answers, are printed in your test booklet. Select the best answer to each question from among the four choices printed and fill in the corresponding circle on your answer sheet.

Question 16

16. Where is this dialogue set?

(A) In a bank
(B) In a shop
(C) In a restaurant
(D) In a school

Question 17

17. What is the relationship between the two people?

(A) Doctor and patient
(B) Colleagues
(C) Husband and wife
(D) Teacher and student

Question 18

18. Which of the following statements is true?

(A) The woman's father is a lawyer.
(B) The woman's father is a banker.
(C) The woman's mother is a housewife.
(D) The woman's parents work at the same location.

Questions 19-20

19. Which of the following is mentioned by the man?
    (A) The cold winter weather
    (B) His broken air conditioner
    (C) The warm summer weather
    (D) Buying a warm coat

20. What is the woman's suggestion?
    (A) They should wait before buying new clothes.
    (B) They do not need to buy a new air conditioner.
    (C) She has a spare heater which they can use.
    (D) They should buy a new electric heater.

Questions 21-22

21. Why does the woman look so tired?
    (A) She has been sick.
    (B) She has been traveling.
    (C) She was looking after her mother last night.
    (D) She has a lot of work to do.

22. What is the possible relationship between the two people?
    (A) Colleagues
    (B) Classmates
    (C) Doctor and patient
    (D) Teacher and student

Question 23

23. Which of the following ice cream flavors is NOT mentioned?
    (A) Coffee
    (B) Banana
    (C) Chocolate
    (D) Vanilla

Questions 24-25

24. What is Zhang's occupation?
    (A) Engineer
    (B) Tour guide
    (C) Professor
    (D) Journalist

25. Where is Zhang going tomorrow?
    (A) Hangzhou
    (B) Shanghai
    (C) Beijing
    (D) Nanjing

Questions 26-27

26. What does the man suggest they do?
    (A) Go to a movie
    (B) Go out to dinner
    (C) Go to a dance
    (D) Go to a concert

27. Why can't the woman go tonight?
    (A) It is her birthday.
    (B) It is her mother's birthday.
    (C) It is her grandmother's birthday.
    (D) It is her grandfather's birthday.

Questions 28-29

28. How many subjects does the woman need to take during this term?

    (A) Four
    (B) Seven
    (C) Eight
    (D) Five

29. Which is her favorite subject?

    (A) Economics
    (B) History
    (C) Mathematics
    (D) Chinese

Question 30

30. What kind of souvenir did the woman buy?

    (A) Scarf
    (B) Hat
    (C) T-shirt
    (D) Chocolates

SECTION II USAGE

Suggested time — 15 minutes
Questions 31 - 55

Part A

Directions:

This section consists of a number of incomplete statements, each of which has four possible completions. Select the word or phrase that best completes the sentence structurally and logically and fill in the corresponding circle on your answer sheet.

This section of the test is presented in four different ways of representing Chinese: traditional characters, simplified characters, pinyin romanization, and the Chinese phonetic alphabet. IT IS RECOMMEMD THAT YOU CHOOSE THE WRITING SYSTEM WITH WHICH YOU ARE MORE FAMILIAR WITH AND **ONLY READ THAT VERSION** AS YOU WORK THROUGH THIS SECTION OF THE TEST.

31. 我____了。
(A) 你已经把书还给
(B) 把书还给你已经
(C) 还给你已经把书
(D) 已经把书还给你

31. 我____了。
(A) 你已經把書還給
(B) 把書還給你已經
(C) 還給你已經把書
(D) 已經把書還給你

31. Wǒ____ le.
(A) nǐ yǐjīng bǎ shū huán gěi
(B) bǎ shū huán gěi nǐ yǐjīng
(C) huán gěi nǐ yǐjīng bǎ shū
(D) yǐjīng bǎ shū huán gěi nǐ

31. ㄨㄛˇ____˙ㄌㄜ。
(A) ㄋㄧˇ ㄧˇ ㄐㄧㄥ ㄅㄚˇ ㄕㄨ ㄏㄨㄢˊ ㄍㄟˇ
(B) ㄅㄚˇ ㄕㄨ ㄏㄨㄢˊ ㄍㄟˇ ㄋㄧˇ ㄧˇ ㄐㄧㄥ
(C) ㄏㄨㄢˊ ㄍㄟˇ ㄋㄧˇ ㄧˇ ㄐㄧㄥ ㄅㄚˇ ㄕㄨ
(D) ㄧˇ ㄐㄧㄥ ㄅㄚˇ ㄕㄨ ㄏㄨㄢˊ ㄍㄟˇ ㄋㄧˇ

32. 我____头晕，得去一趟医院拿点儿药。
(A) 一点儿
(B) 稍微
(C) 很大
(D) 有点儿

32. 我____頭暈，得去一趟醫院拿點兒藥。
(A) 一點兒
(B) 稍微
(C) 很大
(D) 有點兒

32. Wǒ ____ tóuyūn, děi qù yí tàng yīyuàn ná diǎnr yào.
(A) yì diǎnr
(B) shāowēi
(C) hěn dà
(D) yǒu diǎnr

32. ㄨㄛˇ____ㄊㄡˊ ㄩㄣ，ㄉㄟˇ ㄑㄩˋ ㄧˊ ㄊㄤˋ ㄧ ㄩㄢˋ ㄋㄚˊ ㄉㄧㄢˇ ˙ㄦ ㄧㄠˋ。
(A) ㄧˋ ㄉㄧㄢˇ ˙ㄦ
(B) ㄕㄠ ㄨㄟˊ
(C) ㄏㄣˇ ㄉㄚˋ
(D) ㄧㄡˇ ㄉㄧㄢˇ ˙ㄦ

33. ____他来说健康最重要。
(A) 在
(B) 向
(C) 对
(D) 按

33. ____他來說健康最重要。
(A) 在
(B) 向
(C) 對
(D) 按

33. ____tā lái shuō jiànkāng zuì zhòng yào.
(A) Zài
(B) Xiàng
(C) Duì
(D) Àn

33. ____ㄊㄚ ㄌㄞˊ ㄕㄨㄛ ㄐㄧㄢˋ ㄎㄤ ㄗㄨㄟˋ ㄓㄨㄥˋ ㄧㄠˋ。
(A) ㄗㄞˋ
(B) ㄒㄧㄤˋ
(C) ㄉㄨㄟˋ
(D) ㄢˋ

34. 他的汉语水平可比不上你，他才刚刚开始学，你都已经学____四年了。
(A) 着
(B) 的
(C) 了
(D) 不

34. 他的漢語水平可比不上你，他才剛剛開始學，你都已經學____四年了。
(A) 著
(B) 的
(C) 了
(D) 不

34. Tā de Hànyǔ shuǐpíng kě bǐ bú shàng nǐ, tā cái gānggāng kāishǐ xué, nǐ dōu yǐjīng xué____sì nián le.
(A) zhe
(B) de
(C) le
(D) bù

34. ㄊㄚ ˙ㄉㄜ ㄏㄢˋ ㄩˇ ㄕㄨㄟˇ ㄆㄧㄥˊ ㄎㄜˇ ㄅㄧˇ ㄅㄨˊ ㄕㄤˋ ㄋㄧˇ，ㄊㄚ ㄘㄞˊ ㄍㄤ ㄍㄤ ㄎㄞ ㄕˇ ㄒㄩㄝˊ，ㄋㄧˇ ㄉㄡ ㄧˇ ㄐㄧㄥ ㄒㄩㄝˊ ____ ㄙˋ ㄋㄧㄢˊ ˙ㄌㄜ。
(A) ˙ㄓㄜ
(B) ˙ㄉㄜ
(C) ˙ㄌㄜ
(D) ㄅㄨˋ

35. 用电子邮件发贺卡，____环保，____方便。
(A) 既 …… 又
(B) 除 …… 都
(C) 边 …… 边
(D) 虽 …… 但

35. 用電子郵件發賀卡，____環保，____方便。
(A) 既 …… 又
(B) 除 …… 都
(C) 邊 …… 邊
(D) 雖 …… 但

35. Yòng diànzǐ yóujiàn fā hèkǎ, ____ huánbǎo, ____ fāngbiàn.
(A) jì …… yòu
(B) chú …… dōu
(C) biān …… biān
(D) suī …… dàn

35. ㄩㄥˋ ㄉㄧㄢˋ ㄗˇ ㄧㄡˊ ㄐㄧㄢˋ ㄈㄚ ㄏㄜˋ ㄎㄚˇ，____ ㄏㄨㄢˊ ㄅㄠˇ，____ ㄈㄤ ㄅㄧㄢˋ。
(A) ㄐㄧˋ …… ㄧㄡˋ
(B) ㄔㄨˊ …… ㄉㄡ
(C) ㄅㄧㄢ …… ㄅㄧㄢ
(D) ㄙㄨㄟ …… ㄉㄢˋ

36. 那里的冬天____很冷，____很干燥。

(A) 如果 …… 那么
(B) 不但 …… 而且
(C) 即使 …… 也
(D) 虽然 …… 但是

36. Nà lǐ de dōngtiān ____ hěn lěng, ____ hěn gānzào.

(A) rúguǒ …… nàme
(B) búdàn …… érqiě
(C) jíshǐ …… yě
(D) suīrán …… dànshì

37. 穿过这____花园，就可以看到湖边美景。

(A) 个
(B) 枝
(C) 束
(D) 朵

37. Chuān guò zhè ____ huāyuán, jiù kěyǐ kàn dào hú biān měi jǐng.

(A) ge
(B) zhī
(C) shù
(D) duǒ

38. ____怎么说，他也不会答应的。

(A) 即使
(B) 假如
(C) 不管
(D) 只管

38. ____zěnme shuō, tā yě bú húì dāying de.

(A) Jíshǐ
(B) Jiǎrú
(C) Bùguǎn
(D) Zhǐguǎn

36. 那裏的冬天____很冷，____很乾燥。

(A) 如果 …… 那麼
(B) 不但 …… 而且
(C) 即使 …… 也
(D) 雖然 …… 但是

36. ㄋㄚˋ ㄌㄧˇ ㄉㄜ˙ ㄉㄨㄥ ㄊㄧㄢ ____ ㄏㄣˇ ㄌㄥˇ，____ ㄏㄣˇ ㄍㄢ ㄗㄠˋ。

(A) ㄖㄨˊ ㄍㄨㄛˇ …… ㄋㄚˋ ㄇㄜ˙
(B) ㄅㄨˊ ㄉㄢˋ …… ㄦˊ ㄑㄧㄝˇ
(C) ㄐㄧˊ ㄕˇ …… ㄧㄝˇ
(D) ㄙㄨㄟ ㄖㄢˊ …… ㄉㄢˋ ㄕˋ

37. 穿過這____花園，就可以看到湖邊美景。

(A) 個
(B) 枝
(C) 束
(D) 朵

37. ㄔㄨㄢ ㄍㄨㄛˋ ㄓㄜˋ ____ ㄏㄨㄚ ㄩㄢˊ，ㄐㄧㄡˋ ㄎㄜˇ ㄧˇ ㄎㄢˋ ㄉㄠˋ ㄏㄨˊ ㄅㄧㄢ ㄇㄟˇ ㄐㄧㄥˇ。

(A) ㄍㄜ˙
(B) ㄓ
(C) ㄕㄨˋ
(D) ㄉㄨㄛˇ

38. ____怎麼說，他也不會答應的。

(A) 即使
(B) 假如
(C) 不管
(D) 只管

38. ____ ㄗㄣˇ ㄇㄜ˙ ㄕㄨㄛ，ㄊㄚ ㄧㄝˇ ㄅㄨˊ ㄏㄨㄟˋ ㄉㄚ ㄧㄥ˙ ㄉㄜ˙。

(A) ㄐㄧˊ ㄕˇ
(B) ㄐㄧㄚˇ ㄖㄨˊ
(C) ㄅㄨˋ ㄍㄨㄢˇ
(D) ㄓˇ ㄍㄨㄢˇ

39. 那个梨他吃了一口____不吃了。
(A) 都
(B) 并
(C) 还
(D) 就

39. 那個梨他吃了一口____不吃了。
(A) 都
(B) 並
(C) 還
(D) 就

39. Nà ge lí tā chīle yì kǒu____bù chīle.
(A) dōu
(B) bìng
(C) hái
(D) jiù

39. ㄋㄚˋ ㄍㄜ˙ ㄌㄧˊ ㄊㄚ ㄔ ㄌㄜ˙ ㄧˋ ㄎㄡˇ ____ ㄅㄨˋ ㄔ ㄌㄜ˙。
(A) ㄉㄡ
(B) ㄅㄧㄥˋ
(C) ㄏㄞˊ
(D) ㄐㄧㄡˋ

40. 你怎么能____做作业，____看电视呢？
(A) 与其 …… 不如
(B) 一边 …… 一边
(C) 不管 …… 都
(D) 又 …… 又

40. 你怎麼能____做作業，____看電視呢？
(A) 與其 …… 不如
(B) 一邊 …… 一邊
(C) 不管 …… 都
(D) 又 …… 又

40. Nǐ zěnme néng____zuò zuòyè, ____ kàn diànshì ne?
(A) yǔqí …… bùrú
(B) yìbiān …… yìbiān
(C) bùguǎn …… dōu
(D) yòu …… yòu

40. ㄋㄧˇ ㄗㄣˇ ㄇㄜ˙ ㄋㄥˊ ____ ㄗㄨㄛˋ ㄗㄨㄛˋ ㄧㄝˋ， ____ ㄎㄢˋ ㄉㄧㄢˋ ㄕˋ ㄋㄜ˙？
(A) ㄩˇ ㄑㄧˊ …… ㄅㄨˋ ㄖㄨˊ
(B) ㄧˋ ㄅㄧㄢ …… ㄧˋ ㄅㄧㄢ
(C) ㄅㄨˋ ㄍㄨㄢˇ …… ㄉㄡ
(D) ㄧㄡˋ …… ㄧㄡˋ

41. 他们家虽然不大，____什么家具都有。
(A) 但
(B) 于是
(C) 所以
(D) 因为

41. 他們家雖然不大，____什麼傢俱都有。
(A) 但
(B) 於是
(C) 所以
(D) 因爲

41. Tāmen jiā suīrán bú dà, ____ shénme jiājù dōu yǒu.
(A) dàn
(B) yúshì
(C) suǒyǐ
(D) yīnwèi

41. ㄊㄚ ㄇㄣ˙ ㄐㄧㄚ ㄙㄨㄟ ㄖㄢˊ ㄅㄨˊ ㄉㄚˋ， ____ ㄕㄣˊ ㄇㄜ˙ ㄐㄧㄚ ㄐㄩˋ ㄉㄡ ㄧㄡˇ。
(A) ㄉㄢˋ
(B) ㄩˊ ㄕˋ
(C) ㄙㄨㄛˇ ㄧˇ
(D) ㄧㄣ ㄨㄟˋ

42. 去年我____ 。
(A) 写给了你三封信
(B) 给你写了三封信
(C) 三封信写了给你
(D) 你写给了三封信

42. Qù nián wǒ ____.
(A) xiě gěi le nǐ sān fēng xìn
(B) gěi nǐ xiě le sān fēng xìn
(C) sān fēng xìn xiě le gěi nǐ
(D) nǐ xiě gěi le sān fēng xìn

43. 课外兴趣小组____同学们的生活更加丰富多彩了。
(A) 把
(B) 使
(C) 给
(D) 被

43. Kèwài xìngqù xiǎozǔ____tóngxuémen de shēnghuó gèngjiā fēngfù duōcǎi le.
(A) bǎ
(B) shǐ
(C) gěi
(D) bèi

44. 你必须在九点前交作业，____就没有成绩。
(A) 因此
(B) 然后
(C) 于是
(D) 否则

44. Nǐ bìxū zài jiǔ diǎn qián jiāo zuòyè, ____jiù méiyǒu chéngjì.
(A) yīncǐ
(B) ránhòu
(C) yúshì
(D) fǒuzé

42. 去年我____ 。
(A) 寫給了你三封信
(B) 給你寫了三封信
(C) 三封信寫了給你
(D) 你寫給了三封信

42. ㄑㄩˋ ㄋㄧㄢˊ ㄨㄛˇ ____ 。
(A) ㄒㄧㄝˇ ㄍㄟˇ ˙ㄌㄜ ㄋㄧˇ ㄙㄢ ㄈㄥ ㄒㄧㄣˋ
(B) ㄍㄟˇ ㄋㄧˇ ㄒㄧㄝˇ ˙ㄌㄜ ㄙㄢ ㄈㄥ ㄒㄧㄣˋ
(C) ㄙㄢ ㄈㄥ ㄒㄧㄣˋ ㄒㄧㄝˇ ˙ㄌㄜ ㄍㄟˇ ㄋㄧˇ
(D) ㄋㄧˇ ㄒㄧㄝˇ ㄍㄟˇ ˙ㄌㄜ ㄙㄢ ㄈㄥ ㄒㄧㄣˋ

43. 課外興趣小組____同學們的生活更加豐富多彩了。
(A) 把
(B) 使
(C) 給
(D) 被

43. ㄎㄜˋ ㄨㄞˋ ㄒㄧㄥˋ ㄑㄩˋ ㄒㄧㄠˇ ㄗㄨˇ ____ ㄊㄨㄥˊ ㄒㄩㄝˊ ˙ㄇㄣ ˙ㄉㄜ ㄕㄥ ㄏㄨㄛˊ ㄍㄥˋ ㄐㄧㄚ ㄈㄥ ㄈㄨˋ ㄉㄨㄛ ㄘㄞˇ ˙ㄌㄜ 。
(A) ㄅㄚˇ
(B) ㄕˇ
(C) ㄍㄟˇ
(D) ㄅㄟˋ

44. 你必須在九點前交作業，____就沒有成績。
(A) 因此
(B) 然後
(C) 於是
(D) 否則

44. ㄋㄧˇ ㄅㄧˋ ㄒㄩ ㄗㄞˋ ㄐㄧㄡˇ ㄉㄧㄢˇ ㄑㄧㄢˊ ㄐㄧㄠ ㄗㄨㄛˋ ㄧㄝˋ ， ____ ㄐㄧㄡˋ ㄇㄟˊ ㄧㄡˇ ㄔㄥˊ ㄐㄧ 。
(A) ㄧㄣ ㄘˇ
(B) ㄖㄢˊ ㄏㄡˋ
(C) ㄩˊ ㄕˋ
(D) ㄈㄡˇ ㄗㄜˊ

45. 你都病了好几天了，怎么还不去医院____？
(A) 吗
(B) 吧
(C) 呢
(D) 啦

45. Nǐ dōu bìngle hǎo jǐ tiān le, zěnme hái bú qù yīyuàn ____？
(A) ma
(B) ba
(C) ne
(D) la

46. 你在家里好好休息，____我有时间，____会去看你的。
(A) 只有 …… 就
(B) 只要 …… 就
(C) 不论 …… 都
(D) 只好 …… 才

46. Nǐ zài jiāli hǎohao xiūxi, ____ wǒ yǒu shíjiān, ____ huì qù kàn nǐ de.
(A) zhǐyǒu …… jiù
(B) zhǐyào …… jiù
(C) búlùn …… dōu
(D) zhǐhǎo …… cái

47. 这种药吃了以后，病____没有好，____比以前更严重了。
(A) 虽然 …… 但是
(B) 虽然 …… 不过
(C) 不但 …… 反而
(D) 因为 …… 所以

47. Zhè zhǒng yào chīle yǐhòu, bìng ____ méiyǒu hǎo, ____ bǐ yǐqián gèng yánzhòng le.
(A) suīrán …… dànshì
(B) suīrán …… búguò
(C) búdàn …… fǎn'ér
(D) yīnwèi …… suǒyǐ

45. 你都病了好幾天了，怎麼還不去醫院____？
(A) 嗎
(B) 吧
(C) 呢
(D) 啦

45. ㄋㄧˇ ㄉㄡ ㄅㄧㄥˋ ˙ㄌㄜ ㄏㄠˇ ㄐㄧˇ ㄊㄧㄢ ˙ㄌㄜ，ㄗㄣˇ ˙ㄇㄜ ㄏㄞˊ ㄅㄨˊ ㄑㄩˋ ㄧ ㄩㄢˋ ____？
(A) ˙ㄇㄚ
(B) ˙ㄅㄚ
(C) ˙ㄋㄜ
(D) ˙ㄌㄚ

46. 你在家裏好好休息，____我有時間，____會去看你的。
(A) 只有 …… 就
(B) 只要 …… 就
(C) 不論 …… 都
(D) 只好 …… 才

46. ㄋㄧˇ ㄗㄞˋ ㄐㄧㄚ ˙ㄌㄧ ㄏㄠˇ ㄏㄠˇ ㄒㄧㄡ ˙ㄒㄧ，____ ㄨㄛˇ ㄧㄡˇ ㄕˊ ㄐㄧㄢ，____ ㄏㄨㄟˋ ㄑㄩˋ ㄎㄢˋ ㄋㄧˇ ˙ㄉㄜ。
(A) ㄓˇ ㄧㄡˇ …… ㄐㄧㄡˋ
(B) ㄓˇ ㄧㄠˋ …… ㄐㄧㄡˋ
(C) ㄅㄨˋ ㄌㄨㄣˋ …… ㄉㄡ
(D) ㄓˇ ㄏㄠˇ …… ㄘㄞˊ

47. 這種藥吃了以後，病____沒有好，____比以前更嚴重了。
(A) 雖然 …… 但是
(B) 雖然 …… 不過
(C) 不但 …… 反而
(D) 因爲 …… 所以

47. ㄓㄜˋ ㄓㄨㄥˇ ㄧㄠˋ ㄔ ˙ㄌㄜ ㄧˇ ㄏㄡˋ，ㄅㄧㄥˋ ____ ㄇㄟˊ ㄧㄡˇ ㄏㄠˇ，____ ㄅㄧˇ ㄧˇ ㄑㄧㄢˊ ㄍㄥˋ ㄧㄢˊ ㄓㄨㄥˋ ˙ㄌㄜ。
(A) ㄙㄨㄟ ㄖㄢˊ …… ㄉㄢˋ ㄕˋ
(B) ㄙㄨㄟ ㄖㄢˊ …… ㄅㄨˊ ㄍㄨㄛˋ
(C) ㄅㄨˊ ㄉㄢˋ …… ㄈㄢˇ ㄦˊ
(D) ㄧㄣ ㄨㄟˋ …… ㄙㄨㄛˇ ㄧˇ

48. 你要吃中餐____西餐？
(A) 还有
(B) 或者
(C) 可能
(D) 还是

48. Nǐ yào chī zhōngcān____xīcān?
(A) háiyǒu
(B) huòzhě
(C) kěnéng
(D) háishì

49. 你去探望外婆时，____替我问候她。
(A) 随便
(B) 以便
(C) 方便
(D) 顺便

49. Nǐ qù tànwàng wàipó shí, ____tì wǒ wènhòu tā.
(A) suíbiàn
(B) yǐbiàn
(C) fāngbiàn
(D) shùnbiàn

50. 听说这____电影很好看。
(A) 本
(B) 部
(C) 间
(D) 家

50. Tīngshuō zhè____diànyǐng hěn hǎokàn.
(A) běn
(B) bù
(C) jiān
(D) jiā

48. 你要吃中餐____西餐？
(A) 還有
(B) 或者
(C) 可能
(D) 還是

48. ㄋㄧˇ ㄧㄠˋ ㄔ ㄓㄨㄥ ㄘㄢ ____ ㄒㄧ ㄘㄢ？
(A) ㄏㄞˊ ㄧㄡˇ
(B) ㄏㄨㄛˋ ㄓㄜˇ
(C) ㄎㄜˇ ㄋㄥˊ
(D) ㄏㄞˊ ㄕˋ

49. 你去探望外婆時，____替我問候她。
(A) 隨便
(B) 以便
(C) 方便
(D) 順便

49. ㄋㄧˇ ㄑㄩˋ ㄊㄢˋ ㄨㄤˋ ㄨㄞˋ ㄆㄛˊ ㄕˊ，____ ㄊㄧˋ ㄨㄛˇ ㄨㄣˋ ㄏㄡˋ ㄊㄚ。
(A) ㄙㄨㄟˊ ㄅㄧㄢˋ
(B) ㄧˇ ㄅㄧㄢˋ
(C) ㄈㄤ ㄅㄧㄢˋ
(D) ㄕㄨㄣˋ ㄅㄧㄢˋ

50. 聽說這____電影很好看。
(A) 本
(B) 部
(C) 間
(D) 家

50. ㄊㄧㄥ ㄕㄨㄛ ㄓㄜˋ ____ ㄉㄧㄢˋ ㄧㄥˇ ㄏㄣˇ ㄏㄠˇ ㄎㄢˋ。
(A) ㄅㄣˇ
(B) ㄅㄨˋ
(C) ㄐㄧㄢ
(D) ㄐㄧㄚ

51. 这么大的房子只你一个人住着，你不害怕____？

(A) 呢
(B) 啊
(C) 吧
(D) 吗

51. 這麼大的房子只你一個人住著，你不害怕____？

(A) 呢
(B) 啊
(C) 吧
(D) 嗎

51. Zhème dà de fángzi zhǐ nǐ yí ge rén zhù zhe, nǐ bú hàipà____ ?

(A) ne
(B) a
(C) ba
(D) ma

51. ㄓㄜˋ ˙ㄇㄜ ㄉㄚˋ ˙ㄉㄜ ㄈㄤˊ ˙ㄗ ㄓˇ ㄋㄧˇ ㄧˊ ˙ㄍㄜ ㄖㄣˊ ㄓㄨˋ ˙ㄓㄜ，ㄋㄧˇ ㄅㄨˊ ㄏㄞˋ ㄆㄚˋ____？

(A) ˙ㄋㄜ
(B) ˙ㄚ
(C) ˙ㄅㄚ
(D) ˙ㄇㄚ

52. 他说的话____很有道理。

(A) 听出来
(B) 听起来
(C) 听下来
(D) 听下去

52. 他說的話____很有道理。

(A) 聽出來
(B) 聽起來
(C) 聽下來
(D) 聽下去

52. Tā shuō de huà ____ hěn yǒu dàolǐ.

(A) tīng chū lai
(B) tīng qǐ lai
(C) tīng xià lai
(D) tīng xià qu

52. ㄊㄚ ㄕㄨㄛ ˙ㄉㄜ ㄏㄨㄚˋ____ㄏㄣˇ ㄧㄡˇ ㄉㄠˋ ㄌㄧˇ。

(A) ㄊㄧㄥ ㄔㄨ ㄌㄞˊ
(B) ㄊㄧㄥ ㄑㄧˇ ㄌㄞˊ
(C) ㄊㄧㄥ ㄒㄧㄚˋ ㄌㄞˊ
(D) ㄊㄧㄥ ㄒㄧㄚˋ ㄑㄩˋ

53. 那____大桥是世界上最长的桥。

(A) 班
(B) 家
(C) 所
(D) 座

53. 那____大橋是世界上最長的橋。

(A) 班
(B) 家
(C) 所
(D) 座

53. Nà____dàqiáo shì shìjiè shàng zuì cháng de qiáo.

(A) bān
(B) jiā
(C) suǒ
(D) zuò

53. ㄋㄚˋ____ㄉㄚˋ ㄑㄧㄠˊ ㄕˋ ㄕˋ ㄐㄧㄝˋ ㄕㄤˋ ㄗㄨㄟˋ ㄔㄤˊ ˙ㄉㄜ ㄑㄧㄠˊ。

(A) ㄅㄢ
(B) ㄐㄧㄚ
(C) ㄙㄨㄛˇ
(D) ㄗㄨㄛˋ

54. ____就出门了。
(A) 都没吃我连早饭
(B) 我都没吃连早饭
(C) 早饭连我都没吃
(D) 我连早饭都没吃

54. ____ jiù chū mén le.
(A) Dōu méi chī wǒ lián zǎofàn
(B) Wǒ dōu méi chī lián zǎofàn
(C) Zǎofàn lián wǒ dōu méi chī
(D) Wǒ lián zǎofàn dōu méi chī

55. 听说小王今年____选为最受欢迎的服务员。
(A) 被
(B) 让
(C) 叫
(D) 请

55. Tīng shuō XiǎoWáng jīnnián ____ xuǎn wéi zuì shòu huānyíng de fúwùyuán .
(A) bèi
(B) ràng
(C) jiào
(D) qǐng

54. ____就出門了。
(A) 都沒吃我連早飯
(B) 我都沒吃連早飯
(C) 早飯連我都沒吃
(D) 我連早飯都沒吃

54. ____ ㄐㄧㄡˋ ㄔㄨ ㄇㄣˊ ˙ㄌㄜ 。
(A) ㄉㄡ ㄇㄟˊ ㄔ ㄨㄛˇ ㄌㄧㄢˊ ㄗㄠˇ ㄈㄢˋ
(B) ㄨㄛˇ ㄉㄡ ㄇㄟˊ ㄔ ㄌㄧㄢˊ ㄗㄠˇ ㄈㄢˋ
(C) ㄗㄠˇ ㄈㄢˋ ㄌㄧㄢˊ ㄨㄛˇ ㄉㄡ ㄇㄟˊ ㄔ
(D) ㄨㄛˇ ㄌㄧㄢˊ ㄗㄠˇ ㄈㄢˋ ㄉㄡ ㄇㄟˊ ㄔ

55. 聽說小王今年____選爲最受歡迎的服務員。
(A) 被
(B) 讓
(C) 叫
(D) 請

55. ㄊㄧㄥ ㄕㄨㄛ ㄒㄧㄠˇ ㄨㄤˊ ㄐㄧㄣ ㄋㄧㄢˊ ____ ㄒㄩㄢˇ ㄨㄟˊ ㄗㄨㄟˋ ㄕㄡˋ ㄏㄨㄢ ㄧㄥˊ ˙ㄉㄜ ㄈㄨˊ ㄨˋ ㄩㄢˊ 。
(A) ㄅㄟˋ
(B) ㄖㄤˋ
(C) ㄐㄧㄠˋ
(D) ㄑㄧㄥˇ

SECTION III
READING COMPREHENSION

Suggested time — 25 minutes
Questions 56 - 85

WHEN YOU BEGIN THIS SECTION, MAKE SURE THAT YOU MARK YOUR ANSWER TO THE FIRST QUESTION BY FILLING IN ONE OF THE CIRCLES NEXT TO NUMBER 56 ON YOUR ANSWER SHEET.

Directions:

Read the following texts carefully for comprehension. Each one is followed by one or more questions or incomplete statements. Select the answer or completion that is best according to the text and fill in the corresponding circle on your answer sheet.

This section of the test is presented in two writing systems: traditional characters and simplified characters. IT IS RECOMMEMD THAT YOU CHOOSE THE WRITING SYSTEM WITH WHICH YOU ARE MORE FAMILIAR WITH AND **ONLY READ THAT VERSION** AS YOU WORK THROUGH THIS SECTION OF THE TEST.

Questions 56-57

中国国家大剧院位于北京天安门广场西侧。设计师为法国建筑师保罗・安德鲁(Paul Andreu)。剧院内含歌剧院、音乐厅和戏剧院，总座席六千多个。其中歌剧院有观众席两千五百座；音乐厅有观众席两千座；戏剧院有观众席一千二百座。

中國國家大劇院位於北京天安門廣場西側。設計師爲法國建築師保羅・安德魯(Paul Andreu)。劇院內含歌劇院、音樂廳和戲劇院，總座席六千多個。其中歌劇院有觀衆席兩千五百座；音樂廳有觀衆席兩千座；戲劇院有觀衆席一千二百座。

56. Where is the Chinese National Theatre located?

(A) East of Tiananmen Square
(B) West of Tiananmen Square
(C) South of Tiananmen Square
(D) North of Tiananmen Square

57. How many seats are there in the music theatre?
    (A) 2,000
    (B) 2,500
    (C) 6,000
    (D) 1,200

Question 58

中国航空公司宣布增加来往中国与日本航班	中國航空公司宣布增加來往中國與日本航班
二零一零年十一月十一日 （本报讯）中国航空公司宣布，增加来往日本的航班。 旅客可联络航空公司或上网查阅最新航班资讯。	二零一零年十一月十一日 （本報訊）中國航空公司宣布，增加來往日本的航班。 旅客可聯絡航空公司或上網查閱最新航班資訊。

58. What is this news report about?
    (A) A new airport in Japan
    (B) Cancellation of ferry services
    (C) A new travel website
    (D) Increase in the number of flights

Question 59

天气预报	天氣預報
未来一周天气寒冷，北京会持续下雨，气温将下降到六度至九度。	未來一週天氣寒冷，北京會持續下雨，氣溫將下降到六度至九度。

59. What is the weather forecast for Beijing for the coming week?
    (A) Hot and rainy
    (B) Fine and hot
    (C) Cold and rainy
    (D) Cloudy with thunderstorms

Question 60

红红喜欢住在上海，因为上海的交通方便，人来人往，十分热闹。而且上海商店林立，购物也十分方便。此外，在上海可以吃到来自世界各地的美食，大饱口福。

紅紅喜歡住在上海，因為上海的交通方便，人來人往，十分熱鬧。而且上海商店林立，購物也十分方便。此外，在上海可以吃到來自世界各地的美食，大飽口福。

60. Which of the following reasons is NOT mentioned?

(A) Convenient transport
(B) Good for shopping
(C) Her family lives there
(D) Cuisine from all around the world

Question 61

请勿攀爬

請勿攀爬

61. What does this sign say?

(A) Do not disturb
(B) Do not touch
(C) Do not spit
(D) Do not climb

Questions 62-63

农历正月初一，是中国传统的春节，又叫“过年”。中国人喜欢在这一天吃年糕、饺子、糖果等。小孩子都很喜欢过春节，除了可以吃很多好吃的东西，还可以穿新衣服、跟大人拿红包。

農曆正月初一，是中國傳統的春節，又叫“過年”。中國人喜歡在這一天吃年糕、餃子、糖果等。小孩子都很喜歡過春節，除了可以吃很多好吃的東西，還可以穿新衣服、跟大人拿紅包。

62. Which of the following is NOT mentioned?
    (A) Lunar new year cake
    (B) Dumplings
    (C) Candies
    (D) Noodles

63. Which of the following is NOT a reason for children enjoying the Lunar new year?
    (A) They do not have to do homework.
    (B) They can have nice food.
    (C) They can wear new clothes.
    (D) They can get red packets.

Question 64

不准携带外来食品	不准攜帶外來食品

64. Which of the following is not allowed?
    (A) Children
    (B) Pets
    (C) Food
    (D) Cameras

Question 65

北海公园	北海公園
六月至八月开放时间： 上午六点至下午十点	六月至八月開放時間： 上午六點至下午十點
门票价格： 二十元，十五元（儿童）	門票價格： 二十元，十五元（兒童）

65. The opening hours from June thru August are

(A) 6A.M. to 5 P.M.
(B) 6A.M. to 8 P.M.
(C) 6A.M. to 9 P.M.
(D) 6A.M. to 10 P.M.

Questions 66-67

来参加我们好玩又有趣的嘉年华吧！置身于中国首个室内动物乐园，父母和小朋友可在这个大型游乐场里感受亲近小动物的乐趣。此外，为使各位来宾尽情投入嘉年华会的热闹气氛，会场亦设有即场表演，包括唱歌、跳舞、话剧表演等。

这次活动将于八月六号于北京广场举行，欢迎各位参与。这次活动费用全免！有兴趣人士请于七月三十号前联络王小姐，电话号码是1234567。

來參加我們好玩又有趣的嘉年華吧！置身於中國首個室內動物樂園，父母和小朋友可在這個大型遊樂場裏感受親近小動物的樂趣。此外，為使各位來賓盡情投入嘉年華會的熱鬧氣氛，會場亦設有即場表演，包括唱歌、跳舞、話劇表演等。

這次活動將於八月六號於北京廣場舉行，歡迎各位參與。這次活動費用全免！有興趣人士請於七月三十號前聯絡王小姐，電話號碼是1234567。

66. Which of the following activities is NOT mentioned?

(A) Singing
(B) Dancing
(C) Drama
(D) Acrobatics

67. Which of the following statements is correct?

(A) This event will be held during the summer.
(B) This event will be held at an outdoor venue.
(C) This event will be held in June.
(D) Each ticket costs $30.

Question 68

禁止左转	禁止左轉

68. What does this sign say?
    (A) No left turn
    (B) Right turn only
    (C) No parking
    (D) Car park

Questions 69-70

为顺应全球汉语热，更好地推广汉语以及中国文化，中央电视台中文国际频道（CCTV-4）全新打造的《快乐学汉语》将从八月三日起在中文国际频道播出，时间是每周一至周五的二十二点四十五分，每期十五分钟。

為順應全球漢語熱，更好地推廣漢語以及中國文化，中央電視臺中文國際頻道（CCTV-4）全新打造的《快樂學漢語》將從八月三日起在中文國際頻道播出，時間是每週一至週五的二十二點四十五分，每期十五分鐘。

69. When will the new version of “Happy Chinese” be shown?
    (A) From August 3rd
    (B) March 8th
    (C) Every Saturday
    (D) Every Sunday

70. How long is each screening of “Happy Chinese”?
    (A) 10 minutes
    (B) 15 minutes
    (C) 22 minutes
    (D) 45 minutes

Question 71

非 卖 品	非 賣 品

71. What does this sign say?
    (A) Not for sale
    (B) Special offer
    (C) Sold out
    (D) Please do not touch

Question 72

优 惠 券	優 惠 券

72. What is this?
    (A) A movie ticket
    (B) A train ticket
    (C) A discount coupon
    (D) A receipt

Question 73

征稿启事

为庆祝我校建校五十年，校报将从下期开始刊登有关校园生活的文章。欢迎广大师生踊跃投稿。

字数：一千五百字左右。

投稿地址：文星楼A3003室

一经采用，即赠样刊

徵稿啟事

為慶祝我校建校五十年，校報將從下期開始刊登有關校園生活的文章。歡迎廣大師生踴躍投稿。

字數：一千五百字左右。

投稿地址：文星樓A3003室

一經採用，即贈樣刊

73. What is this notice about?
   (A) The contribution of articles
   (B) Lost items
   (C) Missing people
   (D) Teacher recruitment

Question 74

游 人 止 步	遊 人 止 步

74. What does this sign say?
   (A) No visitors
   (B) No smoking
   (C) Do not disturb
   (D) Keep quiet

Questions 75-76

《知识改变了我》是现在最流行的书，很多人看完以后都说很好看。《知识改变了我》是一个真实的故事，作者是著名的教育家陈建明博士。此书记录了他如何从贫穷的家庭长大、如何努力学习，到最后成为全国最出名的教育家的过程。作者认为知识是最重要的，不论你是贫穷还是富贵，只要你肯努力学习，就能得到知识，有了知识，你的人生就会变得更美丽。

《知識改變了我》是現在最流行的書，很多人看完以後都說很好看。《知識改變了我》是一個真實的故事，作者是著名的教育家陳建明博士。此書記錄了他如何從貧窮的家庭長大、如何努力學習，到最後成為全國最出名的教育家的過程。作者認為知識是最重要的，不論你是貧窮還是富貴，只要你肯努力學習，就能得到知識，有了知識，你的人生就會變得更美麗。

75. Who wrote this book?
   (A) A doctor
   (B) A lawyer
   (C) An educator
   (D) A banker

76. According to the author, which of the following is most important?
   (A) Knowledge
   (B) Wealth
   (C) Love
   (D) Friendship

Question 77

上海位于中国大陆海岸线中部的长江口，拥有中国最大的工业基地、最大的外贸港口。人口超过两千万，通行吴语上海话。

上海位於中國大陸海岸線中部的長江口，擁有中國最大的工業基地、最大的外貿港口。人口超過兩千萬，通行吳語上海話。

77. Which of the following statements is true according to the article?
   (A) Shanghai has a population of two million.
   (B) Shanghai is the largest city in China.
   (C) Shanghai is the largest trading port in China.
   (D) Shanghai is located in the middle of mainland China.

Question 78

请假条

李老师：

我今天感冒发烧了，不能来上课，请假一天，望予批准。

学生：王小明
十二月六日

請假條

李老師：

我今天感冒發燒了，不能來上課，請假一天，望予批准。

學生：王小明
十二月六日

78. What is this note about?

(A) Test results
(B) Sick leave
(C) School application
(D) A new school timetable

Question 79

请给有需要的人让座	請給有需要的人讓座

79. What does this sign say?

(A) Please offer your seat to those who are in need
(B) Take your seat according to the number on your ticket
(C) This train is full
(D) Please reserve your seat

Question 80

银圆餐厅 午餐特价 随餐附送咖啡或汽水	銀圓餐廳 午餐特價 隨餐附送咖啡或汽水

80. Where would this notice most likely be found?

(A) In a cinema
(B) In a restaurant
(C) In a supermarket
(D) In a bank

Question 81

未成年人禁入	未成年人禁入

81. What does this sign say?
    (A) Adults only
    (B) No entry
    (C) No smoking
    (D) No pets allowed

Questions 82-83

香蕉不但方便进食，而且适合所有人食用。食香蕉时还可以和面包或牛奶一起吃，这样会更健康及美味。虽然香蕉又便宜又好吃，但是也不应该吃得太多，因为吃得太多就会变胖，所以专家建议每人每日最多只可以吃一根香蕉。

香蕉不但方便進食，而且適合所有人食用。食香蕉時還可以和麵包或牛奶一起吃，這樣會更健康及美味。雖然香蕉又便宜又好吃，但是也不應該吃得太多，因為吃得太多就會變胖，所以專家建議每人每日最多只可以吃一根香蕉。

82. Which of the following advantages is NOT mentioned?
    (A) Healthy
    (B) Tasty
    (C) Cheap
    (D) Helps digestion

83. Which of the following statements is NOT true?
    (A) Bananas are suitable for people of all ages.
    (B) Bananas can be eaten together with bread and milk.
    (C) Eating too many bananas can cause obesity.
    (D) Experts suggest eating at least one banana everyday.

Question 84

欢迎再次光临

歡迎再次光臨

84. What does this sign say?

    (A) Thank you for visiting
    (B) Please come again
    (C) Please do not enter
    (D) No visitors allowed

Question 85

禁 止 饮 食

禁 止 飲 食

85. What does this sign say?

    (A) No smoking
    (B) No visitors
    (C) No shouting
    (D) No eating or drinking

SAT Chinese Practice Test — Four
SAT 中文模拟试题 — 第四套
SAT 中文模擬試題 — 第四套

听力材料
聽力材料
LISTENING TEST MATERIAL

Part A

Simplified Characters

Question 1

A： 他才刚刚开始学，你应该多鼓励他。

(A) 刚刚下雪了。
(B) 天气很冷。
(C) 你说得对，我不应该对他要求太高。

Question 2

A： 奇怪，你也来了？你不是不喜欢参加这种聚会的吗？

(A) 我没见过你 。
(B) 我想多认识些朋友。
(C) 你很奇怪。

Question 3

A： 你好，你去哪？

(A) 天气真好。
(B) 我不知道。
(C) 我去银行，你呢？

Question 4

A： 这是你新买的衣服吗？真漂亮啊。

(A) 哪里哪里，过奖了。
(B) 这件衣服真便宜。
(C) 我的衣服很贵。

Question 5

A： 时间不早了，该睡觉了。

B： 明天就要考试了，我还没复习完呢。

(A) 你这么早睡觉啊？
(B) 我的脚受伤了
(C) 那你复习完就马上睡觉吧！

Question 6

A： 李老师，好好休息，我们会常来看你的。

(A) 你们下次还来吗？
(B) 今天我很开心，谢谢你们。
(C) 我最近很忙，可能没有时间。

Question 7

A： 你喜欢吃梨吗?

(A) 我最喜欢吃苹果。
(B) 这个橘子真甜啊。
(C) 跟我妈妈一样，我特别爱吃梨。

Question 8

A： 怎么又忘记带铅笔了？下次不能再忘记了！

(A) 我没有忘记带红笔。
(B) 我下次一定带来。
(C) 我做事很认真。

Question 9

A： 你们店里什么菜最有名？

(A) 我们店里的每个菜都有名字的啊。
(B) 西红柿炒鸡蛋，这个是我们的招牌菜。
(C) 菜名都在菜单上写着呢。

Question 10

A： 他明天会来吗？

B： 应该会来吧。

(A) 他不知道今天星期几。
(B) 他今天来了。
(C) 那实在太好了。

Question 11

A：你上次申请的结果出来了吗？

B：唉，我没能被录取。

(A) 祝贺你。
(B) 不客气。
(C) 别灰心。

Question 12

A：他说出这样的话来真是太过分了！

(A) 他真不应该这样说话。
(B) 他的发音很不标准。
(C) 我听不懂他在说什么。

Question 13

A：不好意思，我要走了。

B：正好，我想跟你一起走。

(A) 好，那一起走吧。
(B) 别担心，现在时间还早。
(C) 我怕时间来不及了。

Question 14

A：我不想吃药。

B：医生说这个药每天都要吃。

(A) 这个糖很好吃。
(B) 那我只好听医生的吩咐了。
(C) 医生叫我星期六再去找他。

Question 15

A： 马上就放假了，你想去哪里玩？

(A) 哪里也不想去，在家呆着吧。
(B) 这个地方我去过了。
(C) 假期太短了。

Part B

Question 16

男：我想取三千元。

女：你要人民币还是美金？

Question 17

男：你看你这个字写错了。

女：老师，谢谢您，我马上就改。

Question 18

男：你爸爸是做什么的？

女：他是医生，每天都很忙。

男：你妈妈呢？

女：我妈妈是护士，她也在我爸爸的医院工作。

Questions 19-20

男：听说今年的冬天很冷，没有暖气怎么行？

女：那我们买个电暖气吧。

Questions 21-22

男：你怎么这么没有精神？是不是生病了？

女：我母亲昨天晚上生病住院了，我一个晚上都在医院照顾她。

男：如果忙的话，告诉我，公司的事情交给我去办。

Question 23

男：请问这几种冰淇淋的价钱一样吗？

女：咖啡味三元；巧克力味的两元；香蕉味的三点五元。

Questions 24-25

男：张教授，又要出差啊？

女：是啊，上星期刚从香港回来，明天又要去北京讲课。

Questions 26-27

男：我们今晚去看电影怎么样？

女：不好意思，今天是我妈妈的生日，晚上我们全家一起出去吃饭。要不，我们明天去看好吗？

男：好，我明天晚上七点半去接你。

Questions 28-29

男：你这学期看起来很忙。

女：是呀，周一到周五天天都有课，除了三门必修课中文、英文、数学外，我还选了历史和经济。

男：怪不得呢。这些课你都喜欢吗？

女：我都喜欢，但我最喜欢的始终是数学。

Question 30

男：谢谢你给我的纪念品。

女：别客气！我原本想买围巾给你，但卖完了，只好买了一顶帽子给你。

Part A

Traditional Characters

Question 1

A： 他才剛剛開始學，你應該多鼓勵他。

(A) 剛剛下雪了。
(B) 天氣很冷。
(C) 你說得對，我不應該對他要求太高。

Question 2

A： 奇怪，你也來了？你不是不喜歡參加這種聚會的嗎？

(A) 我沒見過你。
(B) 我想多認識些朋友。
(C) 你很奇怪。

Question 3

A： 你好，你去哪？

(A) 天氣真好。
(B) 我不知道。
(C) 我去銀行，你呢？

Question 4

A： 這是你新買的衣服嗎？真漂亮啊。

(A) 哪裏哪裏，過獎了。
(B) 這件衣服真便宜。
(C) 我的衣服很貴。

Question 5

A： 時間不早了，該睡覺了。

B： 明天就要考試了，我還沒複習完呢。

(A) 你這麼早睡覺啊？
(B) 我的腳受傷了。
(C) 那你複習完就馬上睡覺吧！

Question 6

A： 李老師，好好休息，我們會常來看你的。

(A) 你們下次還來嗎？
(B) 今天我很開心，謝謝你們。
(C) 我最近很忙，可能沒有時間。

Question 7

A： 你喜歡吃梨嗎?

(A) 我最喜歡吃蘋果。
(B) 這個橘子真甜啊。
(C) 跟我媽媽一樣，我特別愛吃梨。

Question 8

A： 怎麼又忘記帶鉛筆了？下次不能再忘記了！

(A) 我沒有忘記帶紅筆。
(B) 我下次一定帶來。
(C) 我做事很認真。

Question 9

A： 你們店裏什麼菜最有名？

(A) 我們店裏的每個菜都有名字的啊。
(B) 西紅柿炒雞蛋，這個是我們的招牌菜。
(C) 菜名都在菜單上寫著呢。

Question 10

A： 他明天會來嗎？

B： 應該會來吧。

(A) 他不知道今天星期幾。
(B) 他今天來了。
(C) 那實在太好了。

Question 11

A： 你上次申請的結果出來了嗎？

B： 唉，我沒能被錄取。

(A) 祝賀你。
(B) 不客氣。
(C) 別灰心。

Question 12

A： 他說出這樣的話來真是太過分了！

(A) 他真不應該這樣說話。
(B) 他的發音很不標準。
(C) 我聽不懂他在說什麼。

Question 13

A： 不好意思，我要走了。

B： 正好，我想跟你一起走。

(A) 好，那一起走吧。
(B) 別擔心，現在時間還早。
(C) 我怕時間來不及了。

Question 14

A： 我不想吃藥。

B： 醫生說這個藥每天都要吃。

(A) 這個糖很好吃。
(B) 那我只好聽醫生的吩咐了。
(C) 醫生叫我星期六再去找他。

Question 15

A：馬上就放假了，你想去哪裏玩？

(A) 哪裏也不想去，在家呆著吧。
(B) 這個地方我去過了。
(C) 假期太短了。

Part B

Question 16

男：我想取三千元。

女：你要人民幣還是美金？

Question 17

男：你看你這個字寫錯了。

女：老師，謝謝您，我馬上就改。

Question 18

男：你爸爸是做什麼的？

女：他是醫生，每天都很忙。

男：你媽媽呢？

女：我媽媽是護士，她也在我爸爸的醫院工作。

Questions 19-20

男：聽說今年的冬天很冷，沒有暖氣怎麼行？

女：那我們買個電暖氣吧。

Questions 21-22

男：你怎麼這麼沒有精神？是不是生病了？

女：我母親昨天晚上生病住院了，我一個晚上都在醫院照顧她。

男：如果忙的話，告訴我，公司的事情交給我去辦。

Question 23

男：請問這幾種冰淇淋的價錢一樣嗎？

女：咖啡味三元；巧克力味的兩元；香蕉味的三點五元。

Questions 24-25

男：張教授，又要出差啊？

女：是啊，上星期剛從香港回來，明天又要去北京講課。

Questions 26-27

男：我們今晚去看電影怎麼樣？

女：不好意思，今天是我媽媽的生日，晚上我們全家一起出去吃飯。要不，我們明天去看好嗎？

男：好，我明天晚上七點半去接你。

Questions 28-29

男：你這學期看起來很忙。

女：是呀，週一到週五天天都有課，除了三門必修課中文、英文、數學外，我還選了歷史和經濟。

男：怪不得呢。這些課你都喜歡嗎？

女：我都喜歡，但我最喜歡的始終是數學。

Question 30

男：謝謝你給我的紀念品。

女：別客氣！我原本想買圍巾給你，但賣完了，只好買了一頂帽子給你。

Part A

Pinyin Romanization

Question 1

A：Tā cái gānggang kāishǐ xué, nǐ yīnggāi duō gǔlì tā.

(A) Gānggang xiàxuě le.
(B) Tiānqì hěn lěng.
(C) Nǐ shuō de duì, wǒ bù yīnggāi duì tā yāoqiú tài gāo.

Question 2

A：Qíguài, nǐ yě lái le? Nǐ bú shì bù xǐhuan cānjiā zhè zhǒng jùhuì de ma?

(A) Wǒ méi jiàn guo nǐ.
(B) Wǒ xiǎng duō rènshi xiē péngyou.
(C) Nǐ hěn qíguài.

Question 3

A：Nǐ hǎo, nǐ qù nǎ?

(A) Tiānqì zhēn hǎo.
(B) Wǒ bù zhīdào.
(C) Wǒ qù yínháng, nǐ ne?

Question 4

A：Zhè shì nǐ xīn mǎi de yīfu ma? Zhēn piàoliang a.

(A) Nǎli nǎli, guòjiǎng le.
(B) Zhè jiàn yīfu zhēn piányi.
(C) Wǒ de yīfu hěn guì.

Question 5

A：Shíjiān bù zǎo le, gāi shuìjiào le.

B：Míngtiān jiù yào kǎoshì le, wǒ hái méi fùxí wán ne.

(A) Nǐ zhème zǎo shuìjiào a?
(B) Wǒ de jiǎo shòushāng le.
(C) Nà nǐ fùxí wán jiù mǎshàng shuìjiào ba!

Question 6

A： Lǐ lǎoshī, hǎohao xiūxi, wǒmen huì cháng lái kàn nǐ de.

(A) Nǐmen xià cì hái lái ma?

(B) Jīntiān wǒ hěn kāixīn, xièxie nǐmen.

(C) Wǒ zuìjìn hěn máng, kěnéng méiyǒu shíjiān.

Question 7

A： Nǐ xǐhuan chī lí ma?

(A) Wǒ zuì xǐhuan chī píngguǒ.

(B) Zhège júzi zhēn tián a.

(C) Gēn wǒ māma yíyàng, wǒ tèbié ài chī lí.

Question 8

A： Zěnme yòu wàngjì dài qiānbǐ le? Xià cì bù néng zài wàngjì le!

(A) Wǒ méiyǒu wàngjì dài hóng bǐ.

(B) Wǒ xià cì yídìng dàilái.

(C) Wǒ zuò shì hěn rènzhēn.

Question 9

A： Nǐmen diàn lǐ shénme cài zuì yǒumíng?

(A) Wǒmen diàn lǐ de měi ge cài dōu yǒu míngzi de a.

(B) Xīhóngshì chǎo jīdàn, zhège shì wǒmen de zhāopaicài.

(C) Càimíng dōu zài càidān shang xiězhe ne.

Question 10

A： Tā míngtiān huì lái ma?

B： Yīnggāi huì lái ba.

(A) Tā bù zhīdào jīntiān xīngqī jǐ.

(B) Tā jīntiān láile.

(C) Nà shízài tài hǎo le.

Question 11

A：Nǐ shàngcì shēnqǐng de jiéguǒ chūlai le ma?

B：Āi, wǒ méi néng bèi lùqǔ.

(A) Zhùhè nǐ.
(B) Bú kèqi.
(C) Bié huīxīn.

Question 12

A：Tā shuō chū zhèyàng de huà lái zhēnshì tài guòfèn le!

(A) Tā zhēn bù yīnggāi zhèyàng shuōhuà.
(B) Tā de fāyīn hěn bù biāozhǔn.
(C) Wǒ tīng bùdǒng tā zài shuō shénme.

Question 13

A：Bùhǎoyìsi, wǒ yào zǒu le.

B：Zhènghǎo, wǒ xiǎng gēn nǐ yìqǐ zǒu.

(A) Hǎo, nà yìqǐ zǒu ba.
(B) Bié dānxīn, xiànzài shíjiān hái zǎo.
(C) Wǒ pà shíjiān láibují le.

Question 14

A：Wǒ bùxiǎng chī yào.

B：Yīshēng shuō zhè ge yào měitiān dōu yào chī.

(A) Zhè ge táng hěn hǎochī.
(B) Nà wǒ zhǐhǎo tīng yīshēng de fēnfù le.
(C) Yīshēng jiào wǒ xīngqī liù zài qù zhǎo tā.

Question 15

A：Mǎshàng jiù fàn jià le, nǐ xiǎng qù nǎ lǐ wán?

(A) Nǎli yě bù xiǎng qù, zài jiā dāi zhe ba.

(B) Zhè ge dìfang wǒ qùguo le.

(C) Jiàqī tài duǎn le.

Part B

Question 16

Nán：Wǒ xiǎng qǔ sānqiān yuán.

Nǚ ：Nǐ yào rénmínbì háishì měijīn?

Question 17

Nán：Nǐ kàn nǐ zhè ge zì xiě cuò le.

Nǚ ：Lǎoshī, xièxie nín, wǒ mǎshàng jiù gǎi.

Question 18

Nán：Nǐ bàba shì zuò shénme de?

Nǚ ：Tā shì yīshēng, měitiān dōu hěn máng.

Nán：Nǐ māma ne?

Nǚ ：Wǒ māma shì hùshi, tā yě zài wǒ bàba de yīyuàn gōngzuò.

Questions 19-20

Nán：Tīng shuō jīnnián de dōngtiān hěn lěng, méiyǒu nuǎnqì zěnme xíng?

Nǚ ：Nà wǒmen mǎi ge diànnuǎnqì ba.

Questions 21-22

Nán：Nǐ zěnme zhème méiyǒu jīngshen? Shì bushì shēngbìng le?

Nǚ ：Wǒ mǔqīn zuótiān wǎnshang shēngbìng zhùyuàn le, wǒ yí ge wǎnshang dōu zài yīyuàn zhàogu tā.

Nán：Rúguǒ máng de huà, gàosu wǒ, gōngsī de shìqing jiāo gěi wǒ qù bàn.

Question 23

Nán : Qǐngwèn zhè jǐ zhǒng bīngqílín de jiàqián yíyàng ma?

Nǚ : Kāfēi wèi sān yuán; qiǎokèlì wèi de liǎng yuán; xiāngjiāo wèi de sān diǎn wǔ yuán.

Questions 24-25

Nán : Zhāng jiàoshòu, yòu yào chūchāi a?

Nǚ : Shì a, shàng xīngqī gāng cóng Xiānggǎng huílai, míngtiān yòu yào qù Běijīng jiǎng kè.

Questions 26-27

Nán : Wǒmen jīnwǎn qù kàn diànyǐng zěnmeyàng?

Nǚ : Bù hǎo yìsi, jīntiān shì wǒ māma de shēngrì, wǎnshang wǒmen quán jiā yìqǐ chūqù chīfàn. Yào bu, wǒmen míngtiān qù kàn hǎo ma?

Nán : Hǎo, wǒ míngtiān wǎnshang qī diǎn bàn qù jiē nǐ.

Questions 28-29

Nán : Nǐ zhè xuéqī kàn qǐlai hěn máng.

Nǚ : Shì yā, zhōu yī dào zhōu wǔ tiān tiān dōu yǒu kè, chúle sān mén bìxiūkè Zhōngwén、Yīngwén、shùxué wài, wǒ hái xuǎnle lìshǐ hé jīngjì.

Nán : Guài budé ne. Zhè xiē kè nǐ dōu xǐhuan ma?

Nǚ : Wǒ dōu xǐhuan, dàn wǒ zuì xǐhuan de shìzhōng shì shùxué.

Question 30

Nán : Xièxie nǐ gěi wǒ de jìniànpǐn.

Nǚ : Biékèqi! wǒ yuánběn xiǎng mǎi wéijīn gěi nǐ, dàn mài wán le, zhǐhǎo mǎile yì dǐng màozi gěi nǐ.

Practice Test Four

1	Ⓐ	Ⓑ	Ⓒ	Ⓓ	31	Ⓐ	Ⓑ	Ⓒ	Ⓓ	56	Ⓐ	Ⓑ	Ⓒ	Ⓓ
2	Ⓐ	Ⓑ	Ⓒ	Ⓓ	32	Ⓐ	Ⓑ	Ⓒ	Ⓓ	57	Ⓐ	Ⓑ	Ⓒ	Ⓓ
3	Ⓐ	Ⓑ	Ⓒ	Ⓓ	33	Ⓐ	Ⓑ	Ⓒ	Ⓓ	58	Ⓐ	Ⓑ	Ⓒ	Ⓓ
4	Ⓐ	Ⓑ	Ⓒ	Ⓓ	34	Ⓐ	Ⓑ	Ⓒ	Ⓓ	59	Ⓐ	Ⓑ	Ⓒ	Ⓓ
5	Ⓐ	Ⓑ	Ⓒ	Ⓓ	35	Ⓐ	Ⓑ	Ⓒ	Ⓓ	60	Ⓐ	Ⓑ	Ⓒ	Ⓓ
6	Ⓐ	Ⓑ	Ⓒ	Ⓓ	36	Ⓐ	Ⓑ	Ⓒ	Ⓓ	61	Ⓐ	Ⓑ	Ⓒ	Ⓓ
7	Ⓐ	Ⓑ	Ⓒ	Ⓓ	37	Ⓐ	Ⓑ	Ⓒ	Ⓓ	62	Ⓐ	Ⓑ	Ⓒ	Ⓓ
8	Ⓐ	Ⓑ	Ⓒ	Ⓓ	38	Ⓐ	Ⓑ	Ⓒ	Ⓓ	63	Ⓐ	Ⓑ	Ⓒ	Ⓓ
9	Ⓐ	Ⓑ	Ⓒ	Ⓓ	39	Ⓐ	Ⓑ	Ⓒ	Ⓓ	64	Ⓐ	Ⓑ	Ⓒ	Ⓓ
10	Ⓐ	Ⓑ	Ⓒ	Ⓓ	40	Ⓐ	Ⓑ	Ⓒ	Ⓓ	65	Ⓐ	Ⓑ	Ⓒ	Ⓓ
11	Ⓐ	Ⓑ	Ⓒ	Ⓓ	41	Ⓐ	Ⓑ	Ⓒ	Ⓓ	66	Ⓐ	Ⓑ	Ⓒ	Ⓓ
12	Ⓐ	Ⓑ	Ⓒ	Ⓓ	42	Ⓐ	Ⓑ	Ⓒ	Ⓓ	67	Ⓐ	Ⓑ	Ⓒ	Ⓓ
13	Ⓐ	Ⓑ	Ⓒ	Ⓓ	43	Ⓐ	Ⓑ	Ⓒ	Ⓓ	68	Ⓐ	Ⓑ	Ⓒ	Ⓓ
14	Ⓐ	Ⓑ	Ⓒ	Ⓓ	44	Ⓐ	Ⓑ	Ⓒ	Ⓓ	69	Ⓐ	Ⓑ	Ⓒ	Ⓓ
15	Ⓐ	Ⓑ	Ⓒ	Ⓓ	45	Ⓐ	Ⓑ	Ⓒ	Ⓓ	70	Ⓐ	Ⓑ	Ⓒ	Ⓓ
16	Ⓐ	Ⓑ	Ⓒ	Ⓓ	46	Ⓐ	Ⓑ	Ⓒ	Ⓓ	71	Ⓐ	Ⓑ	Ⓒ	Ⓓ
17	Ⓐ	Ⓑ	Ⓒ	Ⓓ	47	Ⓐ	Ⓑ	Ⓒ	Ⓓ	72	Ⓐ	Ⓑ	Ⓒ	Ⓓ
18	Ⓐ	Ⓑ	Ⓒ	Ⓓ	48	Ⓐ	Ⓑ	Ⓒ	Ⓓ	73	Ⓐ	Ⓑ	Ⓒ	Ⓓ
19	Ⓐ	Ⓑ	Ⓒ	Ⓓ	49	Ⓐ	Ⓑ	Ⓒ	Ⓓ	74	Ⓐ	Ⓑ	Ⓒ	Ⓓ
20	Ⓐ	Ⓑ	Ⓒ	Ⓓ	50	Ⓐ	Ⓑ	Ⓒ	Ⓓ	75	Ⓐ	Ⓑ	Ⓒ	Ⓓ
21	Ⓐ	Ⓑ	Ⓒ	Ⓓ	51	Ⓐ	Ⓑ	Ⓒ	Ⓓ	76	Ⓐ	Ⓑ	Ⓒ	Ⓓ
22	Ⓐ	Ⓑ	Ⓒ	Ⓓ	52	Ⓐ	Ⓑ	Ⓒ	Ⓓ	77	Ⓐ	Ⓑ	Ⓒ	Ⓓ
23	Ⓐ	Ⓑ	Ⓒ	Ⓓ	53	Ⓐ	Ⓑ	Ⓒ	Ⓓ	78	Ⓐ	Ⓑ	Ⓒ	Ⓓ
24	Ⓐ	Ⓑ	Ⓒ	Ⓓ	54	Ⓐ	Ⓑ	Ⓒ	Ⓓ	79	Ⓐ	Ⓑ	Ⓒ	Ⓓ
25	Ⓐ	Ⓑ	Ⓒ	Ⓓ	55	Ⓐ	Ⓑ	Ⓒ	Ⓓ	80	Ⓐ	Ⓑ	Ⓒ	Ⓓ
26	Ⓐ	Ⓑ	Ⓒ	Ⓓ						81	Ⓐ	Ⓑ	Ⓒ	Ⓓ
27	Ⓐ	Ⓑ	Ⓒ	Ⓓ						82	Ⓐ	Ⓑ	Ⓒ	Ⓓ
28	Ⓐ	Ⓑ	Ⓒ	Ⓓ						83	Ⓐ	Ⓑ	Ⓒ	Ⓓ
29	Ⓐ	Ⓑ	Ⓒ	Ⓓ						84	Ⓐ	Ⓑ	Ⓒ	Ⓓ
30	Ⓐ	Ⓑ	Ⓒ	Ⓓ						85	Ⓐ	Ⓑ	Ⓒ	Ⓓ

SAT Chinese Practice Test — Five
SAT 中文模拟试题 — 第五套
SAT 中文模擬試題 — 第五套

Time — 1 hour
Questions 1 - 85

PLEASE NOTE THAT YOUR ANSWER SHEET HAS FOUR ANSWER POSITIONS, MARKED A, B, C, AND D, WHILE THE QUESTIONS THROUGHOUT THIS TEST CONTAIN EITHER THREE OR FOUR ANSWER CHOICES. BE SURE NOT TO MARK YOUR ANSWERS IN COLUMN D IF THERE ARE ONLY THREE CHOICES GIVEN.

SECTION I
LISTENING

Approximate time — 20 minutes
Questions 1 - 30

Part A

Directions:

In this part of the test, you will hear short questions, statements, or commands in Mandarin Chinese, followed by three responses in Mandarin Chinese, designated (A), (B), and (C). You will hear the questions or statements, as well as the responses, only once, and they are not printed in your test booklet. Therefore, you must listen very carefully. Select the best response and fill in the corresponding circle on your answer sheet.

Question 1 Mark your answer on your answer sheet.

Question 2 Mark your answer on your answer sheet.

Question 3 Mark your answer on your answer sheet.

Question 4 Mark your answer on your answer sheet.

Question 5 Mark your answer on your answer sheet.

Question 6 Mark your answer on your answer sheet.

Question 7 Mark your answer on your answer sheet.

Question 8 Mark your answer on your answer sheet.

Question 9 Mark your answer on your answer sheet.

Question 10 Mark your answer on your answer sheet.

Question 11 Mark your answer on your answer sheet.

Question 12 Mark your answer on your answer sheet.

Question 13 Mark your answer on your answer sheet.

Question 14 Mark your answer on your answer sheet.

Question 15 Mark your answer on your answer sheet.

Part B

Directions:

You will now hear a series of dialogues. You will hear them only once, and they are not printed in your test booklet. After each selection, you will be asked to answer one or more questions about what you have just heard. These questions, each with four possible answers, are printed in your test booklet. Select the best answer to each question from among the four choices printed and fill in the corresponding circle on your answer sheet.

Question 16

16. Why is the woman unwilling to sing at the ball?

(A) She cannot sing well.
(B) She does not have time to practice.
(C) She is afraid to sing in front of many people.
(D) She cannot attend the ball.

Question 17

17. What is the woman's response?

(A) She is very busy at the moment.
(B) She needs to go to Beijing.
(C) She also needs to go to the national theatre.
(D) She has also just arrived in Beijing.

Question 18

18. Where is the dialogue set?

(A) In a post office
(B) In a photo studio
(C) In a bookstore
(D) In a supermarket

Question 19

19. Where is the dialogue set?
    (A) On a bus
    (B) In a hospital
    (C) In a shop
    (D) In a post office

Question 20

20. What kind of movie does the man like to watch?
    (A) Romance
    (B) Science fiction
    (C) Martial arts
    (D) Comedy

Question 21

21. At what time can books be returned?
    (A) Between 8 A.M. and 3 P.M.
    (B) Between 8 A.M. and 5 P.M.
    (C) Between 9 A.M. and 5 P.M.
    (D) Anytime before 5 P.M.

Question 22

22. What is the man's biggest worry about the house?
    (A) The location
    (B) The price
    (C) The interior
    (D) The size

Questions 23-24

23. Why is the woman late?
    (A) She went shopping.
    (B) She met Xiao Li on her way back.
    (C) She missed the bus.
    (D) She had an accident on her way back.

24. What did the man ask the woman to do?
    (A) Buy something for him
    (B) Come home early
    (C) Post a letter
    (D) Close the door

Question 25

25. What does the woman order?
    (A) Cake and coffee
    (B) Stir-fried vegetables and rice
    (C) Dumplings and tea
    (D) Noodles and fruit juice

Questions 26-27

26. The man
    (A) has a stomachache
    (B) has a headache
    (C) lost his wallet
    (D) wants to buy some food

27. What did the man have for dinner last night?
    (A) Rice and salad
    (B) Beef and noodles
    (C) Chicken and rice
    (D) Steak and salad

Question 28

28. What are the two people going to do tomorrow?
    - (A) Go hiking
    - (B) Go to the movies
    - (C) Go for a walk
    - (D) Go swimming

Questions 29-30

29. Where does the woman want to live?
    - (A) Near her school
    - (B) Near her office
    - (C) Near the hospital
    - (D) Near her mother's house

30. Why does the woman want to move?
    - (A) The rent is too expensive.
    - (B) The surroundings are too noisy.
    - (C) Public transport is not convenient.
    - (D) Her apartment is too small.

SECTION II
USAGE

Suggested time — 15 minutes
Questions 31 - 55

Part A

Directions:

This section consists of a number of incomplete statements, each of which has four possible completions. Select the word or phrase that best completes the sentence structurally and logically and fill in the corresponding circle on your answer sheet.

This section of the test is presented in four different ways of representing Chinese: traditional characters, simplified characters, pinyin romanization, and the Chinese phonetic alphabet. IT IS RECOMMEMD THAT YOU CHOOSE THE WRITING SYSTEM WITH WHICH YOU ARE MORE FAMILIAR WITH AND **ONLY READ THAT VERSION** AS YOU WORK THROUGH THIS SECTION OF THE TEST.

31. 他____迟到，是因为堵车。
(A) 由于
(B) 只有
(C) 之所以
(D) 可是

31. 他____遲到，是因爲堵車。
(A) 由於
(B) 只有
(C) 之所以
(D) 可是

31. Tā____chídào, shì yīnwèi dǔchē.
(A) yóuyú
(B) zhǐyǒu
(C) zhī suǒyǐ
(D) kěshì

31. ㄊㄚ ____ ㄔˊ ㄉㄠˋ，ㄕˋ ㄧㄣ ㄨㄟˋ ㄉㄨˇ ㄔㄜ 。
(A) ㄧㄡˊ ㄩˊ
(B) ㄓˇ ㄧㄡˇ
(C) ㄓ ㄙㄨㄛˇ ㄧˇ
(D) ㄎㄜˇ ㄕˋ

32. 他欺骗了太多人，____没有人再相信他。
(A) 接着
(B) 于是
(C) 即使
(D) 既然

32. 他欺騙了太多人，____沒有人再相信他。
(A) 接著
(B) 於是
(C) 即使
(D) 既然

32. Tā qīpiàn le tài duō rén, ____ méiyǒu rén zài xiāngxìn tā.
(A) jiēzhe
(B) yúshì
(C) jíshǐ
(D) jìrán

32. ㄊㄚ ㄑㄧ ㄆㄧㄢˋ ㄌㄜ˙ ㄊㄞˋ ㄉㄨㄛ ㄖㄣˊ，____ ㄇㄟˊ ㄧㄡˇ ㄖㄣˊ ㄗㄞˋ ㄒㄧㄤ ㄒㄧㄣˋ ㄊㄚ 。
(A) ㄐㄧㄝ ㄓㄜ˙
(B) ㄩˊ ㄕˋ
(C) ㄐㄧˊ ㄕˇ
(D) ㄐㄧˋ ㄖㄢˊ

33. ____ 我们一起努力，才能把这件事情完成。

(A) 只要
(B) 只有
(C) 只好
(D) 只是

33. ____ 我們一起努力，才能把這件事情完成。

(A) 只要
(B) 只有
(C) 只好
(D) 只是

33. ____ wǒmen yìqǐ nǔlì, cáinéng bǎ zhè jiàn shìqing wánchéng.

(A) Zhǐyào
(B) Zhǐyǒu
(C) Zhǐhǎo
(D) Zhǐshì

33. ____ ㄨㄛˇ ㄇㄣ˙ ㄧˋ ㄑㄧˇ ㄋㄨˇ ㄌㄧˋ，ㄘㄞˊ ㄋㄥˊ ㄅㄚˇ ㄓㄜˋ ㄕˋ ㄑㄧㄥˊ ㄨㄢˊ ㄔㄥˊ。

(A) ㄓˇ ㄧㄠˋ
(B) ㄓˇ ㄧㄡˇ
(C) ㄓˇ ㄏㄠˇ
(D) ㄓˇ ㄕˋ

34. 他____ 医生，____ 老师。

(A) 不是 …… 而是
(B) 不但 …… 而且
(C) 尽管 …… 但是
(D) 因为 …… 所以

34. 他____ 醫生，____ 老師。

(A) 不是 …… 而是
(B) 不但 …… 而且
(C) 儘管 …… 但是
(D) 因爲 …… 所以

34. Tā ____ yīshēng, ____ lǎoshī.

(A) búshì …… érshì
(B) búdàn …… érqiě
(C) jǐnguǎn …… dànshì
(D) yīnwèi …… suǒyǐ

34. ㄊㄚ ____ ㄧ ㄕㄥ，____ ㄌㄠˇ ㄕ 。

(A) ㄅㄨˊ ㄕˋ ㄦˊ ㄕˋ
(B) ㄅㄨˊ ㄉㄢˋ ㄦˊ ㄑㄧㄝˇ
(C) ㄐㄧㄣˇ ㄍㄨㄢˇ ㄉㄢˋ ㄕˋ
(D) ㄧㄣ ㄨㄟˋ ㄙㄨㄛˇ ㄧˇ

35. 你得到这次难得的机会，____ 如何都要尽力完成。

(A) 至于
(B) 与其
(C) 无论
(D) 反正

35. 你得到這次難得的機會，____ 如何都要盡力完成。

(A) 至於
(B) 與其
(C) 無論
(D) 反正

35. Nǐ dédào zhè cì nándé de jīhuì, ____ rúhé dōu yào jìnlì wánchéng.

(A) zhìyú
(B) yǔqí
(C) wúlùn
(D) fǎnzhèng

35. ㄋㄧˇ ㄉㄜˊ ㄉㄠˋ ㄓㄜˋ ㄘˋ ㄋㄢˊ ㄉㄜˊ ㄉㄜ˙ ㄐㄧ ㄏㄨㄟˋ，____ ㄖㄨˊ ㄏㄜˊ ㄉㄡ ㄧㄠˋ ㄐㄧㄣˋ ㄌㄧˋ ㄨㄢˊ ㄔㄥˊ。

(A) ㄓˋ ㄩˊ
(B) ㄩˇ ㄑㄧˊ
(C) ㄨˊ ㄌㄨㄣˋ
(D) ㄈㄢˇ ㄓㄥˋ

36. ____你肯改过，老师就一定会原谅你。

(A) 如果
(B) 为何
(C) 为了
(D) 由于

36. ____nǐ kěn gǎiguò, lǎoshī jiù yídìng huì yuánliàng nǐ.

(A) Rúguǒ
(B) Wèihé
(C) Wèile
(D) Yóuyú

37. 你考试怎么会不及格____？

(A) 吗
(B) 呢
(C) 啊
(D) 咦

37. Nǐ kǎoshì zěnme huì bù jígé____？

(A) ma
(B) ne
(C) a
(D) yí

38. 做运动时一定要注意安全，____受伤。

(A) 以便
(B) 以免
(C) 以及
(D) 以致

38. Zuò yùndòng shí yídìng yào zhùyì ānquán, ____shòushāng.

(A) yǐbiàn
(B) yǐmiǎn
(C) yǐjí
(D) yǐzhì

36. ____你肯改過，老師就一定會原諒你。

(A) 如果
(B) 爲何
(C) 爲了
(D) 由於

36. ____ㄋㄧˇ ㄎㄣˇ ㄍㄞˇ ㄍㄨㄛˋ，ㄌㄠˇ ㄕ ㄐㄧㄡˋ ㄧˊ ㄉㄧㄥˋ ㄏㄨㄟˋ ㄩㄢˊ ㄌㄧㄤˋ ㄋㄧˇ。

(A) ㄖㄨˊ ㄍㄨㄛˇ
(B) ㄨㄟˋ ㄏㄜˊ
(C) ㄨㄟˋ ˙ㄌㄜ
(D) ㄧㄡˊ ㄩˊ

37. 你考試怎麼會不及格____？

(A) 嗎
(B) 呢
(C) 啊
(D) 咦

37. ㄋㄧˇ ㄎㄠˇ ㄕˋ ㄗㄣˇ ˙ㄇㄜ ㄏㄨㄟˋ ㄅㄨˋ ㄐㄧˊ ㄍㄜˊ____？

(A) ㄇㄚ
(B) ㄋㄜ
(C) ˙ㄚ
(D) ㄧˊ

38. 做運動時一定要注意安全，____受傷。

(A) 以便
(B) 以免
(C) 以及
(D) 以致

38. ㄗㄨㄛˋ ㄩㄣˋ ㄉㄨㄥˋ ㄕˊ ㄧˊ ㄉㄧㄥˋ ㄧㄠˋ ㄓㄨˋ ㄧˋ ㄢ ㄑㄩㄢˊ，____ㄕㄡˋ ㄕㄤ。

(A) ㄧˇ ㄅㄧㄢˋ
(B) ㄧˇ ㄇㄧㄢˇ
(C) ㄧˇ ㄐㄧˊ
(D) ㄧˇ ㄓˋ

39. 他什么都不会，只会____别人的毛病。
(A) 选
(B) 挑
(C) 拿
(D) 执

39. 他什麼都不會，只會____別人的毛病。
(A) 選
(B) 挑
(C) 拿
(D) 執

39. Tā shénme dōu bú huì, zhǐ huì ____ biérén de máobìng.
(A) xuǎn
(B) tiāo
(C) ná
(D) zhí

39. ㄊㄚ ㄕㄣˊ ㄇㄜ˙ ㄉㄡ ㄅㄨˊ ㄏㄨㄟˋ，ㄓˇ ㄏㄨㄟˋ ____ ㄅㄧㄝˊ ㄖㄣˊ ㄉㄜ˙ ㄇㄠˊ ㄅㄧㄥˋ。
(A) ㄒㄩㄢˇ
(B) ㄊㄧㄠ
(C) ㄋㄚˊ
(D) ㄓˊ

40. 昨天，老师跟我说他要去美国一____。
(A) 条
(B) 趟
(C) 场
(D) 会

40. 昨天，老師跟我說他要去美國一____。
(A) 條
(B) 趟
(C) 場
(D) 會

40. Zuótiān, lǎoshī gēn wǒ shuō tā yào qù Měiguó yī ____.
(A) tiáo
(B) tàng
(C) chǎng
(D) huì

40. ㄗㄨㄛˊ ㄊㄧㄢ，ㄌㄠˇ ㄕ ㄍㄣ ㄨㄛˇ ㄕㄨㄛ ㄊㄚ ㄧㄠˋ ㄑㄩˋ ㄇㄟˇ ㄍㄨㄛˊ ㄧ ____。
(A) ㄊㄧㄠˊ
(B) ㄊㄤˋ
(C) ㄔㄤˇ
(D) ㄏㄨㄟˋ

41. 他不是不想专心听课，____有点儿累。
(A) 不是
(B) 只能
(C) 只是
(D) 只好

41. 他不是不想專心聽課，____有點兒累。
(A) 不是
(B) 只能
(C) 只是
(D) 只好

41. Tā bú shì bù xiǎng zhuānxīn tīngkè, ____ yǒu diǎnr lèi.
(A) búshì
(B) zhǐnéng
(C) zhǐshì
(D) zhǐhǎo

41. ㄊㄚ ㄅㄨˊ ㄕˋ ㄅㄨˋ ㄒㄧㄤˇ ㄓㄨㄢ ㄒㄧㄣ ㄊㄧㄥ ㄎㄜˋ，____ ㄧㄡˇ ㄉㄧㄢˇ ㄦˊ ㄌㄟˋ。
(A) ㄅㄨˊ ㄕˋ
(B) ㄓˇ ㄋㄥˊ
(C) ㄓˇ ㄕˋ
(D) ㄓˇ ㄏㄠˇ

42. ＿＿在比赛中得到好成绩，他每天都努力练习跑步。

(A) 为
(B) 为了
(C) 为此
(D) 为的是

42. ＿＿在比賽中得到好成績，他每天都努力練習跑步。

(A) 爲
(B) 爲了
(C) 爲此
(D) 爲的是

42. ＿＿zài bǐsài zhōng dédào hǎo chéngjì, tā měitiān dōu nǔlì liànxí pǎobù.

(A) Wéi
(B) Wèile
(C) Wèicǐ
(D) Wéideshì

42. ＿＿ㄗㄞˋ ㄅㄧˇ ㄙㄞˋ ㄓㄨㄥ ㄉㄜˊ ㄉㄠˋ ㄏㄠˇ ㄔㄥˊ ㄐㄧˋ，ㄊㄚ ㄇㄟˇ ㄊㄧㄢ ㄉㄡ ㄋㄨˇ ㄌㄧˋ ㄌㄧㄢˋ ㄒㄧˊ ㄆㄠˇ ㄅㄨˋ。

(A) ㄨㄟˋ
(B) ㄨㄟˋ ˙ㄌㄜ
(C) ㄨㄟˋ ㄘˇ
(D) ㄨㄟˋ ˙ㄉㄜ ㄕˋ

43. ＿＿你想欺骗我到什么时候呢？

(A) 既然
(B) 究竟
(C) 无论
(D) 真的是

43. ＿＿你想欺騙我到什麼時候呢？

(A) 既然
(B) 究竟
(C) 無論
(D) 真的是

43. ＿＿nǐ xiǎng qīpiàn wǒ dào shénme shíhou ne？

(A) Jìrán
(B) Jiūjìng
(C) Wúlùn
(D) Zhēndeshì

43. ＿＿ㄋㄧˇ ㄒㄧㄤˇ ㄑㄧ ㄆㄧㄢˋ ㄨㄛˇ ㄉㄠˋ ㄕㄣˊ ˙ㄇㄜ ㄕˊ ㄏㄡˋ ˙ㄋㄜ？

(A) ㄐㄧˋ ㄖㄢˊ
(B) ㄐㄧㄡ ㄐㄧㄥˋ
(C) ㄨˊ ㄌㄨㄣˋ
(D) ㄓㄣ ˙ㄉㄜ ㄕˋ

44. 农历新年时，到处都＿＿，欢天喜地。

(A) 热热闹闹
(B) 热闹热闹
(C) 闹闹热热
(D) 闹热闹热

44. 農曆新年時，到處都＿＿，歡天喜地。

(A) 熱熱鬧鬧
(B) 熱鬧熱鬧
(C) 鬧鬧熱熱
(D) 鬧熱鬧熱

44. Nónglí xīnnián shí, dàochù dōu ＿＿, huāntiānxǐdì.

(A) rè re nāo nāo
(B) rè nao rè nao
(C) nào nao rè re
(D) nào re nào re

44. ㄋㄨㄥˊ ㄌㄧˋ ㄒㄧㄣ ㄋㄧㄢˊ ㄕˊ，ㄉㄠˋ ㄔㄨˋ ㄉㄡ ＿＿，ㄏㄨㄢ ㄊㄧㄢ ㄒㄧˇ ㄉㄧˋ。

(A) ㄖㄜˋ ㄖㄜˋ ㄋㄠˋ ㄋㄠˋ
(B) ㄖㄜˋ ㄋㄠˋ ㄖㄜˋ ㄋㄠˋ
(C) ㄋㄠˋ ㄋㄠˋ ㄖㄜˋ ㄖㄜˋ
(D) ㄋㄠˋ ㄖㄜˋ ㄋㄠˋ ㄖㄜˋ

45. 她哭着告诉了我她 ____ 骗的经过。
(A) 由
(B) 以
(C) 把
(D) 被

45. Tā kūzhe gàosu le wǒ tā ____ piàn de jīngguò.
(A) yóu
(B) yǐ
(C) bǎ
(D) bèi

46. 我很喜欢你送给我的那 ____ 钢笔。
(A) 个
(B) 枝
(C) 根
(D) 条

46. Wǒ hěn xǐhuan nǐ sònggěi wǒ de nà ____ gāngbǐ.
(A) ge
(B) zhī
(C) gēn
(D) tiáo

47. 这件事 ____ 我去办，我一定会尽力而为。
(A) 把
(B) 被
(C) 由
(D) 于

47. Zhè jiàn shì ____ wǒ qù bàn, wǒ yídìng huì jìnlì’ érwéi.
(A) bǎ
(B) bèi
(C) yóu
(D) yú

45. 她哭著告訴了我她 ____ 騙的經過。
(A) 由
(B) 以
(C) 把
(D) 被

45. ㄊㄚ ㄎㄨ ˙ㄓㄜ ㄍㄠˋ ㄙㄨˋ ˙ㄌㄜ ㄨㄛˇ ㄊㄚ ____ ㄆㄧㄢˋ ˙ㄉㄜ ㄐㄧㄥ ㄍㄨㄛˋ。
(A) ㄧㄡˊ
(B) ㄧˇ
(C) ㄅㄚˇ
(D) ㄅㄟˋ

46. 我很喜歡你送給我的那 ____ 鋼筆。
(A) 個
(B) 枝
(C) 根
(D) 條

46. ㄨㄛˇ ㄏㄣˇ ㄒㄧˇ ㄏㄨㄢ ㄋㄧˇ ㄙㄨㄥˋ ㄍㄟˇ ㄨㄛˇ ˙ㄉㄜ ㄋㄚˋ ____ ㄍㄤ ㄅㄧˇ。
(A) ˙ㄍㄜ
(B) ㄓ
(C) ㄍㄣ
(D) ㄊㄧㄠˊ

47. 這件事 ____ 我去辦，我一定會盡力而爲。
(A) 把
(B) 被
(C) 由
(D) 於

47. ㄓㄜˋ ㄐㄧㄢˋ ㄕˋ ____ ㄨㄛˇ ㄑㄩˋ ㄅㄢˋ，ㄨㄛˇ ㄧˊ ㄉㄧㄥˋ ㄏㄨㄟˋ ㄐㄧㄣˋ ㄌㄧˋ ㄦˊ ㄨㄟˊ。
(A) ㄅㄚˇ
(B) ㄅㄟˋ
(C) ㄧㄡˊ
(D) ㄩˊ

48. ____ 去爬山，不如去游泳。
(A) 因为
(B) 与其
(C) 既然
(D) 即使

48. ____ qù páshān, bùrú qù yóuyǒng.
(A) Yīnwèi
(B) Yǔqí
(C) Jìrán
(D) Jíshǐ

49. 每天吃蔬果，____ 有益健康，____ 可以预防疾病。
(A) 不但 …… 而且
(B) 虽然 …… 但是
(C) 一边 …… 一边
(D) 不但不 …… 反而

49. Měitiān chī shūguǒ, ____ yǒuyì jiànkāng, ____ kěyǐ yùfáng jíbìng.
(A) búdàn …… érqiě
(B) suīrán …… dànshì
(C) yìbiān …… yìbiān
(D) búdànbù …… fǎn'ér

50. ____ 那次考试不及格，他比以前更努力学习了。
(A) 假如
(B) 自从
(C) 已经
(D) 刚才

50. ____ nà cì kǎoshì bù jígé, tā bǐ yǐqián gèng nǔlì xuéxí le.
(A) Jiǎrú
(B) Zìcóng
(C) Yǐjīng
(D) Gāngcái

48. ____ 去爬山，不如去游泳。
(A) 因爲
(B) 與其
(C) 既然
(D) 即使

48. ____ ㄑㄩˋ ㄆㄚˊ ㄕㄢ，ㄅㄨˋ ㄖㄨˊ ㄑㄩˋ ㄧㄡˊ ㄩㄥˇ。
(A) ㄧㄣ ㄨㄟˋ
(B) ㄩˇ ㄑㄧˊ
(C) ㄐㄧˋ ㄖㄢˊ
(D) ㄐㄧˊ ㄕˇ

49. 每天吃蔬果，____ 有益健康，____ 可以預防疾病。
(A) 不但 …… 而且
(B) 雖然 …… 但是
(C) 一邊 …… 一邊
(D) 不但不 …… 反而

49. ㄇㄟˇ ㄊㄧㄢ ㄔ ㄕㄨ ㄍㄨㄛˇ，____ ㄧㄡˇ ㄧˋ ㄐㄧㄢˋ ㄎㄤ，____ ㄎㄜˇ ㄧˇ ㄩˋ ㄈㄤˊ ㄐㄧˊ ㄅㄧㄥˋ。
(A) ㄅㄨˊ ㄉㄢˋ …… ㄦˊ ㄑㄧㄝˇ
(B) ㄙㄨㄟ ㄖㄢˊ …… ㄉㄢˋ ㄕˋ
(C) ㄧˋ ㄅㄧㄢ …… ㄧˋ ㄅㄧㄢ
(D) ㄅㄨˊ ㄉㄢˋ ㄅㄨˋ …… ㄈㄢˇ ㄦˊ

50. ____ 那次考試不及格，他比以前更努力學習了。
(A) 假如
(B) 自從
(C) 已經
(D) 剛才

50. ____ ㄋㄚˋ ㄘˋ ㄎㄠˇ ㄕˋ ㄅㄨˋ ㄐㄧˊ ㄍㄜˊ，ㄊㄚ ㄅㄧˇ ㄧˇ ㄑㄧㄢˊ ㄍㄥˋ ㄋㄨˇ ㄌㄧˋ ㄒㄩㄝˊ ㄒㄧˊ ㄌㄜ˙。
(A) ㄐㄧㄚˇ ㄖㄨˊ
(B) ㄗˋ ㄘㄨㄥˊ
(C) ㄧˇ ㄐㄧㄥ
(D) ㄍㄤ ㄘㄞˊ

51. 这个地方____ 。
(A) 最近游客很受欢迎。
(B) 最近很受游客欢迎。
(C) 游客最近很受欢迎。
(D) 很受欢迎最近游客。

51. Zhè ge dìfāng ____.
(A) zuìjìn yóukè hěn shòu huānyíng.
(B) zuìjìn hěn shòu yóukè huānyíng.
(C) yóukè zuìjìn hěn shòu huānyíng.
(D) hěn shòu huānyíng zuìjìn yóukè.

52. 这个收费包括了住宿，饮食不包括____ 。
(A) 在外
(B) 在内
(C) 以外
(D) 以内

52. Zhè ge shōufèi bāokuò le zhùsù, yǐnshí bù bāokuò____.
(A) zàiwài
(B) zàinèi
(C) yǐwài
(D) yǐnèi

53. 我想找一本____历史的书。
(A) 对于
(B) 关于
(C) 终于
(D) 始终

53. Wǒ xiǎng zhǎo yì běn____lìshǐ de shū.
(A) duìyú
(B) guānyú
(C) zhōngyú
(D) shǐzhōng

51. 這個地方____ 。
(A) 最近遊客很受歡迎。
(B) 最近很受遊客歡迎。
(C) 遊客最近很受歡迎。
(D) 很受歡迎最近遊客。

51. ㄓㄜˋ ㄍㄜˋ ㄉㄧˋ ㄈㄤ ____ 。
(A) ㄗㄨㄟˋ ㄐㄧㄣˋ ㄧㄡˊ ㄎㄜˋ ㄏㄣˇ ㄕㄡˋ ㄏㄨㄢ ㄧㄥˊ。
(B) ㄗㄨㄟˋ ㄐㄧㄣˋ ㄏㄣˇ ㄕㄡˋ ㄧㄡˊ ㄎㄜˋ ㄏㄨㄢ ㄧㄥˊ。
(C) ㄧㄡˊ ㄎㄜˋ ㄗㄨㄟˋ ㄐㄧㄣˋ ㄏㄣˇ ㄕㄡˋ ㄏㄨㄢ ㄧㄥˊ。
(D) ㄏㄣˇ ㄕㄡˋ ㄏㄨㄢ ㄧㄥˊ ㄗㄨㄟˋ ㄐㄧㄣˋ ㄧㄡˊ ㄎㄜˋ。

52. 這個收費包括了住宿，飲食不包括____ 。
(A) 在外
(B) 在內
(C) 以外
(D) 以內

52. ㄓㄜˋ ㄍㄜˋ ㄕㄡ ㄈㄟˋ ㄅㄠ ㄎㄨㄛˋ ㄌㄜ˙ ㄓㄨˋ ㄙㄨˋ，ㄧㄣˇ ㄕˊ ㄅㄨˋ ㄅㄠ ㄎㄨㄛˋ ____ 。
(A) ㄗㄞˋ ㄨㄞˋ
(B) ㄗㄞˋ ㄋㄟˋ
(C) ㄧˇ ㄨㄞˋ
(D) ㄧˇ ㄋㄟˋ

53. 我想找一本____歷史的書。
(A) 對於
(B) 關於
(C) 終於
(D) 始終

53. ㄨㄛˇ ㄒㄧㄤˇ ㄓㄠˇ ㄧˋ ㄅㄣˇ ____ ㄌㄧˋ ㄕˇ ㄉㄜ˙ ㄕㄨ 。
(A) ㄉㄨㄟˋ ㄩˊ
(B) ㄍㄨㄢ ㄩˊ
(C) ㄓㄨㄥ ㄩˊ
(D) ㄕˇ ㄓㄨㄥ

54. 每个人都应该尽力____ 。
(A) 做自己好的工作
(B) 做好自己的工作
(C) 好做自己的工作
(D) 工作自己做好的

54. 每個人都應該盡力____ 。
(A) 做自己好的工作
(B) 做好自己的工作
(C) 好做自己的工作
(D) 工作自己做好的

54. Měi ge rén dōu yīnggāi jìnlì ____.
(A) zuò zìjǐ hǎo de gōngzuò
(B) zuò hǎo zìjǐ de gōngzuò
(C) hǎo zuò zìjǐ de gōngzuò
(D) gōngzuò zìjǐ zuò hǎo de

54. ㄇㄟˇ ˙ㄍㄜ ㄖㄣˊ ㄉㄡ ㄧㄥ ㄍㄞ ㄐㄧㄣˋ ㄌㄧˋ____ 。
(A) ㄗㄨㄛˋ ㄗˋ ㄐㄧˇ ㄏㄠˇ ˙ㄉㄜ ㄍㄨㄥ ㄗㄨㄛˋ
(B) ㄗㄨㄛˋ ㄏㄠˇ ㄗˋ ㄐㄧˇ ˙ㄉㄜ ㄍㄨㄥ ㄗㄨㄛˋ
(C) ㄏㄠˇ ㄗㄨㄛˋ ㄗˋ ㄐㄧˇ ˙ㄉㄜ ㄍㄨㄥ ㄗㄨㄛˋ
(D) ㄍㄨㄥ ㄗㄨㄛˋ ㄗˋ ㄐㄧˇ ㄗㄨㄛˋ ㄏㄠˇ ˙ㄉㄜ

55. 虽然那个地方很危险，但他____要去。
(A) 不过
(B) 而且
(C) 也不
(D) 还是

55. 雖然那個地方很危險，但他____要去。
(A) 不過
(B) 而且
(C) 也不
(D) 還是

55. Suīrán nà ge dìfāng hěn wēixiǎn, dàn tā____ yào qù.
(A) búguò
(B) érqiě
(C) yěbù
(D) háishì

55. ㄙㄨㄟ ㄖㄢˊ ㄋㄚˋ ˙ㄍㄜ ㄉㄧˋ ㄈㄤ ㄏㄣˇ ㄨㄟ ㄒㄧㄢˇ，ㄉㄢˋ ㄊㄚ ____ ㄧㄠˋ ㄑㄩˋ。
(A) ㄅㄨˋ ㄍㄨㄛˋ
(B) ㄦˊ ㄑㄧㄝˇ
(C) ㄧㄝˇ ㄅㄨˋ
(D) ㄏㄞˊ ㄕˋ

SECTION III
READING COMPREHENSION

Suggested time — 25 minutes
Questions 56 - 85

WHEN YOU BEGIN THIS SECTION, MAKE SURE THAT YOU MARK YOUR ANSWER TO THE FIRST QUESTION BY FILLING IN ONE OF THE CIRCLES NEXT TO NUMBER 56 ON YOUR ANSWER SHEET.

Directions:

Read the following texts carefully for comprehension. Each one is followed by one or more questions or incomplete statements. Select the answer or completion that is best according to the text and fill in the corresponding circle on your answer sheet.

This section of the test is presented in two writing systems: traditional characters and simplified characters. IT IS RECOMMEMD THAT YOU CHOOSE THE WRITING SYSTEM WITH WHICH YOU ARE MORE FAMILIAR WITH AND **ONLY READ THAT VERSION** AS YOU WORK THROUGH THIS SECTION OF THE TEST.

Questions 56-57

一九九零年九月二十二日至十月七日，第十一届亚运会在中国北京举办，这是中国第一次举办综合性国际体育大赛，也是自亚运会诞生以来第一次由中国承办。有三十七个国家和地区的四千六百八十四名运动员参赛。二零一零年十一月十二日至二十七日，第十六届亚运会在中国广州举办，这是中国第二次举办亚运会，有来自亚洲四十五个国家和地区的一万零一百五十六名运动员参赛，是参赛人数最多的一届亚运会。

一九九零年九月二十二日至十月七日，第十一屆亞運會在中國北京舉辦，這是中國第一次舉辦綜合性國際體育大賽，也是自亞運會誕生以來第一次由中國承辦。有三十七個國家和地區的四千六百八十四名運動員參賽。二零一零年十一月十二日至二十七日，第十六屆亞運會在中國廣州舉辦，這是中國第二次舉辦亞運會，有來自亞洲四十五個國家和地區的一萬零一百五十六名運動員參賽，是參賽人數最多的一屆亞運會。

56. Which of the following statements is correct?
    (A) China hosted the Asian Games for the first time in 1990.
    (B) The 16th Asian Games was held in Beijing.
    (C) Athletes from 40 countries and territories participated in the 1990 Asian Games.
    (D) Athletes from 50 countries and territories participated in the 16th Asian Games.

57. How many athletes took part in the 16th Asian Games?
    (A) 4684
    (B) 4864
    (C) 10156
    (D) 11056

Question 58

减价物品，一经售出， 恕不退换	減價物品，一經售出， 恕不退換

58. What does this sign say?
    (A) Please do not touch the merchandize
    (B) No exchange or return of goods after they are sold
    (C) Goods can be exchanged but cannot be returned after they are sold
    (D) Big bargain on all goods

Question 59

上车投币 不设找赎	上車投幣 不設找贖

59. Where would this sign most likely be found?
    (A) On a bus
    (B) In a supermarket
    (C) On an airplane
    (D) In a bank

Question 60

上海复旦大学五楼一室

吴海 教授 收

北京大学 李寄

上海復旦大學五樓一室

吳海 教授 收

北京大學 李寄

60. Who is the recipient of this letter?
    - (A) A doctor
    - (B) A manager
    - (C) A student
    - (D) A professor

Question 61

上海火车站列车时刻表

车次	起点—终点	车型	发车时间	到站时间
5054	上海—南京	普通无空调	两点五十五分	七点五十八分
T138	上海—西安	新空调特快	十五点十五分	次日八点零六分
T22	上海—北京	新空调特快	十八点零八分	次日八点零八分

上海火車站列車時刻表

車次	起點—終點	車型	發車時間	到站時間
5054	上海—南京	普通無空調	兩點五十五分	七點五十八分
T138	上海—西安	新空調特快	十五點十五分	次日八點零六分
T22	上海—北京	新空調特快	十八點零八分	次日八點零八分

61. Which train will depart from Shanghai at 6:08 P.M.?
    - (A) 5054
    - (B) T138
    - (C) T22
    - (D) None of the three

Question 62

遗失物处理中心	遺失物處理中心
服务电话：3669-2731	服務電話：3669-2731
服务时间：星期一至星期六（假日除外）上午九点-下午五点	服務時間：星期一至星期六（假日除外）上午九點-下午五點
服务地点：武汉火车站地下二楼一号询问处旁	服務地點：武漢火車站地下二樓一號詢問處旁

62. This notice is about a
    (A) travel agency
    (B) cell phone shop
    (C) ticket office
    (D) lost and found

Question 63

雨天路滑，注意安全	雨天路滑，注意安全

63. Under what kind of weather condition would you see this sign?
    (A) Rainy
    (B) Foggy
    (C) Cloudy
    (D) Windy

Questions 64-65

第二届中国名家书画展	第二屆中國名家書畫展
将于2010年8月1日—15日在中国美术学院展览厅举行。	將於2010年8月1日—15日在中國美術學院展覽廳舉行。
欢迎广大师生前来参观！	歡迎廣大師生前來參觀！
如果你想订票或了解更多关于此次活动的详情	如果你想訂票或了解更多關於此次活動的詳情
请拨打4008009999或登陆www.zhanlan.com	請撥打4008009999或登陸www.zhanlan.com

64. What kind of exhibition is this?
 (A) Calligraphy
 (B) Historical artifact
 (C) Photography
 (D) Sculpture

65. According to the advertisement, how can tickets be booked?
 (A) By telephone
 (B) By fax
 (C) By mail
 (D) At the exhibition hall

Question 66

美国心理学家说，下午五时至七时是一天中谈论家事极易产生冲突的时刻。因为此时刚上完一天班，十分疲倦。晚上八时是最适宜谈论家事的时间。因为此时已吃过晚饭，精神饱满，心情愉快。

美國心理學家說，下午五時至七時是一天中談論家事極易產生衝突的時刻。因為此時剛上完一天班，十分疲倦。晚上八時是最適宜談論家事的時間。因為此時已吃過晚飯，精神飽滿，心情愉快。

66. Discussing family matters at what time during the day is most likely to cause conflict?
 (A) 4 P.M.
 (B) 6 P.M.
 (C) 8 P.M.
 (D) 9 P.M.

Question 67

小 心 玻 璃

小 心 玻 璃

67. What does this sign say?
    (A) Beware of glass
    (B) Beware of waves
    (C) Do not touch
    (D) Beware of slippery floor

Question 68

寻找游伴

我叫大卫，今年暑假想去中国旅游，想找一位懂中文的朋友与我一起同行。我们可以一起计划这次中国之行。如果你感兴趣，请联系我：

电话：52536667

电邮：david@hotmail.com

尋找遊伴

我叫大衛，今年暑假想去中國旅遊，想找一位懂中文的朋友與我一起同行。我們可以一起計劃這次中國之行。如果你感興趣，請聯繫我：

電話：52536667

電郵：david@hotmail.com

68. What does David want to do this summer?
    (A) Learn Chinese
    (B) Travel to China
    (C) Write about his travel experiences
    (D) Teach his friend Chinese

Question 69

请 勿 大 声 喧 哗

請 勿 大 聲 喧 嘩

69. What does this sign say?
    (A) Do not enter
    (B) No smoking
    (C) No spitting
    (D) No shouting

Questions 70-71

中国国家旅行社	中國國家旅行社
西安二日游	西安二日遊
每周二、四、六发团	每週二、四、六發團
费用：成人一千九百九十九元/人	費用：成人一千九百九十九元/人
十二岁以下儿童半价	十二歲以下兒童半價
（包括来回机票、景点门票、住宿费及午餐、晚餐，早餐自理）	（包括來回機票、景點門票、住宿費及午餐、晚餐，早餐自理）

70. How often does this tour depart?
    (A) Twice a week
    (B) Only on Tuesdays
    (C) Only on Thursdays
    (D) Three times a week

71. Which one of the following is incorrect?
    (A) The cost is $1999 per adult.
    (B) Breakfast is not included.
    (C) Lunch is not included.
    (D) Children receive a 50% discount.

Questions 72-73

我的房间不大，里面有一张床、一个书柜、一把椅子、一张书桌。书桌上有一台电脑，我很喜欢用它来上网找资料，每天做完功课后我还喜欢用它来跟朋友聊天。我的房间还有一个大书柜，书柜里放着各种各样的书，有我的课本、参考书、词典、小说和杂志。这些书里面我最喜欢看的是小说。

我的房間不大，裏面有一張床、一個書櫃、一把椅子、一張書桌。書桌上有一台電腦，我很喜歡用它來上網找資料，每天做完功課後我還喜歡用它來跟朋友聊天。我的房間還有一個大書櫃，書櫃裏放著各種各樣的書，有我的課本、參考書、詞典、小說和雜誌。這些書裏面我最喜歡看的是小說。

72. Which of the following items is NOT placed in the room?
    (A) Television
    (B) Bookcase
    (C) Desk
    (D) Chair

73. Which of the following activities is NOT mentioned?
    (A) Search for information on the Internet
    (B) Chat with friends on the Internet
    (C) Watch movies
    (D) Read books

Question 74

全 场 五 折 起	全 場 五 折 起

74. What is this sign about?
    (A) Discount on offer
    (B) Opening hours
    (C) Ticket sales
    (D) Time of flight departure

Questions 75-76

我们学校附近新开了一家超级市场，里面有很多日用品和文具。日用品有牙膏、牙刷和毛巾；文具有橡皮、铅笔、尺子和本子等等。这个超级市场还卖牛奶、面包、水果、饼干等等，方便了我们的日常生活。

我們學校附近新開了一家超級市場，裏面有很多日用品和文具。日用品有牙膏、牙刷和毛巾；文具有橡皮、鉛筆、尺子和本子等等。這個超級市場還賣牛奶、麵包、水果、餅乾等等，方便了我們的日常生活。

75. Which item of stationery is NOT mentioned?
    (A) Ball pen
    (B) Pencil
    (C) Ruler
    (D) Notebook

76. Which of the following items is sold at this supermarket?
   (A) Magazine
   (B) Newspaper
   (C) Milk
   (D) Ice cream

Questions 77-78

主题：面试的准备技巧

申请美国大学的过程中，部分学校会要求申请者参加面试或是电话口试，这常常让同学们十分伤脑筋，不知该如何准备。本场讲座将告诉你如何准备面试，以及面试时应该注意的事项，进而提高获录取的机会！

地点： 北京大学图书馆
日期： 十二月二十日(四)
时间： 十七点三十分至十八点三十分

主題：面試的準備技巧

申請美國大學的過程中，部分學校會要求申請者參加面試或是電話口試，這常常讓同學們十分傷腦筋，不知該如何準備。本場講座將告訴你如何準備面試，以及面試時應該注意的事項，進而提高獲錄取的機會！

地點： 北京大學圖書館
日期： 十二月二十日(四)
時間： 十七點三十分至十八點三十分

77. What is this talk mainly about?
   (A) A brief introduction to Beijing University
   (B) University application criteria
   (C) Skills in preparing for university interviews
   (D) Library regulations

78. Which of the following statements is NOT true?
   (A) This talk is held in the library.
   (B) This talk is held on a Thursday.
   (C) Some universities will require applicants to participate in a phone interview as part of the application process.
   (D) All universities will require applicants to attend an interview in person as part of the application process.

Question 79

实用初级汉语会话

- 介绍口语语法及基本句型
- 日常生活的常见词汇
- 十课课文包括：你好、星期几、茶点、我的教室、我的家庭、我的好友、打电话、日期和时间、购物
- 附送录音光碟一张

實用初級漢語會話

- 介紹口語語法及基本句型
- 日常生活的常見詞彙
- 十課課文包括：你好、星期幾、茶點、我的教室、我的家庭、我的好友、打電話、日期和時間、購物
- 附送錄音光碟一張

79. What is this advertisement about?

(A) Chinese music
(B) Chinese cooking
(C) How to become a Chinese teacher
(D) Chinese conversation book

Question 80

航天博物馆

开放时间：星期二至星期日
下午一时至
下午七时
公众假期照常开放
短片放映：周六下午五时至
六时

航天博物館

開放時間：星期二至星期日
下午一時至
下午七時
公眾假期照常開放
短片放映：週六下午五時至
六時

80. When is this museum closed?

(A) On public holidays
(B) Everyday between 5 P.M. and 6 P.M.
(C) Saturdays
(D) Mondays

Questions 81-82

天皇娱乐群星演唱会	天皇娛樂群星演唱會
日期：二零一零年三月九日(二)	日期：二零一零年三月九日(二)
时间：晚上八时正	時間：晚上八時正
地点：亚洲国际博览馆	地點：亞洲國際博覽館
票价：六百八十元	票價：六百八十元
注意事项:	**注意事項:**
1. 适合任何年龄观众	1. 適合任何年齡觀眾
2. 一人一票	2. 一人一票
3. 亚洲国际博览馆范围内严禁吸烟，不准携带外来食品及饮品进入博览馆	3. 亞洲國際博覽館範圍內嚴禁吸煙，不准攜帶外來食品及飲品進入博覽館
4. 表演场内严禁未获授权的摄影或录音	4. 表演場內嚴禁未獲授權的攝影或錄音

81. What is this advertisement about?
    (A) A new movie
    (B) A photography competition
    (C) A concert
    (D) A singing contest

82. Which of the following is NOT mentioned?
    (A) Location of the event
    (B) Regulations about photography
    (C) Ticket prices
    (D) No children allowed

Question 83

北京是中国的首都，也是全国的政治和文化中心。中国其他重要城市主要集中于东部和南部。	北京是中國的首都，也是全國的政治和文化中心。中國其他重要城市主要集中於東部和南部。

83. Which of the following is NOT mentioned?

(A) Beijing is the capital of China.
(B) Beijing is the political and cultural center of China.
(C) The major cities in China are concentrated in the east and the south.
(D) Beijing is located in the north of China.

Question 84

新春优惠　外套四折
裤子六折

新春優惠　外套四折
褲子六折

84. What discount is available on trousers?

(A) 40% off
(B) 60% off
(C) 30% off
(D) 70% off

Question 85

澳门观光塔+旋转餐厅套票
(平日/假日)

价格:

午餐　一百四十元/一百六十元
下午茶 一百九十五元/二百一十元
晚餐　二百二十元/二百五十元

查询热线: 12345678

澳門觀光塔+旋轉餐廳套票
(平日/假日)

價格:

午餐　一百四十元/一百六十元
下午茶 一百九十五元/二百一十元
晚餐　二百二十元/二百五十元

查詢熱線: 12345678

85. How much is afternoon tea on a weekday?

(A) $160
(B) $195
(C) $210
(D) $220

SAT Chinese Practice Test — Five
SAT 中文模拟试题 — 第五套
SAT 中文模擬試題 — 第五套

听力材料
聽力材料
LISTENING TEST MATERIAL

Part A

Simplified Characters

Question 1

A： 请问由上海来的SH5899次航班什么时候到？

(A) 候机室在那边。
(B) 飞机九点起飞。
(C) 大概下午三点到达。

Question 2

A： 你看那条裙子好看吗？

(A) 很好看，就是价钱有点贵。
(B) 我不喜欢穿裙子。
(C) 可以给我换条大号的吗？

Question 3

A： 周末的中文课你报名了吗？

(A) 你的妈妈是中文老师吗？
(B) 已经报了，下周日去上第一堂课。
(C) 他很喜欢中文。

Question 4

A： 你春节打算在哪里过？

(A) 他春节打算去上海。
(B) 你打算去北京吗？
(C) 还不知道去上海，还是去北京好呢！

Question 5

A： 我今晚加班，不回来吃饭了。

(A) 你今晚要回来吃饭吗？
(B) 你今天为什么不上班？
(C) 那我不等你吃饭了。

Question 6

A： 你刚搬来不久，地方还不太熟吧？

(A) 菜煮得太熟不好吃。
(B) 我跟班上的同学不熟。
(C) 是呀！我连菜市场在哪也不知道！

Question 7

A： 这条鱼怎么样？

(A) 味道还不错。
(B) 我们去饭店吃鱼吧。
(C) 我喜欢钓鱼。

Question 8

A： 你暑假打算做什么？

B： 我先去北京旅行，再去香港购物，然后坐飞机回美国。

(A) 你为什么不去香港？
(B) 坐火车真有意思！
(C) 你的假期真丰富！

Question 9

A： 你昨天去参加晚会了吗？

(A) 那里人太多了，我们还是走吧。
(B) 我昨天一天都在家里休息。
(C) 晚会是晚上八点开始的。

Question 10

A： 你的功课做得怎么样？

(A) 我学过功夫。
(B) 这样做的后果很严重。
(C) 已经做完了。

Question 11

A： 这件衣服是你自己的吗？怎么看起来这么大？

(A) 我哥哥的衣服被淋湿了。
(B) 我感冒了。
(C) 这是我哥哥的衣服。

Question 12

A： 今天星期几？

(A) 今天是九号。
(B) 我今天去新加坡。
(C) 今天是星期三。

Question 13

A： 同事要结婚了，送点什么好呢？

(A) 不送了，请慢走。
(B) 可以买点有纪念意义的东西。
(C) 婚礼在哪里举行？

Question 14

A： 最近考试特别多，忙得我没时间睡觉了。

(A) 你要注意身体呀！
(B) 你去考试吧！
(C) 你今天这么早睡觉呀？

Question 15

A： 请问你要点什么？

B： 我要一碗面条，谢谢。

(A) 慢慢来。
(B) 对不起。
(C) 别客气。

Part B

Question 16

男：今年的晚会上你唱首歌吧？大家都说你唱得不错。

女：不行，不行，人一多我就唱不出来了。

男：就唱一首嘛！

Question 17

男：你好，请问国家大剧院怎么走？

女：真对不起，我也刚来北京。

Question 18

男：请问照片最快什么时候可以取？

女：最早也要明天下午一点以后。

Question 19

男：我身体不舒服。

女：哪里不舒服？

男：肚子疼，想吐。

Question 20

男：你喜欢看电影吗？

女：很喜欢，我最喜欢看爱情片。

男：我比较喜欢看功夫片。

Question 21

男：请问还书处是在这里吗？

女：还书处在三楼，但是现在已经下班了，工作时间是早上八点到下午三点。

Question 22

男：我们的房子不能离父母家太远，万一爸爸生病了，我们也好照顾他。

女：那我们就住在爸爸家附近吧。

Questions 23-24

男：怎么现在才回来？

女：我刚才在路上碰见了小李，聊了几句。

男：我让你买的东西买回来了吗？

女：啊！我忘了，我现在去买！

Question 25

男：请问您要点什么？

女：我要一碗面条和一杯果汁。

Questions 26-27

女：你什么时候开始肚子疼的？

男：昨天半夜。

女：你昨天晚上吃了什么？

男：吃了沙律和牛排。

Question 28

男：明天可能会下雨，你还去爬山吗？

女：不去了，我们去看电影吧？

男：好吧，就听你的。

Questions 29-30

女：我觉得这里的交通很不方便，我想搬家。

男：你想搬去哪里？

女：我想住在学校附近，方便上学，又可以节省车费。

男：好主意！

Part A

Traditional Characters

Question 1

A： 請問由上海來的SH5899次航班什麼時候到？

(A) 候機室在那邊。
(B) 飛機九點起飛。
(C) 大概下午三點到達。

Question 2

A： 你看那條裙子好看嗎？

(A) 很好看，就是價錢有點貴。
(B) 我不喜歡穿裙子。
(C) 可以給我換條大號的嗎？

Question 3

A： 週末的中文課你報名了嗎？

(A) 你的媽媽是中文老師嗎？
(B) 已經報了，下週日去上第一堂課。
(C) 他很喜歡中文。

Question 4

A： 你春節打算在哪裏過？

(A) 他春節打算去上海。
(B) 你打算去北京嗎？
(C) 還不知道去上海，還是去北京好呢！

Question 5

A： 我今晚加班，不回來吃飯了。

(A) 你今晚要回來吃飯嗎？
(B) 你今天爲什麼不上班？
(C) 那我不等你吃飯了。

Question 6

A： 你剛搬來不久，地方還不太熟吧？

(A) 菜煮得太熟不好吃。
(B) 我跟班上的同學不熟。
(C) 是呀！我連菜市場在哪也不知道！

Question 7

A： 這條魚怎麼樣？

(A) 味道還不錯。
(B) 我們去飯店吃魚吧。
(C) 我喜歡釣魚。

Question 8

A： 你暑假打算做什麼？

B： 我先去北京旅行，再去香港購物，然後坐飛機回美國。

(A) 你爲什麼不去香港？
(B) 坐火車真有意思！
(C) 你的假期真豐富！

Question 9

A： 你昨天去參加晚會了嗎？

(A) 那裏人太多了，我們還是走吧。
(B) 我昨天一天都在家裏休息。
(C) 晚會是晚上八點開始的。

Question 10

A： 你的功課做得怎麼樣？

(A) 我學過功夫。
(B) 這樣做的後果很嚴重。
(C) 已經做完了。

Question 11

A： 這件衣服是你自己的嗎？怎麼看起來這麼大？

(A) 我哥哥的衣服被淋濕了。
(B) 我感冒了。
(C) 這是我哥哥的衣服。

Question 12

A： 今天星期幾？

(A) 今天是九號。
(B) 我今天去新加坡。
(C) 今天是星期三。

Question 13

A： 同事要結婚了，送點什麼好呢？

(A) 不送了，請慢走。
(B) 可以買點有紀念意義的東西。
(C) 婚禮在哪裏舉行？

Question 14

A： 最近考試特別多，忙得我沒時間睡覺了。

(A) 你要注意身體呀！
(B) 你去考試吧！
(C) 你今天這麼早睡覺呀？

Question 15

A： 請問你要點什麼？

B： 我要一碗麵條，謝謝。

(A) 慢慢來。
(B) 對不起。
(C) 別客氣。

Part B

Question 16

男：今年的晚會上你唱首歌吧？大家都說你唱得不錯。

女：不行，不行，人一多我就唱不出來了。

男：就唱一首嘛！

Question 17

男：你好，請問國家大劇院怎麼走？

女：真對不起，我也剛來北京。

Question 18

男：請問照片最快什麼時候可以取？

女：最早也要明天下午一點以後。

Question 19

男：我身體不舒服。

女：哪裏不舒服？

男：肚子疼，想吐。

Question 20

男：你喜歡看電影嗎？

女：很喜歡，我最喜歡看愛情片。

男：我比較喜歡看功夫片。

Question 21

男：請問還書處是在這裏嗎？

女：還書處在三樓，但是現在已經下班了，工作時間是早上八點到下午三點。

Question 22

男：我們的房子不能離父母家太遠，萬一爸爸生病了，我們也好照顧他。

女：那我們就住在爸爸家附近吧。

Questions 23-24

男：怎麼現在才回來？

女：我剛才在路上碰見了小李，聊了幾句 。

男：我讓你買的東西買回來了嗎？

女：啊！我忘了，我現在去買！

Question 25

男：請問您要點什麼？

女：我要一碗麵條和一杯果汁。

Questions 26-27

女：你什麼時候開始肚子疼的？

男：昨天半夜。

女：你昨天晚上吃了什麼？

男：吃了沙律和牛排。

Question 28

男：明天可能會下雨，你還去爬山嗎？

女：不去了，我們去看電影吧？

男：好吧，就聽你的。

Questions 29-30

女：我覺得這裏的交通很不方便，我想搬家。

男：你想搬去哪裏？

女：我想住在學校附近，方便上學，又可以節省車費。

男：好主意！

Part A

Pinyin Romanization

Question 1

A： Qǐngwèn yóu Shànghǎi lái de SH5899 cì hángbān shénme shíhou dào？

(A) Hòujīshì zài nàbian.
(B) Fēijī jiǔ diǎn qǐfēi.
(C) Dàgài xiàwǔ sān diǎn dàodá.

Question 2

A： Nǐ kàn nà tiáo qúnzi hǎokàn ma？

(A) Hěn hǎokàn, jiùshì jiàqián yǒudiǎn guì.
(B) Wǒ bù xǐhuan chuān qúnzi.
(C) Kěyǐ gěi wǒ huàn tiáo dàhào de ma？

Question 3

A： Zhōumò de Zhōngwén kè nǐ bàomíng le ma？

(A) Nǐ de māma shì Zhōngwén lǎoshī ma？
(B) Yǐjīng bào le, xià zhōurì qù shàng dìyī táng kè.
(C) Tā hěn xǐhuan Zhōngwén.

Question 4

A： Nǐ Chūn Jié dǎsuan zài nǎli guò？

(A) Tā Chūn Jié dǎsuan qù Shànghǎi.
(B) Nǐ dǎsuan qù Běijīng ma？
(C) Hái bù zhīdào qù Shànghǎi, háishì qù Běijīng hǎo ne！

Question 5

A： Wǒ jīnwǎn jiābān, bù huílái chīfàn le.

(A) Nǐ jīnwǎn yào huílái chīfàn ma？
(B) Nǐ jīntiān wèi shénme bú shàngbān？
(C) Nà wǒ bù děng nǐ chīfàn le.

Question 6

A：Nǐ gāng bān lái bùjiǔ, dìfāng hái bú tài shú ba？

(A) Cài zhǔ de tài shú bù hǎo chī.

(B) Wǒ gēn bān shàng de tóngxué bù shú.

(C) Shì ya！Wǒ lián càishìchǎng zài nǎ yě bù zhīdào.

Question 7

A：Zhè tiáo yú zěnmeyàng？

(A) Wèidao hái búcuò.

(B) Wǒmen qù fàndiàn chīyú ba.

(C) Wǒ xǐhuan diàoyú.

Question 8

A：Nǐ shǔjià dǎsuan zuò shénme？

B：Wǒ xiān qù Běijīng lǚxíng, zài qù Xiānggǎng gòuwù, ránhòu zuò fēijī huí Měiguó.

(A) Nǐ wèi shénme bú qù Xiānggǎng？

(B) Zuò huǒchē zhēn yǒu yìsi！

(C) Nǐ de jiàqī zhēn fēngfù！

Question 9

A：Nǐ zuótiān qù cānjiā wǎnhuì le ma？

(A) Nàli rén tài duō le, wǒmen háishi zǒu ba.

(B) Wǒ zuótiān yì tiān dōu zài jiā lǐ xiūxi.

(C) Wǎnhuì shì wǎnshang bā diǎn kāishǐ de.

Question 10

A：Nǐ de gōngkè zuò de zěnmeyàng？

(A) Wǒ xué guo gōngfu.

(B) Zhèyàng zuò de hòuguǒ hěn yánzhòng.

(C) Yǐjīng zuò wán le.

Question 11

A：Zhè jiàn yīfu shì nǐ zìjǐ de ma？Zěnme kàn qǐlai zhème dà？

(A) Wǒ gēge de yīfu bèi lín shī le.
(B) Wǒ gǎnmào le.
(C) Zhè shì wǒ gēge de yīfu.

Question 12

A：Jīntiān xīngqī jǐ？

(A) Jīntiān shì jiǔ hào.
(B) Wǒ jīntiān qù Xīnjiāpō.
(C) Jīntiān shì xīngqī sān.

Question 13

A：Tóngshì yào jiéhūn le, sòng diǎn shénme hǎo ne？

(A) Bú sòng le, qǐng màn zǒu.
(B) Kěyǐ mǎi diǎn yǒu jìniàn yìyì de dōngxi.
(C) Hūnlǐ zài nǎli jǔxíng？

Question 14

A：Zuìjìn kǎoshì tèbié duō, máng de wǒ méi shíjiān shuìjiào le.

(A) Nǐ yào zhùyì shēntǐ ya！
(B) Nǐ qù kǎoshì ba！
(C) Nǐ jīntiān zhème zǎo shuìjiào ya？

Question 15

A：Qǐngwèn nǐ yào diǎn shénme？

B：Wǒ yào yì wǎn miàntiáo, xièxie.

(A) Mànmàn lái.
(B) Duì bu qǐ.
(C) Bié kèqi.

Part B

Question 16

Nán : Jīnnián de wǎnhuì shàng nǐ chàng shǒu gē ba? Dàjiā dōu shuō nǐ chàng de bú cuò.

Nǚ : Bùxíng, bùxíng, rén yì duō wǒ jiù chàng bù chūlai le.

Nán : Jiù chàng yì shǒu ma!

Question 17

Nán : Nǐ hǎo, Qǐngwèn guójiā dàjùyuàn zěnme zǒu?

Nǚ : Zhēn duìbuqǐ, wǒ yě gāng lái Běijīng.

Question 18

Nán : Qǐngwèn zhàopiàn zuì kuài shénme shíhou kěyǐ qǔ?

Nǚ : Zuì zǎo yě yào míngtiān xiàwǔ yì diǎn yǐhòu.

Question 19

Nán : Wǒ shēntǐ bù shūfu.

Nǚ : Nǎli bù shūfu?

Nán : Dùzi téng, xiǎng tù.

Question 20

Nán : Nǐ xǐhuan kàn diànyǐng ma?

Nǚ : Hěn xǐhuan, wǒ zuì xǐhuan kàn àiqíngpiàn.

Nán : Wǒ bǐjiào xǐhuan kàn gōngfupiàn.

Question 21

Nán : Qǐngwèn huánshūchù shì zài zhèli ma?

Nǚ : Huánshūchù zài sān lóu, dànshì xiànzài yǐjīng xiàbān le, gōngzuò shíjiān shì zǎoshang bā diǎn dào xiàwǔ sān diǎn.

Question 22

Nán : Wǒmen de fángzi bù néng lí fùmǔ jiā tài yuǎn, wànyī bàba shēngbìng le, wǒmen yě hǎo zhàogù tā.

Nǚ : Nà wǒmen jiù zhù zài bàba jiā fùjìn ba.

Questions 23-24

Nán : Zěnme xiànzài cái huílai ?

Nǚ : Wǒ gāngcái zài lùshang pèngjiànle Xiǎo Lǐ, liáo le jǐ jù.

Nán : Wǒ ràng nǐ mǎi de dōngxi mǎi huílai le ma ?

Nǚ : A ! Wǒ wàngle, wǒ xiànzài qù mǎi !

Question 25

Nán : Qǐngwèn nín yào diǎn shénme ?

Nǚ : Wǒ yào yì wǎn miàntiáo hé yì bēi guǒzhī.

Questions 26-27

Nǚ : Nǐ shénme shíhou kāishǐ dùzi téng de ?

Nán : Zuótiān bànyè.

Nǚ : Nǐ zuótiān wǎnshang chīle shénme ?

Nán : Chīle shālǜ hé niúpái.

Question 28

Nán : Míngtiān kěnéng huì xiàyǔ, nǐ hái qù páshān ma ?

Nǚ : Bú qù le, wǒmen qù kàn diànyǐng ba ?

Nán : Hǎo ba, jiù tīng nǐ de.

Questions 29-30

Nǚ : Wǒ juéde zhèli de jiāotōng hěn bù fāngbiàn, wǒ xiǎng bānjiā.

Nán : Nǐ xiǎng bān qù nǎli ?

Nǚ : Wǒ xiǎng zhù zài xuéxiào fùjìn, fāngbiàn shàngxué, yòu kěyǐ jiéshěng chēfèi.

Nán : Hǎo zhǔyi !

Practice Test Five

1	Ⓐ	Ⓑ	Ⓒ	Ⓓ	31	Ⓐ	Ⓑ	Ⓒ	Ⓓ	56	Ⓐ	Ⓑ	Ⓒ	Ⓓ
2	Ⓐ	Ⓑ	Ⓒ	Ⓓ	32	Ⓐ	Ⓑ	Ⓒ	Ⓓ	57	Ⓐ	Ⓑ	Ⓒ	Ⓓ
3	Ⓐ	Ⓑ	Ⓒ	Ⓓ	33	Ⓐ	Ⓑ	Ⓒ	Ⓓ	58	Ⓐ	Ⓑ	Ⓒ	Ⓓ
4	Ⓐ	Ⓑ	Ⓒ	Ⓓ	34	Ⓐ	Ⓑ	Ⓒ	Ⓓ	59	Ⓐ	Ⓑ	Ⓒ	Ⓓ
5	Ⓐ	Ⓑ	Ⓒ	Ⓓ	35	Ⓐ	Ⓑ	Ⓒ	Ⓓ	60	Ⓐ	Ⓑ	Ⓒ	Ⓓ
6	Ⓐ	Ⓑ	Ⓒ	Ⓓ	36	Ⓐ	Ⓑ	Ⓒ	Ⓓ	61	Ⓐ	Ⓑ	Ⓒ	Ⓓ
7	Ⓐ	Ⓑ	Ⓒ	Ⓓ	37	Ⓐ	Ⓑ	Ⓒ	Ⓓ	62	Ⓐ	Ⓑ	Ⓒ	Ⓓ
8	Ⓐ	Ⓑ	Ⓒ	Ⓓ	38	Ⓐ	Ⓑ	Ⓒ	Ⓓ	63	Ⓐ	Ⓑ	Ⓒ	Ⓓ
9	Ⓐ	Ⓑ	Ⓒ	Ⓓ	39	Ⓐ	Ⓑ	Ⓒ	Ⓓ	64	Ⓐ	Ⓑ	Ⓒ	Ⓓ
10	Ⓐ	Ⓑ	Ⓒ	Ⓓ	40	Ⓐ	Ⓑ	Ⓒ	Ⓓ	65	Ⓐ	Ⓑ	Ⓒ	Ⓓ
11	Ⓐ	Ⓑ	Ⓒ	Ⓓ	41	Ⓐ	Ⓑ	Ⓒ	Ⓓ	66	Ⓐ	Ⓑ	Ⓒ	Ⓓ
12	Ⓐ	Ⓑ	Ⓒ	Ⓓ	42	Ⓐ	Ⓑ	Ⓒ	Ⓓ	67	Ⓐ	Ⓑ	Ⓒ	Ⓓ
13	Ⓐ	Ⓑ	Ⓒ	Ⓓ	43	Ⓐ	Ⓑ	Ⓒ	Ⓓ	68	Ⓐ	Ⓑ	Ⓒ	Ⓓ
14	Ⓐ	Ⓑ	Ⓒ	Ⓓ	44	Ⓐ	Ⓑ	Ⓒ	Ⓓ	69	Ⓐ	Ⓑ	Ⓒ	Ⓓ
15	Ⓐ	Ⓑ	Ⓒ	Ⓓ	45	Ⓐ	Ⓑ	Ⓒ	Ⓓ	70	Ⓐ	Ⓑ	Ⓒ	Ⓓ
16	Ⓐ	Ⓑ	Ⓒ	Ⓓ	46	Ⓐ	Ⓑ	Ⓒ	Ⓓ	71	Ⓐ	Ⓑ	Ⓒ	Ⓓ
17	Ⓐ	Ⓑ	Ⓒ	Ⓓ	47	Ⓐ	Ⓑ	Ⓒ	Ⓓ	72	Ⓐ	Ⓑ	Ⓒ	Ⓓ
18	Ⓐ	Ⓑ	Ⓒ	Ⓓ	48	Ⓐ	Ⓑ	Ⓒ	Ⓓ	73	Ⓐ	Ⓑ	Ⓒ	Ⓓ
19	Ⓐ	Ⓑ	Ⓒ	Ⓓ	49	Ⓐ	Ⓑ	Ⓒ	Ⓓ	74	Ⓐ	Ⓑ	Ⓒ	Ⓓ
20	Ⓐ	Ⓑ	Ⓒ	Ⓓ	50	Ⓐ	Ⓑ	Ⓒ	Ⓓ	75	Ⓐ	Ⓑ	Ⓒ	Ⓓ
21	Ⓐ	Ⓑ	Ⓒ	Ⓓ	51	Ⓐ	Ⓑ	Ⓒ	Ⓓ	76	Ⓐ	Ⓑ	Ⓒ	Ⓓ
22	Ⓐ	Ⓑ	Ⓒ	Ⓓ	52	Ⓐ	Ⓑ	Ⓒ	Ⓓ	77	Ⓐ	Ⓑ	Ⓒ	Ⓓ
23	Ⓐ	Ⓑ	Ⓒ	Ⓓ	53	Ⓐ	Ⓑ	Ⓒ	Ⓓ	78	Ⓐ	Ⓑ	Ⓒ	Ⓓ
24	Ⓐ	Ⓑ	Ⓒ	Ⓓ	54	Ⓐ	Ⓑ	Ⓒ	Ⓓ	79	Ⓐ	Ⓑ	Ⓒ	Ⓓ
25	Ⓐ	Ⓑ	Ⓒ	Ⓓ	55	Ⓐ	Ⓑ	Ⓒ	Ⓓ	80	Ⓐ	Ⓑ	Ⓒ	Ⓓ
26	Ⓐ	Ⓑ	Ⓒ	Ⓓ						81	Ⓐ	Ⓑ	Ⓒ	Ⓓ
27	Ⓐ	Ⓑ	Ⓒ	Ⓓ						82	Ⓐ	Ⓑ	Ⓒ	Ⓓ
28	Ⓐ	Ⓑ	Ⓒ	Ⓓ						83	Ⓐ	Ⓑ	Ⓒ	Ⓓ
29	Ⓐ	Ⓑ	Ⓒ	Ⓓ						84	Ⓐ	Ⓑ	Ⓒ	Ⓓ
30	Ⓐ	Ⓑ	Ⓒ	Ⓓ						85	Ⓐ	Ⓑ	Ⓒ	Ⓓ

SAT Chinese Practice Test — Six

SAT 中文模拟试题 — 第六套

SAT 中文模擬試題 — 第六套

Time — 1 hour

Questions 1 - 85

PLEASE NOTE THAT YOUR ANSWER SHEET HAS FOUR ANSWER POSITIONS, MARKED A, B, C, AND D, WHILE THE QUESTIONS THROUGHOUT THIS TEST CONTAIN EITHER THREE OR FOUR ANSWER CHOICES. BE SURE NOT TO MARK YOUR ANSWERS IN COLUMN D IF THERE ARE ONLY THREE CHOICES GIVEN.

SECTION I
LISTENING

Approximate time — 20 minutes
Questions 1 - 30

Part A

Directions:

In this part of the test, you will hear short questions, statements, or commands in Mandarin Chinese, followed by three responses in Mandarin Chinese, designated (A), (B), and (C). You will hear the questions or statements, as well as the responses, only once, and they are not printed in your test booklet. Therefore, you must listen very carefully. Select the best response and fill in the corresponding circle on your answer sheet.

Question 1 Mark your answer on your answer sheet.

Question 2 Mark your answer on your answer sheet.

Question 3 Mark your answer on your answer sheet.

Question 4 Mark your answer on your answer sheet.

Question 5 Mark your answer on your answer sheet.

Question 6 Mark your answer on your answer sheet.

Question 7 Mark your answer on your answer sheet.

Question 8 Mark your answer on your answer sheet.

Question 9 Mark your answer on your answer sheet.

Question 10 Mark your answer on your answer sheet.

Question 11 Mark your answer on your answer sheet.

Question 12 Mark your answer on your answer sheet.

Question 13 Mark your answer on your answer sheet.

Question 14 Mark your answer on your answer sheet.

Question 15 Mark your answer on your answer sheet.

Part B

Directions:

You will now hear a series of dialogues. You will hear them only once, and they are not printed in your test booklet. After each selection, you will be asked to answer one or more questions about what you have just heard. These questions, each with four possible answers, are printed in your test booklet. Select the best answer to each question from among the four choices printed and fill in the corresponding circle on your answer sheet.

Question 16

16. Why was the woman late for work today?
    (A) She woke up late.
    (B) Her alarm clock was broken.
    (C) She was not feeling well.
    (D) She was stuck in traffic.

Questions 17-18

17. When is the first train of Beijing Subway line 1?
    (A) 11:00 A.M.
    (B) 5:00 A.M.
    (C) 5:30 A.M.
    (D) 6:30 A.M.

18. Which line can passengers interchange at the next station?
    (A) Line 2
    (B) Line 3
    (C) Line 4
    (D) Line 5

Questions 19-20

19. What does the man ask the woman to do?
    (A) Help him with directions
    (B) Help him book a tour
    (C) Take a photo for him
    (D) Help him choose a souvenir

20. What are the man's friends doing?
    (A) Buying souvenirs
    (B) Buying tickets
    (C) Buying drinks
    (D) Taking photos

Question 21

21. Who is the woman currently living with?
    (A) Her sister
    (B) Her parents
    (C) Her grandmother
    (D) She is living alone.

Questions 22-23

22. What kind of restaurant is mentioned by the man?
    (A) Chinese
    (B) Japanese
    (C) Italian
    (D) French

23. Why hasn't the man visited the restaurant yet?
    (A) The food is not tasty.
    (B) He does not know the way.
    (C) The service is poor.
    (D) He has been busy with revision.

Question 24

24. What drink does the woman order in the end?

(A) Orange juice
(B) Apple juice
(C) Watermelon juice
(D) She does not order a drink.

Question 25

25. What did the woman buy?

(A) Children's story book
(B) Cookbook
(C) Travel guide
(D) Map

Question 26

26. On which day of the week is this year's Mid-autumn Festival?

(A) Sunday
(B) Monday
(C) Wednesday
(D) Friday

Question 27

27. What are the two people planning to do?

(A) Watch a movie
(B) Buy some water
(C) Go to a concert
(D) Catch a train

Question 28

28. Where is the library?
    (A) Next to the post office
    (B) Next to the park
    (C) Next to the swimming pool
    (D) Next to the fairground

Question 29

29. What has the woman been busy with recently?
    (A) Writing a book
    (B) Revising for exams
    (C) Looking for a job
    (D) Traveling

Question 30

30. Which of the following activities does the woman mention?
    (A) Hiking
    (B) Soccer
    (C) Dancing
    (D) Badminton

SECTION II USAGE

Suggested time — 15 minutes

Questions 31 - 55

Part A

Directions:

This section consists of a number of incomplete statements, each of which has four possible completions. Select the word or phrase that best completes the sentence structurally and logically and fill in the corresponding circle on your answer sheet.

This section of the test is presented in four different ways of representing Chinese: traditional characters, simplified characters, pinyin romanization, and the Chinese phonetic alphabet. IT IS RECOMMEMD THAT YOU CHOOSE THE WRITING SYSTEM WITH WHICH YOU ARE MORE FAMILIAR WITH AND **ONLY READ THAT VERSION** AS YOU WORK THROUGH THIS SECTION OF THE TEST.

31. 他的样子____总是很生气似的。
    (A) 其实
    (B) 实际
    (C) 看上去
    (D) 说得倒

31. 他的樣子____總是很生氣似的。
    (A) 其實
    (B) 實際
    (C) 看上去
    (D) 說得倒

31. Tā de yàngzi ____zǒngshì hěn shēngqì shìde.
    (A) qíshí
    (B) shíjì
    (C) kàn shàngqu
    (D) shuō de dào

31. ㄊㄚ ˙ㄉㄜ ㄧㄤˋ ˙ㄗ ____ ㄗㄨㄥˇ ㄕˋ ㄏㄣˇ ㄕㄥ ㄑㄧˋ ㄙˋ ˙ㄉㄜ。
    (A) ㄑㄧˊ ㄕˊ
    (B) ㄕˊ ㄐㄧˋ
    (C) ㄎㄢˋ ㄕㄤˋ ㄑㄩˋ
    (D) ㄕㄨㄛ ㄉㄜˊ ㄉㄠˋ

32. 他已经欺骗过我太多次了，所以____他怎么说，我都不会再相信。
    (A) 尤其
    (B) 凡是
    (C) 无论
    (D) 关于

32. 他已經欺騙過我太多次了，所以____他怎麼說，我都不會再相信。
    (A) 尤其
    (B) 凡是
    (C) 無論
    (D) 關於

32. Tā yǐjīng qīpiànguo wǒ tài duō cì le, suǒyǐ____tā zěnme shuō, wǒ dōu bú huì zài xiāngxìn.
    (A) yóuqí
    (B) fánshì
    (C) wúlùn
    (D) guānyú

32. ㄊㄚ ㄧˇ ㄐㄧㄥ ㄑㄧ ㄆㄧㄢˋ ㄍㄨㄛˋ ㄨㄛˇ ㄊㄞˋ ㄉㄨㄛ ㄘˋ ˙ㄌㄜ，ㄙㄨㄛˇ ㄧˇ ____ ㄊㄚ ㄗㄜˇ ˙ㄇㄜ ㄕㄨㄛ，ㄨㄛˇ ㄉㄡ ㄅㄨˊ ㄏㄨㄟˋ ㄗㄞˋ ㄒㄧㄤ ㄒㄧㄣˋ。
    (A) ㄧㄡˊ ㄑㄧˊ
    (B) ㄈㄢˊ ㄕˋ
    (C) ㄨˊ ㄌㄨㄣˋ
    (D) ㄍㄨㄢ ㄩˊ

33. 他之所以成功，是____得到了大家的帮忙。
(A) 因为
(B) 因而
(C) 为了
(D) 即使

33. 他之所以成功，是____得到了大家的幫忙。
(A) 因爲
(B) 因而
(C) 爲了
(D) 即使

33. Tā zhīsuǒyǐ chénggōng, shì____ dédào le dàjiā de bāngmáng.
(A) yīnwèi
(B) yīn'ér
(C) wèile
(D) jíshǐ

33. ㄊㄚ ㄓ ㄙㄨㄛˇ ㄧˇ ㄔㄥˊ ㄍㄨㄥ，ㄕˋ ____ ㄉㄜˊ ㄉㄠˋ ˙ㄌㄜ ㄉㄚˋ ㄐㄧㄚ ˙ㄉㄜ ㄅㄤ ㄇㄤˊ。
(A) ㄧㄣ ㄨㄟˋ
(B) ㄧㄣ ㄦˊ
(C) ㄨㄟˋ ˙ㄌㄜ
(D) ㄐㄧˊ ㄕˇ

34. 这家百货公司关门的原因是____？
(A) 怎样
(B) 如何
(C) 什么
(D) 为什么

34. 這家百貨公司關門的原因是____？
(A) 怎樣
(B) 如何
(C) 什麼
(D) 爲什麼

34. Zhè jiā bǎihuògōngsī guānmén de yuányīn shì____？
(A) zěnyàng
(B) rúhé
(C) shénme
(D) wèishénme

34. ㄓㄜˋ ㄐㄧㄚ ㄅㄞˇ ㄏㄨㄛˋ ㄍㄨㄥ ㄙ ㄍㄨㄢ ㄇㄣˊ ˙ㄉㄜ ㄩㄢˊ ㄧㄣ ㄕˋ ____？
(A) ㄗㄣˇ ㄧㄤˋ
(B) ㄖㄨˊ ㄏㄜˊ
(C) ㄕㄣˊ ˙ㄇㄜ
(D) ㄨㄟˋ ㄕㄣˊ ˙ㄇㄜ

35. ____想在考试中获取理想的成绩，____要用功读书。
(A) 为了 …… 也
(B) 如果 …… 就
(C) 无论 …… 都
(D) 只要 …… 哪怕

35. ____想在考試中獲取理想的成績，____要用功讀書。
(A) 爲了 …… 也
(B) 如果 …… 就
(C) 無論 …… 都
(D) 只要 …… 哪怕

35. ____xiǎng zài kǎoshì zhōng huòqǔ lǐxiǎng de chéngjì, ____ yào yònggōng dúshū.
(A) Wèile …… yě
(B) Rúguǒ …… jiù
(C) Wúlùn …… dōu
(D) Zhǐyào …… nǎpà

35. ____ ㄒㄧㄤˇ ㄗㄞˋ ㄎㄠˇ ㄕˋ ㄓㄨㄥ ㄏㄨㄛˋ ㄑㄩˇ ㄌㄧˇ ㄒㄧㄤˇ ˙ㄉㄜ ㄔㄥˊ ㄐㄧ，____ ㄧㄠˋ ㄩㄥˋ ㄍㄨㄥ ㄉㄨˊ ㄕㄨ。
(A) ㄨㄟˋ ˙ㄌㄜ …… ㄧㄝˇ
(B) ㄖㄨˊ ㄍㄨㄛˇ …… ㄐㄧㄡˋ
(C) ㄨˊ ㄌㄨㄣˋ …… ㄉㄡ
(D) ㄓˇ ㄧㄠˋ …… ㄋㄚˇ ㄆㄚˋ

36. ____五月起，这里的学费改为五百元。
(A) 就
(B) 到
(C) 从
(D) 以

36. ____wŭyuè qĭ, zhè li de xuéfèi găi wéi 500 yuán.
(A) Jiù
(B) Dào
(C) Cóng
(D) Yĭ

37. 他想考上大学，____努力地温习。
(A) 可见
(B) 无疑
(C) 因此
(D) 尤其

37. Tā xiăng kăo shàng dàxué, ____ nŭlì de wēnxí.
(A) kějiàn
(B) wúyí
(C) yīncĭ
(D) yóuqí

38. 我喜欢运动，____是篮球。
(A) 尽管
(B) 尤其
(C) 显然
(D) 总之

38. Wŏ xĭhuan yùndòng, ____shì lánqiú.
(A) jĭnguăn
(B) yóuqí
(C) xiănrán
(D) zŏngzhī

36. ____五月起，這裏的學費改爲五百元。
(A) 就
(B) 到
(C) 從
(D) 以

36. ____ㄨˇ ㄩㄝˋ ㄑㄧˇ，ㄓㄜˋ ㄌㄧ ㄉㄜ ㄒㄩㄝˊ ㄈㄟˋ ㄍㄞˇ ㄨㄟˊ ㄨˇ ㄅㄞˇ ㄩㄢˊ。
(A) ㄐㄧㄡˋ
(B) ㄉㄠˋ
(C) ㄘㄨㄥˊ
(D) ㄧˇ

37. 他想考上大學，____努力地溫習。
(A) 可見
(B) 無疑
(C) 因此
(D) 尤其

37. ㄊㄚ ㄒㄧㄤˇ ㄎㄠˇ ㄕㄤˋ ㄉㄚˋ ㄒㄩㄝˊ，____ ㄋㄨˇ ㄌㄧˋ ㄉㄜ ㄨㄣ ㄒㄧˊ。
(A) ㄎㄜˇ ㄐㄧㄢˋ
(B) ㄨˊ ㄧˊ
(C) ㄧㄣ ㄘˇ
(D) ㄧㄡˊ ㄑㄧˊ

38. 我喜歡運動，____是籃球。
(A) 儘管
(B) 尤其
(C) 顯然
(D) 總之

38. ㄨㄛˇ ㄒㄧˇ ㄏㄨㄢ ㄩㄣˋ ㄉㄨㄥˋ，____ ㄕˋ ㄌㄢˊ ㄑㄧㄡˊ。
(A) ㄐㄧㄣˇ ㄍㄨㄢˇ
(B) ㄧㄡˊ ㄑㄧˊ
(C) ㄒㄧㄢˇ ㄖㄢˊ
(D) ㄗㄨㄥˇ ㄓ

39. 这____相片里的人是我妈妈。

(A) 张
(B) 块
(C) 件
(D) 部

39. 這____相片裏的人是我媽媽。

(A) 張
(B) 塊
(C) 件
(D) 部

39. Zhè ____ xiàngpiàn li de rén shì wǒ māma.

(A) zhāng
(B) kuài
(C) jiàn
(D) bù

39. ㄓㄜˋ ____ ㄒㄧㄤˋ ㄆㄧㄢˋ ㄌㄧˇ ˙ㄉㄜ ㄖㄣˊ ㄕˋ ㄨㄛˇ ㄇㄚ ˙ㄇㄚ。

(A) ㄓㄤ
(B) ㄎㄨㄞˋ
(C) ㄐㄧㄢˋ
(D) ㄅㄨˋ

40. 我习惯每晚睡觉前喝一____牛奶。

(A) 番
(B) 瓶
(C) 片
(D) 头

40. 我習慣每晚睡覺前喝一____牛奶。

(A) 番
(B) 瓶
(C) 片
(D) 頭

40. Wǒ xíguàn měiwǎn shuìjiào qián hē yī ____ niúnǎi.

(A) fān
(B) píng
(C) piàn
(D) tóu

40. ㄨㄛˇ ____ ㄒㄧˊ ㄍㄨㄢˋ ㄇㄟˇ ㄨㄢˇ ㄕㄨㄟˋ ㄐㄧㄠˋ ㄑㄧㄢˊ ㄏㄜ ㄧ ____ ㄋㄧㄡˊ ㄋㄞˇ。

(A) ㄈㄢ
(B) ㄆㄧㄥˊ
(C) ㄆㄧㄢˋ
(D) ㄊㄡˊ

41. 他没把工作做完，____离开了。

(A) 而
(B) 还
(C) 就
(D) 才

41. 他沒把工作做完，____離開了。

(A) 而
(B) 還
(C) 就
(D) 才

41. Tā méi bǎ gōngzuò zuò wán, ____ líkāi le.

(A) ér
(B) hái
(C) jiù
(D) cái

41. ㄊㄚ ㄇㄟˊ ㄅㄚˇ ㄍㄨㄥ ㄗㄨㄛˋ ㄗㄨㄛˋ ㄨㄢˊ，____ ㄌㄧˊ ㄎㄞ ˙ㄌㄜ。

(A) ㄦˊ
(B) ㄏㄞˊ
(C) ㄐㄧㄡˋ
(D) ㄘㄞˊ

42. 这部电影真精彩，我想再看一____。
(A) 个
(B) 条
(C) 遍
(D) 篇

42. Zhè bù diànyǐng zhēn jīngcǎi, wǒ xiǎng zài kàn yī____.
(A) ge
(B) tiáo
(C) biàn
(D) piān

42. 這部電影真精彩，我想再看一____。
(A) 個
(B) 條
(C) 遍
(D) 篇

42. ㄓㄜˋ ㄅㄨˋ ㄉㄧㄢˋ ㄧㄥˇ ㄓㄣ ㄐㄧㄥ ㄘㄞˇ，ㄨㄛˇ ㄒㄧㄤˇ ㄗㄞˋ ㄎㄢˋ ㄧ ____。
(A) ˙ㄍㄜ
(B) ㄊㄧㄠˊ
(C) ㄅㄧㄢˋ
(D) ㄆㄧㄢ

43. 弟弟考试不及格，____爸爸并没有责怪他。
(A) 所以
(B) 刚才
(C) 然而
(D) 然后

43. Dìdi kǎoshì bù jígé, ____bàba bìng méiyǒu zéguài tā.
(A) suǒyǐ
(B) gāngcái
(C) rán'ér
(D) ránhòu

43. 弟弟考試不及格，____爸爸並沒有責怪他。
(A) 所以
(B) 剛才
(C) 然而
(D) 然後

43. ㄉㄧˋ ˙ㄉㄧ ㄎㄠˇ ㄕˋ ㄅㄨˋ ㄐㄧˊ ㄍㄜˊ，____ ㄅㄚˋ ˙ㄅㄚ ㄅㄧㄥˋ ㄇㄟˊ ㄧㄡˇ ㄗㄜˊ ㄍㄨㄞˋ ㄊㄚ。
(A) ㄙㄨㄛˇ ㄧˇ
(B) ㄍㄤ ㄘㄞˊ
(C) ㄖㄢˊ ㄦˊ
(D) ㄖㄢˊ ㄏㄡˋ

44. 他只是不小心犯错，你____生气呢？
(A) 于是
(B) 何必
(C) 不过
(D) 但是

44. Tā zhǐshì bù xiǎoxīn fàncuò, nǐ ____shēngqì ne？
(A) yúshì
(B) hébì
(C) búguò
(D) dànshì

44. 他只是不小心犯錯，你____生氣呢？
(A) 於是
(B) 何必
(C) 不過
(D) 但是

44. ㄊㄚ ㄓˇ ㄕˋ ㄅㄨˋ ㄒㄧㄠˇ ㄒㄧㄣ ㄈㄢˋ ㄘㄨㄛˋ，ㄋㄧˇ ____ ㄕㄥ ㄑㄧˋ ˙ㄋㄜ？
(A) ㄩˊ ㄕˋ
(B) ㄏㄜˊ ㄅㄧˋ
(C) ㄅㄨˊ ㄍㄨㄛˋ
(D) ㄉㄢˋ ㄕˋ

45. 他的中文____我好得多。
(A) 和
(B) 比
(C) 更
(D) 不

45. Tā de Zhōngwén____wǒ hǎo de duō.
(A) hé
(B) bǐ
(C) gèng
(D) bù

46. 到外地生活，____。
(A) 懂得照顾自己你要
(B) 你懂得要自己照顾
(C) 你要懂得照顾自己
(D) 懂得要照顾你自己

46. Dào wàidì shēnghuó, ____.
(A) dǒngde zhàogu zìjǐ nǐ yào
(B) nǐ dǒngde yào zìjǐ zhàogu
(C) nǐ yào dǒngde zhàogu zìjǐ
(D) dǒngde yào zhàogu nǐ zìjǐ

47. 我的房间挂着一____画。
(A) 枝
(B) 件
(C) 条
(D) 幅

47. Wǒ de fángjiān guàzhe yī____huà.
(A) zhī
(B) jiàn
(C) tiáo
(D) fú

45. 他的中文____我好得多。
(A) 和
(B) 比
(C) 更
(D) 不

45. ㄊㄚ ˙ㄉㄜ ㄓㄨㄥ ㄨㄣˊ ____ ㄨㄛˇ ㄏㄠˇ ˙ㄉㄜ ㄉㄨㄛ 。
(A) ㄏㄜˊ
(B) ㄅㄧˇ
(C) ㄍㄥˋ
(D) ㄅㄨˋ

46. 到外地生活，____。
(A) 懂得照顧自己你要
(B) 你懂得要自己照顧
(C) 你要懂得照顧自己
(D) 懂得要照顧你自己

46. ㄉㄠˋ ㄨㄞˋ ㄉㄧˋ ㄕㄥ ㄏㄨㄛˊ， ____ 。
(A) ㄉㄨㄥˇ ㄉㄜˊ ㄓㄠˋ ㄍㄨˋ ㄗˋ ㄐㄧˇ ㄋㄧˇ ㄧㄠˋ
(B) ㄋㄧˇ ㄉㄨㄥˇ ㄉㄜˊ ㄧㄠˋ ㄗˋ ㄐㄧˇ ㄓㄠˋ ㄍㄨˋ
(C) ㄋㄧˇ ㄧㄠˋ ㄉㄨㄥˇ ㄉㄜˊ ㄓㄠˋ ㄍㄨˋ ㄗˋ ㄐㄧˇ
(D) ㄉㄨㄥˇ ㄉㄜˊ ㄧㄠˋ ㄓㄠˋ ㄍㄨˋ ㄋㄧˇ ㄗˋ ㄐㄧˇ

47. 我的房間掛著一____畫。
(A) 枝
(B) 件
(C) 條
(D) 幅

47. ㄨㄛˇ ˙ㄉㄜ ㄈㄤˊ ㄐㄧㄢ ㄍㄨㄚˋ ˙ㄓㄜ ㄧ ㄏㄨㄚˋ 。
(A) ㄓ
(B) ㄐㄧㄢˋ
(C) ㄊㄧㄠˊ
(D) ㄈㄨˊ

48. 昨天天气____转凉，他就生病了。
(A) 立即
(B) 突然
(C) 一直
(D) 偶然

48. Zuótiān tiānqì ____ zhuǎn liáng, tā jiù shēngbìng le.
(A) lìjí
(B) tūrán
(C) yìzhí
(D) ǒurán

49. 听音乐会____。
(A) 舒服很让人感到
(B) 感到让人很舒服
(C) 很舒服感到让人
(D) 让人感到很舒服

49. Tīng yīnyuè huì ____ .
(A) shūfu hěn ràng rén gǎndào
(B) gǎndào ràng rén hěn shūfu
(C) hěn shūfu gǎndào ràng rén
(D) ràng rén gǎndào hěn shūfu

50. ____他失败了很多次，____他仍然继续努力。
(A) 因为 …… 所以
(B) 无论 …… 都
(C) 尽管 …… 但是
(D) 不但 …… 而且

50. ____ tā shībài le hěnduō cì, ____ tā réngrán jìxù nǔlì.
(A) Yīnwèi …… suǒyǐ
(B) Wúlùn …… dōu
(C) Jǐnguǎn …… dànshì
(D) Búdàn …… érqiě

48. 昨天天氣____轉涼，他就生病了。
(A) 立即
(B) 突然
(C) 一直
(D) 偶然

48. ㄗㄨㄛˊ ㄊㄧㄢ ㄊㄧㄢ ㄑㄧˋ ____ ㄓㄨㄢˇ ㄌㄧㄤˊ，ㄊㄚ ㄐㄧㄡˋ ㄕㄥ ㄅㄧㄥˋ ˙ㄌㄜ。
(A) ㄌㄧˋ ㄐㄧˊ
(B) ㄊㄨˊ ㄖㄢˊ
(C) ㄧˋ ㄓˊ
(D) ㄡˇ ㄖㄢˊ

49. 聽音樂會____。
(A) 舒服很讓人感到
(B) 感到讓人很舒服
(C) 很舒服感到讓人
(D) 讓人感到很舒服

49. ㄊㄧㄥ ㄧㄣ ㄩㄝˋ ㄏㄨㄟˋ ____。
(A) ㄕㄨ ㄈㄨˊ ㄏㄣˇ ㄖㄤˋ ㄖㄣˊ ㄍㄢˇ ㄉㄠˋ
(B) ㄍㄢˇ ㄉㄠˋ ㄖㄤˋ ㄖㄣˊ ㄏㄣˇ ㄕㄨ ㄈㄨˊ
(C) ㄏㄣˇ ㄕㄨ ㄈㄨˊ ㄍㄢˇ ㄉㄠˋ ㄖㄤˋ ㄖㄣˊ
(D) ㄖㄤˋ ㄖㄣˊ ㄍㄢˇ ㄉㄠˋ ㄏㄣˇ ㄕㄨ ㄈㄨˊ

50. ____他失敗了很多次，____他仍然繼續努力。
(A) 因為 …… 所以
(B) 無論 …… 都
(C) 儘管 …… 但是
(D) 不但 …… 而且

50. ____ ㄊㄚ ㄕ ㄅㄞˋ ˙ㄌㄜ ㄏㄣˇ ㄉㄨㄛ ㄘˋ，____ ㄊㄚ ㄖㄥˊ ㄖㄢˊ ㄐㄧˋ ㄒㄩˋ ㄋㄨˇ ㄌㄧˋ。
(A) ㄧㄣ ㄨㄟˋ …… ㄙㄨㄛˇ ㄧˇ
(B) ㄨˊ ㄌㄨㄣˋ …… ㄉㄡ
(C) ㄐㄧㄣˇ ㄍㄨㄢˇ …… ㄉㄢˋ ㄕˋ
(D) ㄅㄨˊ ㄉㄢˋ …… ㄦˊ ㄑㄧㄝˇ

51. 我不是不知道，____忘记了。
(A) 但是
(B) 而是
(C) 不是
(D) 可是

51. Wǒ bú shì bù zhīdào, ____wàngjìle.
(A) dànshì
(B) érshì
(C) búshì
(D) kěshì

52. 你已经____，该休息一下了。
(A) 看了一整天书
(B) 一整天看了书
(C) 看书了一整天
(D) 书一整天看了

52. Nǐ yǐjīng ____, gāi xiūxi yí xià le.
(A) kànle yì zhěngtiān shū
(B) yì zhěngtiān kànle shū
(C) kàn shū le yì zhěngtiān
(D) shū yì zhěngtiān kànle

53. 既然你不相信我，____我再说你也不会相信。
(A) 即使
(B) 除非
(C) 既然
(D) 无论

53. Jìrán nǐ bù xiāngxìn wǒ, ____ wǒ zài shuō nǐ yě bú huì xiāngxìn.
(A) jíshǐ
(B) chúfēi
(C) jìrán
(D) wúlùn

51. 我不是不知道，____忘記了。
(A) 但是
(B) 而是
(C) 不是
(D) 可是

51. ㄨㄛˇ ㄅㄨˊ ㄕˋ ㄅㄨˋ ㄓ ㄉㄠˋ，____ ㄨㄤˋ ㄐㄧˋ ˙ㄌㄜ。
(A) ㄐㄧㄡˋ ㄕˋ
(B) ㄦˊ ㄕˋ
(C) ㄅㄨˊ ㄕˋ
(D) ㄎㄜˇ ㄕˋ

52. 你已經____，該休息一下了。
(A) 看了一整天書
(B) 一整天看了書
(C) 看書了一整天
(D) 書一整天看了

52. ㄋㄧˇ ㄧˇ ㄐㄧㄥ ____，ㄍㄞ ㄒㄧㄡ ㄒㄧˊ ㄧˊ ㄒㄧㄚˋ ˙ㄌㄜ。
(A) ㄎㄢˋ ˙ㄌㄜ ㄧˋ ㄓㄥˇ ㄊㄧㄢ ㄕㄨ
(B) ㄧˋ ㄓㄥˇ ㄊㄧㄢ ㄎㄢˋ ˙ㄌㄜ ㄕㄨ
(C) ㄎㄢˋ ㄕㄨ ˙ㄌㄜ ㄧˋ ㄓㄥˇ ㄊㄧㄢ
(D) ㄕㄨ ㄧˋ ㄓㄥˇ ㄊㄧㄢ ㄎㄢˋ ˙ㄌㄜ

53. 既然你不相信我，____我再說你也不會相信。
(A) 即使
(B) 除非
(C) 既然
(D) 無論

53. ㄐㄧˋ ㄖㄢˊ ㄋㄧˇ ㄅㄨˋ ㄒㄧㄤ ㄒㄧㄣˋ ㄨㄛˇ，____ ㄨㄛˇ ㄗㄞˋ ㄕㄨㄛ ㄋㄧˇ ㄧㄝˇ ㄅㄨˊ ㄏㄨㄟˋ ㄒㄧㄤ ㄒㄧㄣˋ。
(A) ㄐㄧˊ ㄕˇ
(B) ㄔㄨˊ ㄈㄟ
(C) ㄐㄧˋ ㄖㄢˊ
(D) ㄨˊ ㄌㄨㄣˋ

54. 做好准备，____能取得最好的成绩。

(A) 也
(B) 才
(C) 却
(D) 而

54. 做好準備，____能取得最好的成績。

(A) 也
(B) 才
(C) 卻
(D) 而

54. Zuò hǎo zhǔnbèi, ____néng qǔdé zuìhǎo de chéngjì.

(A) yě
(B) cái
(C) què
(D) ér

54. ㄗㄨㄛˋ ㄏㄠˇ ㄓㄨㄣˇ ㄅㄟˋ，____ ㄋㄥˊ ㄑㄩˇ ㄉㄜˊ ㄗㄨㄟˋ ㄏㄠˇ ˙ㄉㄜ ㄔㄥˊ ㄐㄧ。

(A) ㄧㄝˇ
(B) ㄘㄞˊ
(C) ㄑㄩㄝˋ
(D) ㄦˊ

55. 你带上这把雨伞吧，____下雨也不会被淋湿。

(A) 一万
(B) 万一
(C) 千万
(D) 万万

55. 你帶上這把雨傘吧，____下雨也不會被淋濕。

(A) 一萬
(B) 萬一
(C) 千萬
(D) 萬萬

55. Nǐ dài shàng zhè bǎ yǔsǎn ba, ____xiàyǔ yě bú huì bèi lín shī.

(A) yīwàn
(B) wànyī
(C) qiānwàn
(D) wànwàn

55. ㄋㄧˇ ㄉㄞˋ ㄕㄤˋ ㄓㄜˋ ㄅㄚˇ ㄩˇ ㄙㄢˇ ˙ㄅㄚ，____ ㄒㄧㄚˋ ㄩˇ ㄧㄝˇ ㄅㄨˊ ㄏㄨㄟˋ ㄅㄟˋ ㄌㄧㄣˊ ㄕ。

(A) ㄧ ㄨㄢˋ
(B) ㄨㄢˋ ㄧ
(C) ㄑㄧㄢ ㄨㄢˋ
(D) ㄨㄢˋ ㄨㄢˋ

SECTION III
READING COMPREHENSION

Suggested time — 25 minutes
Questions 56 - 85

WHEN YOU BEGIN THIS SECTION, MAKE SURE THAT YOU MARK YOUR ANSWER TO THE FIRST QUESTION BY FILLING IN ONE OF THE CIRCLES NEXT TO NUMBER 56 ON YOUR ANSWER SHEET.

Directions:

Read the following texts carefully for comprehension. Each one is followed by one or more questions or incomplete statements. Select the answer or completion that is best according to the text and fill in the corresponding circle on your answer sheet.

This section of the test is presented in two writing systems: traditional characters and simplified characters. IT IS RECOMMEMD THAT YOU CHOOSE THE WRITING SYSTEM WITH WHICH YOU ARE MORE FAMILIAR WITH AND **ONLY READ THAT VERSION** AS YOU WORK THROUGH THIS SECTION OF THE TEST.

Question 56

男 宾 止 步	男 賓 止 步

56. What does this sign mean?
    (A) Male visitors only
    (B) Female visitors only
    (C) No visitors
    (D) No eating

Question 57

本地投寄免贴邮票

本地投寄免貼郵票

57. What does this sign say?
   (A) Stamp required
   (B) Home delivery
   (C) Free local postage
   (D) Stamps are sold out

Question 58

好好超市售货小票

2010-11-3

品名	单价(元)	数量	总价(元)
可乐	7.5	1	7.5
面包	3.8	2	7.6
乐事薯片	6.2	1	6.2
合计		4	21.3
实收			25
找零			3.7

好好超市售貨小票

2010-11-3

品名	單價(元)	數量	總價(元)
可樂	7.5	1	7.5
麵包	3.8	2	7.6
樂事薯片	6.2	1	6.2
合計		4	21.3
實收			25
找零			3.7

58. This is
   (A) a receipt
   (B) a menu
   (C) a shopping list
   (D) an advertisement

Question 59

禁止吸烟 | 禁止吸煙

59. What does this sign say?
    - (A) No eating or drinking
    - (B) No smoking
    - (C) No naked flames
    - (D) No fireworks allowed

Question 60

请勿拍照 | 請勿拍照

60. This sign means
    - (A) do not touch
    - (B) no photography
    - (C) no visitors
    - (D) no parking

Questions 61-62

优惠价　抢购
女袜四双仅售三十六元
二零一零年三月十一日起

優惠價　搶購
女襪四雙僅售三十六元
二零一零年三月十一日起

61. What is this advertisement about?
    - (A) A new product
    - (B) A fashion show
    - (C) A special offer
    - (D) The opening of a new shop

62. Which of the following items is mentioned?
   (A) Children's T-shirts
   (B) Women's shoes
   (C) Women's socks
   (D) Men's shoes

Questions 63-64

我的第一位英文老师叫保罗（Paul），是英国人，不过他从小就住在美国。他是位年轻的美国学生，刚来中国的时候一句中文也不会，可是在中国当了两年英文老师后，他已经会说一口流利的中文了。

我的第一位英文老師叫保羅（Paul），是英國人，不過他從小就住在美國。他是位年輕的美國學生，剛來中國的時候一句中文也不會，可是在中國當了兩年英文老師後，他已經會說一口流利的中文了。

63. Why did Paul come to China?
   (A) To travel
   (B) To learn Chinese
   (C) To teach Chinese
   (D) To teach English

64. Which of the following statements is NOT true?
   (A) Paul wrote this passage.
   (B) Paul studied in the US.
   (C) Paul could not speak Chinese when he first arrived in China.
   (D) Paul has been in China for at least two years.

Question 65

一周计划表	
星期一	完成计划书
星期二	跟经理开会
星期三	购买机票
星期四	去银行取钱及购买旅行支票
星期五	付房租
星期六	收拾行李、检查签证和护照
星期日	去美国

一週計劃表	
星期一	完成計劃書
星期二	跟經理開會
星期三	購買機票
星期四	去銀行取錢及購買旅行支票
星期五	付房租
星期六	收拾行李、檢查簽證和護照
星期日	去美國

65. On which day does the writer plan to buy travelers checks?
    (A) Wednesday
    (B) Thursday
    (C) Friday
    (D) Saturday

Question 66

退烧药水

每四小时喝一次
每次喝一格
每天最多喝四次
如果不退烧，请立即就医

退燒藥水

每四小時喝一次
每次喝一格
每天最多喝四次
如果不退燒，請立即就醫

66. This drug is for
    (A) headaches
    (B) travel sickness
    (C) stomachaches
    (D) fevers

Questions 67-68

校庆纪念日活动通知

本月十六日(周五)为本校建校三十周年纪念日，现通知庆祝活动的详情如下：

一、当日上午九时，在本校礼堂举行庆祝大会，全校师生一律准时参加；

二、当日晚上八时，在本校操场举行晚会，欢迎各学生家长携同亲友参加。

香城中学校长张国强
二零一零年十一月一日

校慶紀念日活動通知

本月十六日(週五)為本校建校三十周年紀念日，現通知慶祝活動的詳情如下：

一、當日上午九時，在本校禮堂舉行慶祝大會，全校師生一律準時參加；

二、當日晚上八時，在本校操場舉行晚會，歡迎各學生家長攜同親友參加。

香城中學校長張國強
二零一零年十一月一日

67. This is an invitation to
    (A) a music festival
    (B) a talent show
    (C) a charity fundraising event
    (D) a school anniversary

68. Who is invited to join the events in the morning?
    (A) Teachers and students
    (B) Students only
    (C) Parents only
    (D) Students, parents and their friends

Question 69

车次	出发—到达	出发时间—到达时间	票价
T50	上海—北京	上午九点二十三分—下午九点四十七分	四百零九元

車次	出發—到達	出發時間—到達時間	票價
T50	上海—北京	上午九點二十三分-下午九點四十七分	四百零九元

69. Where would this message most likely appear?
    (A) On an air ticket
    (B) On a train ticket
    (C) On a movie ticket
    (D) On a concert ticket

Questions 70-71

电影《我的父亲母亲》
场次：十二点三十分　十五点
　　　二十点　二十一点三十分
成人票价：六十元
儿童票价：四十元
日期：一月二十日

電影《我的父親母親》
場次：十二點三十分　十五點
　　　二十點　二十一點三十分
成人票價：六十元
兒童票價：四十元
日期：一月二十日

70. What information is NOT given?
    (A) Screening times
    (B) Movie title
    (C) Length of movie
    (D) Screening date

71. How much is a child ticket?

(A) $60
(B) $40
(C) $30
(D) $20

Question 72

诚信广告公司	誠信廣告公司
本公司成立于一九九五年，多年来一直致力为各大小商务机构及政府部门制作各类型的广告设计。本公司能配合顾客的不同需要，给予专业的意见，提供优质服务。	本公司成立於一九九五年，多年來一直致力為各大小商務機構及政府部門製作各類型的廣告設計。本公司能配合顧客的不同需要，給予專業的意見，提供優質服務。

72. What does this company specialize in?

(A) Trading
(B) Advertising
(C) Technology
(D) Education

Question 73

请 关 掉 手 机	請 關 掉 手 機

73. What does this sign say?

(A) Please keep quiet
(B) Please switch off cell phones
(C) Please close the door
(D) Please switch off engine

Question 74

网上广告比传统广告更具互动性，不受时间、地域限制，每日二十四小时无间断地将宣传讯息传递到世界各地。网上广告价钱较传统广告便宜，有效节省制作成本，并得到更佳的宣传效果。

網上廣告比傳統廣告更具互動性，不受時間、地域限制，每日二十四小時無間斷地將宣傳訊息傳遞到世界各地。網上廣告價錢較傳統廣告便宜，有效節省製作成本，並得到更佳的宣傳效果。

74. This passage is about
   (A) Internet advertising
   (B) telephone service
   (C) satellite television
   (D) courier service

Question 75

一律四折

一律四折

75. What does this sign say?
   (A) 60% off
   (B) 40% off
   (C) Buy 4 get 1 free
   (D) $4 each

Question 76

《剑桥百科全书》
电子字典

《剑桥百科全书》由百多名学者精心编撰，拥有庞大的学术字库。字典中收录近四百万字，涵盖一万六千个主题，包括自然科学、社会科学、文学艺术等多个学术范畴，而且图文兼备，为学习增添趣味。

《劍橋百科全書》
電子字典

《劍橋百科全書》由百多名學者精心編撰，擁有龐大的學術字庫。字典中收錄近四百萬字，涵蓋一萬六千個主題，包括自然科學、社會科學、文學藝術等多個學術範疇，而且圖文兼備，為學習增添趣味。

76. Which of the following is NOT a feature of the electronic encyclopedia?
  (A) Compiled by hundreds of scholars
  (B) Covers 160,000 themes
  (C) Covers the vocabularies of many academic areas
  (D) Includes text and illustrations

Question 77

地下铁失物认领中心

服务电话：123456

服务时间：星期一至星期六
（假日休息）
中午十二时至
晚上九时

服务地点：北京四合路三楼四室

地下鐵失物認領中心

服務電話：123456

服務時間：星期一至星期六
（假日休息）
中午十二時至
晚上九時

服務地點：北京四合路三樓四室

77. Where would this sign be found?
  (A) In a restaurant
  (B) At a post office
  (C) At a box office
  (D) In a subway station

Question 78

电车租车服务		
类型	费用	载客量
古典开蓬电车	一千二百元/小时	十五/人
古典电车	一千元/小时	二十五/人
普通电车	七百五十元/小时	三十五/人

電車租車服務		
類型	費用	載客量
古典開蓬電車	一千二百元/小時	十五/人
古典電車	一千元/小時	二十五/人
普通電車	七百五十元/小時	三十五/人

78. This advertisement is about renting
   (A) motorcycles
   (B) trams
   (C) buses
   (D) boats

Question 79

出　租

一房一厅，三百八十呎，月租四千五百元，包家电、家具（冰箱、洗衣机、单人床、餐桌、沙发）

代理：龙凤地产

联络人：谢小姐

电话：12345678

出　租

一房一廳，三百八十呎，月租四千五百元，包家電、傢俱（冰箱、洗衣機、單人床、餐桌、沙發）

代理：龍鳳地產

聯絡人：謝小姐

電話：12345678

79. What is this advertisement about?
   (A) House for sale
   (B) Refrigerator repairs
   (C) Furniture for sale
   (D) Apartment for rent

Question 80

小心地滑

小心地滑

80. What does this sign say?
    (A) Landslide warning
    (B) Beware of slippery floor
    (C) Ski slope closed
    (D) Take care when using the children's slide

Question 81

互联网对学生的好处是多不胜数的。第一、在互联网上，学生可以认识世界各地发生的大事，增广见闻，建立敏锐的时事触觉；第二、学生可在网上与同学交流意见和进行讨论，提高思辩能力；第三、互联网为学生提供了很多娱乐和资讯，一方面可纾缓他们的学习压力，另一方面可为他们与朋友交谈时提供源源不绝的话题。

互聯網對學生的好處是多不勝數的。第一、在互聯網上，學生可以認識世界各地發生的大事，增廣見聞，建立敏銳的時事觸覺；第二、學生可在網上與同學交流意見和進行討論，提高思辯能力；第三、互聯網為學生提供了很多娛樂和資訊，一方面可紓緩他們的學習壓力，另一方面可為他們與朋友交談時提供源源不絕的話題。

81. Which of the following benefits is NOT mentioned?
    (A) Broadens students' horizon
    (B) Allows discussions and exchanges with friends
    (C) Provides opportunuties to buy discounted products
    (D) Provides entertainment and information

Questions 82-83

中美女排大战 国际排球比赛	中美女排大戰 國際排球比賽
七月十五日星期日晚上八时	七月十五日星期日晚上八時
香港红磡体育馆	香港紅磡體育館
票价:一百八十元 二百五十元 三百六十元	票價:一百八十元 二百五十元 三百六十元
当日早上十时售票	當日早上十時售票

82. This is an advertisement for
    (A) a basketball game
    (B) a volleyball game
    (C) a soccer game
    (D) a baseball game

83. Which of the following statements is NOT true?
    (A) The game will take place on July 15th.
    (B) The game will be a men's game.
    (C) The most expensive tickets cost $360 each.
    (D) Tickets can only be purchased on the day.

Question 84

是日精选(二十八元/份)	是日精選(二十八元/份)
A、鸡翼煎双蛋饭	A、雞翼煎雙蛋飯
B、粟米鱼块饭	B、粟米魚塊飯
C、猪排饭	C、豬排飯
D、牛排饭	D、牛排飯
附送:	附送:
餐汤或热饮(冷饮加两元)	餐湯或熱飲(冷飲加兩元)

84. Which of the following is NOT on the menu?
   (A) Chicken wings and fried egg with rice
   (B) Roast duck with rice
   (C) Beef steak with rice
   (D) Pork chops with rice

Question 85

支　票　　号码：114379
二零一零年十一月七日
受款人：黄静
金　额：美金八百七十元五角七分
汇通银行
付款人：李子明

支　票　　號碼：114379
二零一零年十一月七日
受款人：黃靜
金　額：美金八百七十元五角七分
匯通銀行
付款人：李子明

85. This is a
   (A) check
   (B) memo
   (C) movie ticket
   (D) train ticket

SAT Chinese Practice Test — Six
SAT 中文模拟试题 — 第六套
SAT 中文模擬試題 — 第六套

听力材料
聽力材料
LISTENING TEST MATERIAL

Part A

Simplified Characters

Question 1

A： 你爷爷、奶奶退休了吗？

(A) 爸爸妈妈都退休了。
(B) 爷爷还在工作。
(C) 奶奶不休息了。

Question 2

A： 请问订这份报纸一年多少钱？

(A) 一份报纸三元。
(B) 报纸是每周一出版的。
(C) 一年一百三十元。

Question 3

A： 我最想去旅行。

(A) 我不想去东京旅行。
(B) 我住在伦敦。
(C) 这个圣诞节一起去吧。

Question 4

A： 请问这件衣服是买给自己穿的吗？

(A) 这是给我妈妈买的。
(B) 这件衣服多少钱？
(C) 我不知道试衣间在哪里。

Question 5

A： 这周三我想请一天假。
B： 你有什么事？

(A) 没事了，不用放在心上。
(B) 我爷爷病了，要送他去看医生。
(C) 我会早点回来帮你做事的。

Question 6

A： 我来帮你拿这杯茶吧。

(A) 我可以自己拿这床被子。
(B) 谢谢，小心烫手。
(C) 这杯是柠檬水。

Question 7

A： 请问你要些什么？

(A) 我要一杯橙汁。
(B) 咖啡卖完了。
(C) 这本书很有意思。

Question 8

A： 最近怎么不去打球了，在忙什么？

B： 我现在每天下午都去跳舞。

(A) 怪不得我最近老是见不到你了。
(B) 明天我们一起去打球吧。
(C) 你的舞跳得真好。

Question 9

A： 最近李强来找过你吗？

(A) 没有，他最近很忙。
(B) 这里有空位。
(C) 李强不过来了。

Question 10

A： 我给他打了好几次电话，都打不通。

B： 你去他家找他吧。

(A) 我买了部新手机。
(B) 电话很贵。
(C) 我不知道他住哪。

Question 11

A： 你吃过什么中国菜？

B： 我吃过北京烤鸭，那你呢？

(A) 北京的天气很好。
(B) 麻婆豆腐。
(C) 我们周末去吃烤鸭好吗？

Question 12

A： 现在可以买十二号的火车票吗？

(A) 提前买飞机票可以有九折优惠。
(B) 今天是七号，十二号的火车票还没出来。
(C) 十二号候车室在那边。

Question 13

A： 谁把音乐开得这么大？吵死了！

(A) 他生病了。
(B) 是新来的邻居在开生日会。
(C) 早上好，你想吃点什么？

Question 14

A： 晚上一起去看电影吧？

B： 我的作业还没做完呢。

(A) 那我们现在去吧。
(B) 那我们改天吧。
(C) 我不想做作业。

Question 15

A： 这种药一天吃几次？

(A) 要记得饭后吃。
(B) 最好是一天三次，严重的话也可以吃四次。
(C) 我不知道这是什么药。

Part B

Question 16

男：你怎么又迟到了？昨天是闹钟坏了，今天又是什么理由？

女：对不起，今天路上堵车了。

Questions 17-18

女：北京地铁一号线的首班时间是几点？

男：早上五点三十分。

女：下一站可以转乘几号线？

男：二号线。

Questions 19-20

男：可以麻烦你帮我照张相吗？

女：没问题。你是一个人来旅游的吗？

男：我和朋友一起来的，不过他们现在去买纪念品了。

Question 21

男：你现在和爸爸妈妈一起住吗？

女：不是，我和奶奶一起住。

Questions 22-23

男：听说学校附近新开了一家意大利餐馆，你去过吗？

女：我昨天刚刚去过，味道很不错。

男：我也很想去，可最近忙着复习考试，没有时间去。

Question 24

男：请问你要些什么？

女：我要一个西红柿炒鸡蛋、一碗米饭 和一杯橙汁。

男：对不起，橙汁已经卖完了，还有苹果汁和西瓜汁，你要什么？

女：那算了，不需要了。

Question 25

男：你买了什么书？

女：买了杂志、儿童故事书，还有一本字典。

Question 26

男：你知道今年的中秋节是哪一天吗？

女：九月二十七日，星期天。

Question 27

男：我们去看电影吧。

女：好的，等会儿在餐厅前面的路口见。

Question 28

男：请问附近的图书馆怎么走？

女：你直走五分钟，就会看到一个公园，图书馆就在它的右边。

Question 29

男：小王，最近忙些什么？

女：下周要考试了，忙着复习。你呢？

Question 30

男：你喜欢做什么运动？

女：打篮球、爬山我都喜欢，但我最喜欢游泳。

Part A

Traditional Characters

Question 1

A： 你爺爺、奶奶退休了嗎？

(A) 爸爸媽媽都退休了。
(B) 爺爺還在工作。
(C) 奶奶不休息了。

Question 2

A： 請問訂這份報紙一年多少錢？

(A) 一份報紙三元。
(B) 報紙是每週一出版的。
(C) 一年一百三十元。

Question 3

A： 我最想去旅行。

(A) 我不想去東京旅行。
(B) 我住在倫敦。
(C) 這個聖誕節一起去吧。

Question 4

A： 請問這件衣服是買給自己穿的嗎？

(A) 這是給我媽媽買的。
(B) 這件衣服多少錢？
(C) 我不知道試衣間在哪裏。

Question 5

A： 這週三我想請一天假。

B： 你有什麼事？

(A) 沒事了，不用放在心上。
(B) 我爺爺病了，要送他去看醫生。
(C) 我會早點回來幫你做事的。

Question 6

A： 我來幫你拿這杯茶吧。

(A) 我可以自己拿這床被子。
(B) 謝謝，小心燙手。
(C) 這杯是檸檬水。

Question 7

A： 請問你要些什麼？

(A) 我要一杯橙汁。
(B) 咖啡賣完了。
(C) 這本書很有意思。

Question 8

A： 最近怎麼不去打球了，在忙什麼？
B： 我現在每天下午都去跳舞。

(A) 怪不得我最近老是見不到你了。
(B) 明天我們一起去打球吧。
(C) 你的舞跳得真好。

Question 9

A： 最近李強來找過你嗎？

(A) 沒有，他最近很忙。
(B) 這裏有空位。
(C) 李強不過來了。

Question 10

A： 我給他打了好幾次電話，都打不通。
B： 你去他家找他吧。

(A) 我買了部新手機。
(B) 電話很貴。
(C) 我不知道他住哪。

Question 11

A： 你吃過什麼中國菜？

B： 我吃過北京烤鴨，那你呢？

(A) 北京的天氣很好。
(B) 麻婆豆腐。
(C) 我們週末去吃烤鴨好嗎？

Question 12

A： 現在可以買十二號的火車票嗎？

(A) 提前買飛機票可以有九折優惠。
(B) 今天是七號，十二號的火車票還沒出來。
(C) 十二號候車室在那邊。

Question 13

A： 誰把音樂開得這麼大？吵死了！

(A) 他生病了。
(B) 是新來的鄰居在開生日會。
(C) 早上好，你想吃點什麼？

Question 14

A： 晚上一起去看電影吧？

B： 我的作業還沒做完呢。

(A) 那我們現在去吧。
(B) 那我們改天吧。
(C) 我不想做作業。

Question 15

A： 這種藥一天吃幾次？

(A) 要記得飯後吃。
(B) 最好是一天三次，嚴重的話也可以吃四次。
(C) 我不知道這是什麼藥。

Part B

Question 16

男：你怎麼又遲到了？昨天是鬧鐘壞了，今天又是什麼理由？

女：對不起，今天路上堵車了。

Questions 17-18

女：北京地鐵一號線的首班時間是幾點？

男：早上五點三十分。

女：下一站可以轉乘幾號線？

男：二號線。

Questions 19-20

男：可以麻煩你幫我照張相嗎？

女：沒問題。你是一個人來旅游的嗎？

男：我和朋友一起來的，不過他們現在去買紀念品了。

Question 21

男：你現在和爸爸媽媽一起住嗎？

女：不是，我和奶奶一起住。

Questions 22-23

男：聽說學校附近新開了一家意大利餐館，你去過嗎？

女：我昨天剛剛去過，味道很不錯。

男：我也很想去，可最近忙著複習考試，沒有時間去。

Question 24

男：請問你要些什麼？

女：我要一個西紅柿炒雞蛋、一碗米飯和一杯橙汁。

男：對不起，橙汁已經賣完了，還有蘋果汁和西瓜汁，你要什麼？

女：那算了，不需要了。

Question 25

男：你買了什麼書？

女：買了雜誌、兒童故事書，還有一本字典。

Question 26

男：你知道今年的中秋節是哪一天嗎？

女：九月二十七日，星期天。

Question 27

男：我們去看電影吧。

女：好的，等會兒在餐廳前面的路口見。

Question 28

男：請問附近的圖書館怎麼走？

女：你直走五分鐘，就會看到一個公園，圖書館就在它的右邊。

Question 29

男：小王，最近忙些什麼？

女：下週要考試了，忙著複習。你呢？

Question 30

男：你喜歡做什麼運動？

女：打籃球、爬山我都喜歡，但我最喜歡游泳。

Part A

Pinyin Romanization

Question 1

A：Nǐ yéye、nǎinai tuìxiū le ma？

(A) Bàba māma dōu tuìxiū le.

(B) Yéye hái zài gōngzuò.

(C) Nǎinai bù xiūxi le.

Question 2

A：Qǐngwèn dìng zhè fèn bàozhǐ yì nián duōshao qián？

(A) Yífèn bàozhǐ sān yuán.

(B) Bàozhǐ shì měi zhōu yī chūbǎn de.

(C) Yì nián yībǎi sānshí yuán.

Question 3

A：Wǒ zuì xiǎng qù lǚxíng.

(A) Wǒ bù xiǎng qù Dōngjīng lǚxíng.

(B) Wǒ zhù zài Lúndūn.

(C) Zhè ge shèngdànjié yìqǐ qù ba.

Question 4

A：Qǐngwèn zhè jiàn yīfu shì mǎi gěi zìjǐ chuān de ma？

(A) Zhè shì gěi wǒ māma mǎi de.

(B) Zhè jiàn yīfu duōshao qián？

(C) Wǒ bù zhīdào shìyījiān zài nǎli.

Question 5

A：Zhè zhōu sān wǒ xiǎng qǐng yì tiān jià.

B：Nǐ yǒu shénme shì？

(A) Méi shì le, búyòng fàng zài xīn shang.

(B) Wǒ yéye bìng le, yào sòng tā qù kàn yīshēng.

(C) Wǒ huì zǎo diǎn huílai bāng nǐ zuò shì de.

Question 6

A：Wǒ lái bāng nǐ ná zhè bēi chá ba.

(A) Wǒ kěyǐ zìjǐ ná zhè chuáng bèizi.

(B) Xièxie, xiǎoxīn tàng shǒu.

(C) Zhè bēi shì níngméng shuǐ.

Question 7

A：Qǐngwèn nǐ yào xiē shénme？

(A) Wǒ yào yì bēi chéngzhī.

(B) Kāfēi mài wán le.

(C) Zhè běn shū hěn yǒu yìsi.

Question 8

A：Zuì jìn zěnme bú qù dǎ qiú le, zài máng shénme？

B：Wǒ xiànzài měitiān xiàwǔ dōu qù tiàowǔ.

(A) Guàibudé wǒ zuìjìn lǎo shì jiànbudào nǐ le.

(B) Míngtiān wǒmen yìqǐ qù dǎ qiú ba.

(C) Nǐ de wǔ tiào de zhēn hǎo.

Question 9

A：Zuìjìn Lǐ Qiáng lái zhǎo guo nǐ ma？

(A) Méiyǒu, tā zuìjìn hěn máng.

(B) Zhèli yǒu kōngwèi.

(C) Lǐ Qiáng bú guòlai le.

Question 10

A：Wǒ gěi tā dǎ le hǎo jǐ cì diànhuà, dōu dǎ bù tōng.

B：Nǐ qù tā jiā zhǎo tā ba.

(A) Wǒ mǎi le bù xīn shǒujī.

(B) Diànhuà hěn guì.

(C) Wǒ bù zhīdao tā zhù nǎ.

Question 11

A： Nǐ chī guo shénme Zhōngguó cài？

B： Wǒ chī guo Běijīng kǎoyā, nà nǐ ne？

(A) Běijīng de tiānqì hěn hǎo.
(B) Mápó dòufǔ.
(C) Wǒmen zhōumò qù chī kǎoyā hǎo ma？

Question 12

A： Xiànzài kěyǐ mǎi shí èr hào de huǒchēpiào ma？

(A) Tíqián mǎi fēijī piào kěyǐ yǒu jiǔzhé yōuhuì.
(B) Jīntiān shì qī hào, shí èr hào de huǒchē piào hái méi chūlai.
(C) Shí èr hào hòuchēshì zài nàbian.

Question 13

A： Shéi bǎ yīnyuè kāi de zhème dà？ Chǎo sǐ le！

(A) Tā shēngbìng le.
(B) Shì xīn lái de línjū zài kāi shēngrìhuì.
(C) Zǎoshang hǎo, nǐ xiǎng chī diǎn shénme？

Question 14

A： Wǎnshang yìqǐ qù kàn diànyǐng ba？

B： Wǒ de zuòyè hái méi zuò wán ne.

(A) Nà wǒmen xiànzài qù ba.
(B) Nà wǒmen gǎi tiān ba.
(C) Wǒ bù xiǎng zuò zuòyè.

Question 15

A： Zhè zhǒng yào yì tiān chī jǐ cì？

(A) Yào jì dé fàn hòu chī.
(B) Zuìhǎo shì yī tiān sān cì, yánzhòng de huà yě kěyǐ chī sì cì.
(C) Wǒ bù zhīdao zhè shì shénme yào.

Part B

Question 16

Nán : Nǐ zěnme yòu chídào le? Zuótiān shì nàozhōng huài le, jīntiān yòu shì shénme lǐyóu?

Nǚ : Duìbuqǐ, jīntiān lù shang dǔchē le.

Questions 17-18

Nǚ : Běijīng dìtiě yī hào xiàn de shǒu bān shíjiān shì jǐ diǎn?

Nán : Zǎoshang wǔ diǎn sānshí fēn.

Nǚ : Xià yí zhàn kěyǐ zhuǎn chéng jǐ hào xiàn?

Nán : Èr hào xiàn.

Questions 19-20

Nán : Kěyǐ máfan nǐ bāng wǒ zhào zhāng xiàng ma?

Nǚ : Méiwèntí. Nǐ shì yí ge rén lái lǚyóu de ma?

Nán : Wǒ hé péngyou yìqǐ lái de, búguò tāmen xiànzài qù mǎi jìniànpǐn le.

Question 21

Nán : Nǐ xiànzài hé bàba māma yìqǐ zhù ma?

Nǚ : Búshì, wǒ hé nǎinai yìqǐ zhù.

Questions 22-23

Nán : Tīngshuō xuéxiào fùjìn xīn kāi le yì jiā Yìdàlì cānguǎn, nǐ qùguo ma?

Nǚ : Wǒ zuótiān gānggāng qùguo, wèidao hěn búcuò.

Nán : Wǒ yě hěn xiǎng qù, kě zuìjìn máng zhe fùxí kǎoshì, méiyǒu shíjiān qù.

Question 24

Nán : Qǐngwèn nǐ yào xiē shénme?

Nǚ : Wǒ yào yí ge xīhóngshì chǎojīdàn、yì wǎn mǐfàn hē yì bēi chéngzhī.

Nán : Duìbuqǐ, chéngzhī yǐjīng mài wán le, háiyǒu píngguǒzhī hé xīguāzhī, nǐ yào shénme?

Nǚ : Nà suàn le, bù xūyào le.

Question 25

Nán : Nǐ mǎi le shénme shū?

Nǚ : Mǎi le zázhì、értóng gùshishū, háiyǒu yì běn zìdiǎn.

Question 26

Nán : Nǐ zhīdào jīnnián de Zhōngqiū Jié shì nǎ yì tiān ma?

Nǚ : Jiǔ yuè èrshí qī rì, xīngqī tiān.

Question 27

Nán : Wǒmen qù kàn diànyǐng ba.

Nǚ : Hǎode, děnghuìér zài cāntīng qiánmiàn de lùkǒu jiàn.

Question 28

Nán : Qǐngwèn fùjìn de túshūguǎn zěnme zǒu?

Nǚ : Nǐ zhí zǒu wǔ fēnzhōng, jiùhuì kàndào yí ge gōngyuán, túshūguǎn jiù zài tā de yòubian.

Question 29

Nán : Xiǎo Wáng, zuìjìn máng xiē shénme?

Nǚ : Xiàzhōu yào kǎoshì le, máng zhe fùxí. Nǐ ne?

Question 30

Nán : Nǐ xǐhuan zuò shénme yùndòng?

Nǚ : Dǎ lánqiú、páshān wǒ dōu xǐhuan, dàn wǒ zuì xǐhuan yóuyǒng.

Practice Test Six

1	Ⓐ	Ⓑ	Ⓒ	Ⓓ	31	Ⓐ	Ⓑ	Ⓒ	Ⓓ	56	Ⓐ	Ⓑ	Ⓒ	Ⓓ
2	Ⓐ	Ⓑ	Ⓒ	Ⓓ	32	Ⓐ	Ⓑ	Ⓒ	Ⓓ	57	Ⓐ	Ⓑ	Ⓒ	Ⓓ
3	Ⓐ	Ⓑ	Ⓒ	Ⓓ	33	Ⓐ	Ⓑ	Ⓒ	Ⓓ	58	Ⓐ	Ⓑ	Ⓒ	Ⓓ
4	Ⓐ	Ⓑ	Ⓒ	Ⓓ	34	Ⓐ	Ⓑ	Ⓒ	Ⓓ	59	Ⓐ	Ⓑ	Ⓒ	Ⓓ
5	Ⓐ	Ⓑ	Ⓒ	Ⓓ	35	Ⓐ	Ⓑ	Ⓒ	Ⓓ	60	Ⓐ	Ⓑ	Ⓒ	Ⓓ
6	Ⓐ	Ⓑ	Ⓒ	Ⓓ	36	Ⓐ	Ⓑ	Ⓒ	Ⓓ	61	Ⓐ	Ⓑ	Ⓒ	Ⓓ
7	Ⓐ	Ⓑ	Ⓒ	Ⓓ	37	Ⓐ	Ⓑ	Ⓒ	Ⓓ	62	Ⓐ	Ⓑ	Ⓒ	Ⓓ
8	Ⓐ	Ⓑ	Ⓒ	Ⓓ	38	Ⓐ	Ⓑ	Ⓒ	Ⓓ	63	Ⓐ	Ⓑ	Ⓒ	Ⓓ
9	Ⓐ	Ⓑ	Ⓒ	Ⓓ	39	Ⓐ	Ⓑ	Ⓒ	Ⓓ	64	Ⓐ	Ⓑ	Ⓒ	Ⓓ
10	Ⓐ	Ⓑ	Ⓒ	Ⓓ	40	Ⓐ	Ⓑ	Ⓒ	Ⓓ	65	Ⓐ	Ⓑ	Ⓒ	Ⓓ
11	Ⓐ	Ⓑ	Ⓒ	Ⓓ	41	Ⓐ	Ⓑ	Ⓒ	Ⓓ	66	Ⓐ	Ⓑ	Ⓒ	Ⓓ
12	Ⓐ	Ⓑ	Ⓒ	Ⓓ	42	Ⓐ	Ⓑ	Ⓒ	Ⓓ	67	Ⓐ	Ⓑ	Ⓒ	Ⓓ
13	Ⓐ	Ⓑ	Ⓒ	Ⓓ	43	Ⓐ	Ⓑ	Ⓒ	Ⓓ	68	Ⓐ	Ⓑ	Ⓒ	Ⓓ
14	Ⓐ	Ⓑ	Ⓒ	Ⓓ	44	Ⓐ	Ⓑ	Ⓒ	Ⓓ	69	Ⓐ	Ⓑ	Ⓒ	Ⓓ
15	Ⓐ	Ⓑ	Ⓒ	Ⓓ	45	Ⓐ	Ⓑ	Ⓒ	Ⓓ	70	Ⓐ	Ⓑ	Ⓒ	Ⓓ
16	Ⓐ	Ⓑ	Ⓒ	Ⓓ	46	Ⓐ	Ⓑ	Ⓒ	Ⓓ	71	Ⓐ	Ⓑ	Ⓒ	Ⓓ
17	Ⓐ	Ⓑ	Ⓒ	Ⓓ	47	Ⓐ	Ⓑ	Ⓒ	Ⓓ	72	Ⓐ	Ⓑ	Ⓒ	Ⓓ
18	Ⓐ	Ⓑ	Ⓒ	Ⓓ	48	Ⓐ	Ⓑ	Ⓒ	Ⓓ	73	Ⓐ	Ⓑ	Ⓒ	Ⓓ
19	Ⓐ	Ⓑ	Ⓒ	Ⓓ	49	Ⓐ	Ⓑ	Ⓒ	Ⓓ	74	Ⓐ	Ⓑ	Ⓒ	Ⓓ
20	Ⓐ	Ⓑ	Ⓒ	Ⓓ	50	Ⓐ	Ⓑ	Ⓒ	Ⓓ	75	Ⓐ	Ⓑ	Ⓒ	Ⓓ
21	Ⓐ	Ⓑ	Ⓒ	Ⓓ	51	Ⓐ	Ⓑ	Ⓒ	Ⓓ	76	Ⓐ	Ⓑ	Ⓒ	Ⓓ
22	Ⓐ	Ⓑ	Ⓒ	Ⓓ	52	Ⓐ	Ⓑ	Ⓒ	Ⓓ	77	Ⓐ	Ⓑ	Ⓒ	Ⓓ
23	Ⓐ	Ⓑ	Ⓒ	Ⓓ	53	Ⓐ	Ⓑ	Ⓒ	Ⓓ	78	Ⓐ	Ⓑ	Ⓒ	Ⓓ
24	Ⓐ	Ⓑ	Ⓒ	Ⓓ	54	Ⓐ	Ⓑ	Ⓒ	Ⓓ	79	Ⓐ	Ⓑ	Ⓒ	Ⓓ
25	Ⓐ	Ⓑ	Ⓒ	Ⓓ	55	Ⓐ	Ⓑ	Ⓒ	Ⓓ	80	Ⓐ	Ⓑ	Ⓒ	Ⓓ
26	Ⓐ	Ⓑ	Ⓒ	Ⓓ						81	Ⓐ	Ⓑ	Ⓒ	Ⓓ
27	Ⓐ	Ⓑ	Ⓒ	Ⓓ						82	Ⓐ	Ⓑ	Ⓒ	Ⓓ
28	Ⓐ	Ⓑ	Ⓒ	Ⓓ						83	Ⓐ	Ⓑ	Ⓒ	Ⓓ
29	Ⓐ	Ⓑ	Ⓒ	Ⓓ						84	Ⓐ	Ⓑ	Ⓒ	Ⓓ
30	Ⓐ	Ⓑ	Ⓒ	Ⓓ						85	Ⓐ	Ⓑ	Ⓒ	Ⓓ

Practice Tests Answers

Practice Test One

1	A	●	C	D	31	A	B	●	D	56	A	B	C	●
2	A	B	●	D	32	A	B	C	●	57	A	B	●	D
3	●	B	C	D	33	A	B	C	●	58	A	B	●	D
4	●	B	C	D	34	A	B	C	●	59	A	B	●	D
5	A	B	●	D	35	●	B	C	D	60	●	B	C	D
6	A	●	C	D	36	A	B	C	●	61	A	B	C	●
7	●	B	C	D	37	A	●	C	D	62	●	B	C	D
8	A	●	C	D	38	A	B	C	●	63	A	●	C	D
9	●	B	C	D	39	A	●	C	D	64	●	B	C	D
10	A	B	●	D	40	A	●	C	D	65	A	●	C	D
11	●	B	C	D	41	A	B	●	D	66	A	B	C	●
12	A	B	●	D	42	A	B	●	D	67	●	B	C	D
13	A	B	●	D	43	A	B	●	D	68	A	●	C	D
14	●	B	C	D	44	A	●	C	D	69	A	B	C	●
15	●	B	C	D	45	A	●	C	D	70	A	●	C	D
16	A	●	C	D	46	A	●	C	D	71	●	B	C	D
17	A	B	●	D	47	A	●	C	D	72	A	●	C	D
18	●	B	C	D	48	A	●	C	D	73	A	B	C	●
19	A	B	C	●	49	A	●	C	D	74	●	B	C	D
20	A	B	C	●	50	A	B	●	D	75	A	B	●	D
21	A	B	●	D	51	A	B	●	D	76	A	B	●	D
22	●	B	C	D	52	A	B	●	D	77	A	B	●	D
23	A	●	C	D	53	●	B	C	D	78	●	B	C	D
24	●	B	C	D	54	A	B	C	●	79	A	●	C	D
25	A	B	●	D	55	A	B	●	D	80	A	●	C	D
26	A	●	C	D						81	A	B	●	D
27	A	B	C	●						82	A	●	C	D
28	A	●	C	D						83	●	B	C	D
29	●	B	C	D						84	A	B	●	D
30	A	●	C	D						85	●	B	C	D

Practice Test Two

1	●	Ⓑ	Ⓒ	Ⓓ	31	Ⓐ	Ⓑ	Ⓒ	●	56	Ⓐ	●	Ⓒ	Ⓓ
2	Ⓐ	Ⓑ	●	Ⓓ	32	●	Ⓑ	Ⓒ	Ⓓ	57	●	Ⓑ	Ⓒ	Ⓓ
3	●	Ⓑ	Ⓒ	Ⓓ	33	Ⓐ	Ⓑ	Ⓒ	●	58	Ⓐ	●	Ⓒ	Ⓓ
4	Ⓐ	Ⓑ	●	Ⓓ	34	●	Ⓑ	Ⓒ	Ⓓ	59	Ⓐ	●	Ⓒ	Ⓓ
5	●	Ⓑ	Ⓒ	Ⓓ	35	Ⓐ	Ⓑ	Ⓒ	●	60	Ⓐ	●	Ⓒ	Ⓓ
6	●	Ⓑ	Ⓒ	Ⓓ	36	Ⓐ	Ⓑ	Ⓒ	●	61	Ⓐ	Ⓑ	●	Ⓓ
7	Ⓐ	Ⓑ	●	Ⓓ	37	Ⓐ	●	Ⓒ	Ⓓ	62	Ⓐ	Ⓑ	●	Ⓓ
8	Ⓐ	●	Ⓒ	Ⓓ	38	Ⓐ	●	Ⓒ	Ⓓ	63	Ⓐ	Ⓑ	●	Ⓓ
9	Ⓐ	●	Ⓒ	Ⓓ	39	Ⓐ	●	Ⓒ	Ⓓ	64	Ⓐ	●	Ⓒ	Ⓓ
10	Ⓐ	●	Ⓒ	Ⓓ	40	Ⓐ	Ⓑ	●	Ⓓ	65	Ⓐ	Ⓑ	Ⓒ	●
11	●	Ⓑ	Ⓒ	Ⓓ	41	Ⓐ	Ⓑ	●	Ⓓ	66	Ⓐ	Ⓑ	●	Ⓓ
12	Ⓐ	●	Ⓒ	Ⓓ	42	●	Ⓑ	Ⓒ	Ⓓ	67	Ⓐ	Ⓑ	Ⓒ	●
13	Ⓐ	Ⓑ	●	Ⓓ	43	Ⓐ	●	Ⓒ	Ⓓ	68	Ⓐ	Ⓑ	●	Ⓓ
14	Ⓐ	Ⓑ	●	Ⓓ	44	●	Ⓑ	Ⓒ	Ⓓ	69	Ⓐ	Ⓑ	●	Ⓓ
15	Ⓐ	●	Ⓒ	Ⓓ	45	Ⓐ	●	Ⓒ	Ⓓ	70	Ⓐ	Ⓑ	Ⓒ	●
16	●	Ⓑ	Ⓒ	Ⓓ	46	●	Ⓑ	Ⓒ	Ⓓ	71	●	Ⓑ	Ⓒ	Ⓓ
17	Ⓐ	Ⓑ	Ⓒ	●	47	Ⓐ	●	Ⓒ	Ⓓ	72	Ⓐ	●	Ⓒ	Ⓓ
18	Ⓐ	Ⓑ	●	Ⓓ	48	Ⓐ	Ⓑ	●	Ⓓ	73	Ⓐ	●	Ⓒ	Ⓓ
19	●	Ⓑ	Ⓒ	Ⓓ	49	Ⓐ	Ⓑ	●	Ⓓ	74	Ⓐ	●	Ⓒ	Ⓓ
20	Ⓐ	Ⓑ	Ⓒ	●	50	●	Ⓑ	Ⓒ	Ⓓ	75	Ⓐ	Ⓑ	●	Ⓓ
21	Ⓐ	Ⓑ	●	Ⓓ	51	●	Ⓑ	Ⓒ	Ⓓ	76	Ⓐ	Ⓑ	●	Ⓓ
22	Ⓐ	Ⓑ	●	Ⓓ	52	Ⓐ	●	Ⓒ	Ⓓ	77	Ⓐ	Ⓑ	●	Ⓓ
23	Ⓐ	Ⓑ	Ⓒ	●	53	Ⓐ	Ⓑ	●	Ⓓ	78	●	Ⓑ	Ⓒ	Ⓓ
24	●	Ⓑ	Ⓒ	Ⓓ	54	Ⓐ	Ⓑ	●	Ⓓ	79	Ⓐ	Ⓑ	●	Ⓓ
25	Ⓐ	Ⓑ	Ⓒ	●	55	Ⓐ	Ⓑ	Ⓒ	●	80	●	Ⓑ	Ⓒ	Ⓓ
26	Ⓐ	Ⓑ	●	Ⓓ						81	●	Ⓑ	Ⓒ	Ⓓ
27	Ⓐ	●	Ⓒ	Ⓓ						82	Ⓐ	Ⓑ	●	Ⓓ
28	Ⓐ	●	Ⓒ	Ⓓ						83	Ⓐ	●	Ⓒ	Ⓓ
29	●	Ⓑ	Ⓒ	Ⓓ						84	Ⓐ	Ⓑ	●	Ⓓ
30	●	Ⓑ	Ⓒ	Ⓓ						85	●	Ⓑ	Ⓒ	Ⓓ

Practice Test Three

1	●	Ⓑ	Ⓒ	Ⓓ	31	Ⓐ	●	Ⓒ	Ⓓ	56	Ⓐ	Ⓑ	Ⓒ	●
2	Ⓐ	●	Ⓒ	Ⓓ	32	Ⓐ	Ⓑ	●	Ⓓ	57	Ⓐ	Ⓑ	●	Ⓓ
3	Ⓐ	Ⓑ	●	Ⓓ	33	●	Ⓑ	Ⓒ	Ⓓ	58	●	Ⓑ	Ⓒ	Ⓓ
4	●	Ⓑ	Ⓒ	Ⓓ	34	●	Ⓑ	Ⓒ	Ⓓ	59	Ⓐ	Ⓑ	Ⓒ	●
5	Ⓐ	●	Ⓒ	Ⓓ	35	Ⓐ	Ⓑ	●	Ⓓ	60	Ⓐ	Ⓑ	●	Ⓓ
6	Ⓐ	●	Ⓒ	Ⓓ	36	Ⓐ	●	Ⓒ	Ⓓ	61	Ⓐ	●	Ⓒ	Ⓓ
7	Ⓐ	●	Ⓒ	Ⓓ	37	Ⓐ	Ⓑ	Ⓒ	●	62	Ⓐ	Ⓑ	Ⓒ	●
8	Ⓐ	Ⓑ	●	Ⓓ	38	●	Ⓑ	Ⓒ	Ⓓ	63	Ⓐ	Ⓑ	Ⓒ	●
9	Ⓐ	Ⓑ	●	Ⓓ	39	Ⓐ	Ⓑ	●	Ⓓ	64	Ⓐ	Ⓑ	●	Ⓓ
10	Ⓐ	●	Ⓒ	Ⓓ	40	●	Ⓑ	Ⓒ	Ⓓ	65	●	Ⓑ	Ⓒ	Ⓓ
11	Ⓐ	●	Ⓒ	Ⓓ	41	Ⓐ	●	Ⓒ	Ⓓ	66	Ⓐ	Ⓑ	Ⓒ	●
12	Ⓐ	●	Ⓒ	Ⓓ	42	●	Ⓑ	Ⓒ	Ⓓ	67	Ⓐ	Ⓑ	●	Ⓓ
13	Ⓐ	Ⓑ	●	Ⓓ	43	Ⓐ	●	Ⓒ	Ⓓ	68	●	Ⓑ	Ⓒ	Ⓓ
14	Ⓐ	Ⓑ	●	Ⓓ	44	Ⓐ	Ⓑ	Ⓒ	●	69	●	Ⓑ	Ⓒ	Ⓓ
15	●	Ⓑ	Ⓒ	Ⓓ	45	Ⓐ	Ⓑ	●	Ⓓ	70	Ⓐ	●	Ⓒ	Ⓓ
16	Ⓐ	Ⓑ	●	Ⓓ	46	●	Ⓑ	Ⓒ	Ⓓ	71	Ⓐ	Ⓑ	●	Ⓓ
17	Ⓐ	●	Ⓒ	Ⓓ	47	Ⓐ	Ⓑ	●	Ⓓ	72	●	Ⓑ	Ⓒ	Ⓓ
18	●	Ⓑ	Ⓒ	Ⓓ	48	●	Ⓑ	Ⓒ	Ⓓ	73	Ⓐ	Ⓑ	●	Ⓓ
19	Ⓐ	Ⓑ	●	Ⓓ	49	Ⓐ	Ⓑ	●	Ⓓ	74	Ⓐ	●	Ⓒ	Ⓓ
20	Ⓐ	Ⓑ	Ⓒ	●	50	Ⓐ	Ⓑ	Ⓒ	●	75	●	Ⓑ	Ⓒ	Ⓓ
21	●	Ⓑ	Ⓒ	Ⓓ	51	Ⓐ	●	Ⓒ	Ⓓ	76	Ⓐ	Ⓑ	●	Ⓓ
22	Ⓐ	Ⓑ	Ⓒ	●	52	Ⓐ	Ⓑ	●	Ⓓ	77	Ⓐ	Ⓑ	Ⓒ	●
23	Ⓐ	Ⓑ	●	Ⓓ	53	Ⓐ	Ⓑ	●	Ⓓ	78	●	Ⓑ	Ⓒ	Ⓓ
24	Ⓐ	●	Ⓒ	Ⓓ	54	●	Ⓑ	Ⓒ	Ⓓ	79	Ⓐ	●	Ⓒ	Ⓓ
25	Ⓐ	Ⓑ	Ⓒ	●	55	Ⓐ	●	Ⓒ	Ⓓ	80	●	Ⓑ	Ⓒ	Ⓓ
26	Ⓐ	Ⓑ	●	Ⓓ						81	Ⓐ	●	Ⓒ	Ⓓ
27	Ⓐ	●	Ⓒ	Ⓓ						82	●	Ⓑ	Ⓒ	Ⓓ
28	Ⓐ	●	Ⓒ	Ⓓ						83	Ⓐ	●	Ⓒ	Ⓓ
29	Ⓐ	●	Ⓒ	Ⓓ						84	●	Ⓑ	Ⓒ	Ⓓ
30	Ⓐ	Ⓑ	●	Ⓓ						85	Ⓐ	●	Ⓒ	Ⓓ

Practice Test Four

1	Ⓐ	Ⓑ	●	Ⓓ	31	Ⓐ	Ⓑ	Ⓒ	●	56	Ⓐ	●	Ⓒ	Ⓓ
2	Ⓐ	●	Ⓒ	Ⓓ	32	Ⓐ	Ⓑ	Ⓒ	●	57	●	Ⓑ	Ⓒ	Ⓓ
3	Ⓐ	Ⓑ	●	Ⓓ	33	Ⓐ	Ⓑ	●	Ⓓ	58	Ⓐ	Ⓑ	Ⓒ	●
4	●	Ⓑ	Ⓒ	Ⓓ	34	Ⓐ	Ⓑ	●	Ⓓ	59	Ⓐ	Ⓑ	●	Ⓓ
5	Ⓐ	Ⓑ	●	Ⓓ	35	●	Ⓑ	Ⓒ	Ⓓ	60	Ⓐ	Ⓑ	●	Ⓓ
6	Ⓐ	●	Ⓒ	Ⓓ	36	Ⓐ	●	Ⓒ	Ⓓ	61	Ⓐ	Ⓑ	Ⓒ	●
7	Ⓐ	Ⓑ	●	Ⓓ	37	●	Ⓑ	Ⓒ	Ⓓ	62	Ⓐ	Ⓑ	Ⓒ	●
8	Ⓐ	●	Ⓒ	Ⓓ	38	Ⓐ	Ⓑ	●	Ⓓ	63	●	Ⓑ	Ⓒ	Ⓓ
9	Ⓐ	●	Ⓒ	Ⓓ	39	Ⓐ	Ⓑ	Ⓒ	●	64	Ⓐ	Ⓑ	●	Ⓓ
10	Ⓐ	Ⓑ	●	Ⓓ	40	Ⓐ	●	Ⓒ	Ⓓ	65	Ⓐ	Ⓑ	Ⓒ	●
11	Ⓐ	Ⓑ	●	Ⓓ	41	●	Ⓑ	Ⓒ	Ⓓ	66	Ⓐ	Ⓑ	Ⓒ	●
12	●	Ⓑ	Ⓒ	Ⓓ	42	Ⓐ	●	Ⓒ	Ⓓ	67	●	Ⓑ	Ⓒ	Ⓓ
13	●	Ⓑ	Ⓒ	Ⓓ	43	Ⓐ	●	Ⓒ	Ⓓ	68	●	Ⓑ	Ⓒ	Ⓓ
14	Ⓐ	●	Ⓒ	Ⓓ	44	Ⓐ	Ⓑ	Ⓒ	●	69	●	Ⓑ	Ⓒ	Ⓓ
15	●	Ⓑ	Ⓒ	Ⓓ	45	Ⓐ	Ⓑ	●	Ⓓ	70	Ⓐ	●	Ⓒ	Ⓓ
16	●	Ⓑ	Ⓒ	Ⓓ	46	Ⓐ	●	Ⓒ	Ⓓ	71	●	Ⓑ	Ⓒ	Ⓓ
17	Ⓐ	Ⓑ	Ⓒ	●	47	Ⓐ	Ⓑ	●	Ⓓ	72	Ⓐ	Ⓑ	●	Ⓓ
18	Ⓐ	Ⓑ	Ⓒ	●	48	Ⓐ	Ⓑ	Ⓒ	●	73	●	Ⓑ	Ⓒ	Ⓓ
19	●	Ⓑ	Ⓒ	Ⓓ	49	Ⓐ	Ⓑ	Ⓒ	●	74	●	Ⓑ	Ⓒ	Ⓓ
20	Ⓐ	Ⓑ	Ⓒ	●	50	Ⓐ	●	Ⓒ	Ⓓ	75	Ⓐ	Ⓑ	●	Ⓓ
21	Ⓐ	Ⓑ	●	Ⓓ	51	Ⓐ	Ⓑ	Ⓒ	●	76	●	Ⓑ	Ⓒ	Ⓓ
22	●	Ⓑ	Ⓒ	Ⓓ	52	Ⓐ	●	Ⓒ	Ⓓ	77	Ⓐ	Ⓑ	●	Ⓓ
23	Ⓐ	Ⓑ	Ⓒ	●	53	Ⓐ	Ⓑ	Ⓒ	●	78	Ⓐ	●	Ⓒ	Ⓓ
24	Ⓐ	Ⓑ	●	Ⓓ	54	Ⓐ	Ⓑ	Ⓒ	●	79	●	Ⓑ	Ⓒ	Ⓓ
25	Ⓐ	Ⓑ	●	Ⓓ	55	●	Ⓑ	Ⓒ	Ⓓ	80	Ⓐ	●	Ⓒ	Ⓓ
26	●	Ⓑ	Ⓒ	Ⓓ						81	●	Ⓑ	Ⓒ	Ⓓ
27	Ⓐ	●	Ⓒ	Ⓓ						82	Ⓐ	Ⓑ	Ⓒ	●
28	Ⓐ	Ⓑ	Ⓒ	●						83	Ⓐ	Ⓑ	Ⓒ	●
29	Ⓐ	Ⓑ	●	Ⓓ						84	Ⓐ	●	Ⓒ	Ⓓ
30	Ⓐ	●	Ⓒ	Ⓓ						85	Ⓐ	Ⓑ	Ⓒ	●

Practice Test Five

1	Ⓐ	Ⓑ	●	Ⓓ	31	Ⓐ	Ⓑ	●	Ⓓ	56	●	Ⓑ	Ⓒ	Ⓓ
2	●	Ⓑ	Ⓒ	Ⓓ	32	Ⓐ	●	Ⓒ	Ⓓ	57	Ⓐ	Ⓑ	●	Ⓓ
3	Ⓐ	●	Ⓒ	Ⓓ	33	Ⓐ	●	Ⓒ	Ⓓ	58	Ⓐ	●	Ⓒ	Ⓓ
4	Ⓐ	Ⓑ	●	Ⓓ	34	●	Ⓑ	Ⓒ	Ⓓ	59	●	Ⓑ	Ⓒ	Ⓓ
5	Ⓐ	Ⓑ	●	Ⓓ	35	Ⓐ	Ⓑ	●	Ⓓ	60	Ⓐ	Ⓑ	Ⓒ	●
6	Ⓐ	Ⓑ	●	Ⓓ	36	●	Ⓑ	Ⓒ	Ⓓ	61	Ⓐ	Ⓑ	●	Ⓓ
7	●	Ⓑ	Ⓒ	Ⓓ	37	Ⓐ	●	Ⓒ	Ⓓ	62	Ⓐ	Ⓑ	Ⓒ	●
8	Ⓐ	Ⓑ	●	Ⓓ	38	Ⓐ	●	Ⓒ	Ⓓ	63	●	Ⓑ	Ⓒ	Ⓓ
9	Ⓐ	●	Ⓒ	Ⓓ	39	Ⓐ	●	Ⓒ	Ⓓ	64	●	Ⓑ	Ⓒ	Ⓓ
10	Ⓐ	Ⓑ	●	Ⓓ	40	Ⓐ	●	Ⓒ	Ⓓ	65	●	Ⓑ	Ⓒ	Ⓓ
11	Ⓐ	Ⓑ	●	Ⓓ	41	Ⓐ	Ⓑ	●	Ⓓ	66	Ⓐ	●	Ⓒ	Ⓓ
12	Ⓐ	Ⓑ	●	Ⓓ	42	Ⓐ	●	Ⓒ	Ⓓ	67	●	Ⓑ	Ⓒ	Ⓓ
13	Ⓐ	●	Ⓒ	Ⓓ	43	Ⓐ	●	Ⓒ	Ⓓ	68	Ⓐ	●	Ⓒ	Ⓓ
14	●	Ⓑ	Ⓒ	Ⓓ	44	●	Ⓑ	Ⓒ	Ⓓ	69	Ⓐ	Ⓑ	Ⓒ	●
15	Ⓐ	Ⓑ	●	Ⓓ	45	Ⓐ	Ⓑ	Ⓒ	●	70	Ⓐ	Ⓑ	Ⓒ	●
16	Ⓐ	Ⓑ	●	Ⓓ	46	Ⓐ	●	Ⓒ	Ⓓ	71	Ⓐ	Ⓑ	●	Ⓓ
17	Ⓐ	Ⓑ	Ⓒ	●	47	Ⓐ	Ⓑ	●	Ⓓ	72	●	Ⓑ	Ⓒ	Ⓓ
18	Ⓐ	●	Ⓒ	Ⓓ	48	Ⓐ	●	Ⓒ	Ⓓ	73	Ⓐ	Ⓑ	●	Ⓓ
19	Ⓐ	●	Ⓒ	Ⓓ	49	●	Ⓑ	Ⓒ	Ⓓ	74	●	Ⓑ	Ⓒ	Ⓓ
20	Ⓐ	Ⓑ	●	Ⓓ	50	Ⓐ	●	Ⓒ	Ⓓ	75	●	Ⓑ	Ⓒ	Ⓓ
21	●	Ⓑ	Ⓒ	Ⓓ	51	Ⓐ	●	Ⓒ	Ⓓ	76	Ⓐ	Ⓑ	●	Ⓓ
22	●	Ⓑ	Ⓒ	Ⓓ	52	Ⓐ	●	Ⓒ	Ⓓ	77	Ⓐ	Ⓑ	●	Ⓓ
23	Ⓐ	●	Ⓒ	Ⓓ	53	Ⓐ	●	Ⓒ	Ⓓ	78	Ⓐ	Ⓑ	Ⓒ	●
24	●	Ⓑ	Ⓒ	Ⓓ	54	Ⓐ	●	Ⓒ	Ⓓ	79	Ⓐ	Ⓑ	Ⓒ	●
25	Ⓐ	Ⓑ	Ⓒ	●	55	Ⓐ	Ⓑ	Ⓒ	●	80	Ⓐ	Ⓑ	Ⓒ	●
26	●	Ⓑ	Ⓒ	Ⓓ						81	Ⓐ	Ⓑ	●	Ⓓ
27	Ⓐ	Ⓑ	Ⓒ	●						82	Ⓐ	Ⓑ	Ⓒ	●
28	Ⓐ	●	Ⓒ	Ⓓ						83	Ⓐ	Ⓑ	Ⓒ	●
29	●	Ⓑ	Ⓒ	Ⓓ						84	●	Ⓑ	Ⓒ	Ⓓ
30	Ⓐ	Ⓑ	●	Ⓓ						85	Ⓐ	●	Ⓒ	Ⓓ

Practice Test Six

1	Ⓐ	●	Ⓒ	Ⓓ	31	Ⓐ	Ⓑ	●	Ⓓ	56	Ⓐ	●	Ⓒ	Ⓓ
2	Ⓐ	Ⓑ	●	Ⓓ	32	Ⓐ	Ⓑ	●	Ⓓ	57	Ⓐ	Ⓑ	●	Ⓓ
3	Ⓐ	Ⓑ	●	Ⓓ	33	●	Ⓑ	Ⓒ	Ⓓ	58	●	Ⓑ	Ⓒ	Ⓓ
4	●	Ⓑ	Ⓒ	Ⓓ	34	Ⓐ	Ⓑ	●	Ⓓ	59	Ⓐ	●	Ⓒ	Ⓓ
5	Ⓐ	●	Ⓒ	Ⓓ	35	Ⓐ	●	Ⓒ	Ⓓ	60	Ⓐ	●	Ⓒ	Ⓓ
6	Ⓐ	●	Ⓒ	Ⓓ	36	Ⓐ	Ⓑ	●	Ⓓ	61	Ⓐ	Ⓑ	●	Ⓓ
7	●	Ⓑ	Ⓒ	Ⓓ	37	Ⓐ	Ⓑ	●	Ⓓ	62	Ⓐ	Ⓑ	●	Ⓓ
8	●	Ⓑ	Ⓒ	Ⓓ	38	Ⓐ	●	Ⓒ	Ⓓ	63	Ⓐ	Ⓑ	Ⓒ	●
9	●	Ⓑ	Ⓒ	Ⓓ	39	●	Ⓑ	Ⓒ	Ⓓ	64	●	Ⓑ	Ⓒ	Ⓓ
10	Ⓐ	Ⓑ	●	Ⓓ	40	Ⓐ	●	Ⓒ	Ⓓ	65	Ⓐ	●	Ⓒ	Ⓓ
11	Ⓐ	●	Ⓒ	Ⓓ	41	Ⓐ	Ⓑ	●	Ⓓ	66	Ⓐ	Ⓑ	Ⓒ	●
12	Ⓐ	●	Ⓒ	Ⓓ	42	Ⓐ	Ⓑ	●	Ⓓ	67	Ⓐ	Ⓑ	Ⓒ	●
13	Ⓐ	●	Ⓒ	Ⓓ	43	Ⓐ	Ⓑ	●	Ⓓ	68	●	Ⓑ	Ⓒ	Ⓓ
14	Ⓐ	●	Ⓒ	Ⓓ	44	Ⓐ	●	Ⓒ	Ⓓ	69	Ⓐ	●	Ⓒ	Ⓓ
15	Ⓐ	●	Ⓒ	Ⓓ	45	Ⓐ	●	Ⓒ	Ⓓ	70	Ⓐ	Ⓑ	●	Ⓓ
16	Ⓐ	Ⓑ	Ⓒ	●	46	Ⓐ	Ⓑ	●	Ⓓ	71	Ⓐ	●	Ⓒ	Ⓓ
17	Ⓐ	Ⓑ	●	Ⓓ	47	Ⓐ	Ⓑ	Ⓒ	●	72	Ⓐ	●	Ⓒ	Ⓓ
18	●	Ⓑ	Ⓒ	Ⓓ	48	Ⓐ	●	Ⓒ	Ⓓ	73	Ⓐ	●	Ⓒ	Ⓓ
19	Ⓐ	Ⓑ	●	Ⓓ	49	Ⓐ	Ⓑ	Ⓒ	●	74	●	Ⓑ	Ⓒ	Ⓓ
20	●	Ⓑ	Ⓒ	Ⓓ	50	Ⓐ	Ⓑ	●	Ⓓ	75	●	Ⓑ	Ⓒ	Ⓓ
21	Ⓐ	Ⓑ	●	Ⓓ	51	Ⓐ	●	Ⓒ	Ⓓ	76	Ⓐ	●	Ⓒ	Ⓓ
22	Ⓐ	Ⓑ	●	Ⓓ	52	●	Ⓑ	Ⓒ	Ⓓ	77	Ⓐ	Ⓑ	Ⓒ	●
23	Ⓐ	Ⓑ	Ⓒ	●	53	●	Ⓑ	Ⓒ	Ⓓ	78	Ⓐ	●	Ⓒ	Ⓓ
24	Ⓐ	Ⓑ	Ⓒ	●	54	Ⓐ	●	Ⓒ	Ⓓ	79	Ⓐ	Ⓑ	Ⓒ	●
25	●	Ⓑ	Ⓒ	Ⓓ	55	Ⓐ	●	Ⓒ	Ⓓ	80	Ⓐ	●	Ⓒ	Ⓓ
26	●	Ⓑ	Ⓒ	Ⓓ						81	Ⓐ	Ⓑ	●	Ⓓ
27	●	Ⓑ	Ⓒ	Ⓓ						82	Ⓐ	●	Ⓒ	Ⓓ
28	Ⓐ	●	Ⓒ	Ⓓ						83	Ⓐ	●	Ⓒ	Ⓓ
29	Ⓐ	●	Ⓒ	Ⓓ						84	Ⓐ	●	Ⓒ	Ⓓ
30	●	Ⓑ	Ⓒ	Ⓓ						85	●	Ⓑ	Ⓒ	Ⓓ

Listening Test Material

CD 1

Track 1	Practice Test 1
Track 2	Practice Test 2
Track 3	Practice Test 3

CD 2

Track 1	Practice Test 4
Track 2	Practice Test 5
Track 3	Practice Test 6

Each track includes the full-length listening section, including appropriate instructions and time gaps for answering.

The transcripts of the listening tests are printed at the end of each test.